The Art of CRM

Proven strategies for modern customer
relationship management

Max Fatouretchi

BIRMINGHAM - MUMBAI

The Art of CRM

Acquisition Editor: Ben Renow-Clarke
Acquisition Editor - Peer Reviews: Suresh Jain
Project Editor: Kishor Rit
Development Editor: Alex Sorrentino
Copy Editor: Joanne Lovell
Technical Editor: Aniket Shetty
Proofreader: Safis Editing
Indexer: Rekha Nair
Graphics: Sandip Tadge
Production Coordinator: Sandip Tadge

First published: May 2019

Production reference: 1200519

Published by Packt Publishing Ltd.
Livery Place
35 Livery Street
Birmingham B3 2PB, UK.

ISBN 978-1-78953-892-2

www.packtpub.com

`mapt.io`

Mapt is an online digital library that gives you full access to over 5,000 books and videos, as well as industry leading tools to help you plan your personal development and advance your career. For more information, please visit our website.

Why subscribe?

- Spend less time learning and more time coding with practical eBooks and Videos from over 4,000 industry professionals
- Learn better with Skill Plans built especially for you
- Get a free eBook or video every month
- Mapt is fully searchable
- Copy and paste, print, and bookmark content

Packt.com

Did you know that Packt offers eBook versions of every book published, with PDF and ePub files available? You can upgrade to the eBook version at `www.Packt.com` and as a print book customer, you are entitled to a discount on the eBook copy. Get in touch with us at `customercare@packtpub.com` for more details.

At `www.Packt.com`, you can also read a collection of free technical articles, sign up for a range of free newsletters, and receive exclusive discounts and offers on Packt books and eBooks.

Contributors

About the author

Max Fatouretchi's CRM journey began some 20 years ago as he started his small software business in Vienna, Austria, developing custom CRM applications for clients in Austria. Some 7 years, later he joined Microsoft's international team as a partner technology specialist and industry manager for Microsoft Dynamics 365 products for the next 13 years.

Throughout these 20 years, he has been engaged in many CRM implementations across the globe. The first one was with his own software company in Vienna, where he developed a CRM system for several banking clients in collaboration with HP (Hewlett Packard). At the same time, he fulfilled a role as a mentor and trainer, teaching CRM classes across Europe. After joining Microsoft, he started working with Microsoft teams across Europe the, Middle East, Africa, the Asia, Pacific, China, and Latin America to develop and deliver CRM projects to enterprise customers. As a lead architect and industry manager with Microsoft, he has participated in many CRM implementations with some 100+ multinational companies, mostly in the financial services industry.

I have much to be thankful for in writing this book, such as all my colleagues, clients, and partners who have given me the opportunity to work with them and learn from them in so many exciting projects; this book is my recognition for them all.

I would also like to express my deep gratitude to some of my colleagues, friends, and partners for their voluntary support in reviewing the contents of the book and for providing valuable feedback and input to improve it. My special thanks go to (in alphabetical order):

- *Erener Ozkan, CEO at VeriPark*
- *Brissaud Philippe, Program Manager - Artificial Intelligence at Microsoft*
- *Fratello Nick, Microsoft Business Applications Solutions Architect*
- *Genov Yuriy, Chief Operation Officer of DSK bank*
- *Jamrik Ferenc, SLA Manager at Emarsys*
- *Khoso Jandost, Group Manager, CRM at Avanade*
- *Slepitsky Andrey, Architect, Business Applications Domain at Microsoft*
- *Venkata-chalam Ganapathy, Senior Program Manager at Microsoft*
- *Verlinden Philip, Architect, Business Applications Domain at Microsoft*
- *Viganò Corrado, Sales Executive - Program Manager Altitudo*
- *Wijns Bert, Architect, Business Applications Domain at Microsoft*

Special thanks also go to Veripark for allowing me to leverage some of their intellectual properties in Chapter 2, Getting to Know Your Customer, and building a comprehensive 360-degree client view. This is one of my favorite solutions with a very rich and easy UI architecture but with a very comprehensive and role-based 360-degree client view.

About the reviewers

Guillermo Barker is an electrical engineer from Universidad de Chile. He is also a CRM consultant and was awarded certifications in Microsoft MCT and MAP last year. Prior to working as support manager at XMS Business Solutions, Guillermo spent almost 30 years in service management with a variety of CRM platforms.

This experience gave him wide knowledge about how to design and configure a Dynamics CRM and how such configurations can impact user adoption. Additionally, he has helped many companies with CRM and its installation, deployment, reporting and configuration.

Guillermo is also a trainer at Golden Training and Comunidad CRM (www.comunidadcrm.com). He is also a frequent contributor to Comunidad CRM on the internet and has reviewed the following books for Packt Publishing:

- Microsoft Dynamics CRM 2011 Applications (MB2-868) Certification Guide.
- Microsoft Dynamics CRM Customization Essentials.
- Building Dynamics CRM 2015 Dashboards.

You can read more about Guillermo at http://www.linkedin.com/ profile/ view?id=32635763&trk=tab_pro. He blogs at http:// www.comunidadcrm.com/ guillermobarker/.

Steve Ivie is an enterprise solutions architect with experience preparing businesses for the cloud. He has expertise in consulting, management, solutions, the cloud, and business development. His major focus is on business technologies for financial services, life sciences, healthcare, professional services, manufacturing, government, and the sports, and entertainment industries.

He is a partner at BluePrint **Business Process Transformation** (**BPT**), which is a Microsoft-focused professional services and independent software vendor with employees throughout the United States. As a value-adding partner to their clients, they provide strategic and tactical business solution advice and services in the areas of sales, customer service, marketing, project and field services, operations, talent, human resources, and financial management.

Steve Ivie authored *Building Dynamics CRM 2015 Dashboards with Power BI*, published by Packt Publishing. This book will provide you with the skills you need to learn how to build and present Dynamics CRM 2015 sales dashboards using Power BI.

TABLE OF CONTENTS

Chapter 4: Architecting Your CRM Solution – Preparing for Today and Tomorrow 139

Chapter 5: Utilizing Artificial Intelligence and Machine Learning in Your CRM Strategy 179

Preface

Customer Relationship Management (**CRM**) systems have delivered huge value to organizations. This book shares proven and cutting-edge techniques to increase the power of CRM even further.

In *The Art of CRM*, Max Fatouretchi shares his decades of experience building successful CRM systems that make a real difference to business performance. Through clear processes, actionable advice, and informative case studies, *The Art of CRM* teaches you how to design successful CRM systems for your clients.

Fatouretchi, the founder of the Academy4CRM institute, draws on his experience of over 20 years and 200 CRM implementations worldwide. Bringing CRM up to date, *The Art of CRM* shows you how to add AI and machine learning to your CRM, ensure compliance with GDPR, and choose between on-premise, cloud, and hybrid hosting solutions.

If you're looking for an expert guide to real-world CRM implementations, this book is for you.

Who this book is for

This book is targeted at all individuals who are involved in implementing or maintaining a CRM system. It involves storytelling, where the author shares some of the lessons that he has learned throughout his 20 years of CRM work in different capacities. You'll find most of the stories to be from the financial services industry, as this was his primary industry, and most of the implementations to be ones for international firms.

The targeted audience includes both business and technical staff, including chief experience officers, business leaders, project managers, architects, consultants, developers, and end users.

What this book covers

Chapter 1, What is CRM?, explores the roles, views, and responsibilities of project members, since CRM matters to everyone in a company and all staff members need to feel the sense of ownership right from the beginning of the CRM journey, though everyone plays a different role in this journey and has a different view of CRM. I will list briefly the important elements of a CRM system, including the operational CRM, analytical CRM, and collaborative CRM. We will also look at five real-life case studies of CRM implementations to compare how the particular business pain points and company strategies will shape functional priorities for your CRM design.

Chapter 2, Getting to Know Your Customer, helps in understanding the customer by maintaining and managing relevant customer information, which is at the heart of any successful business. Customer knowledge is perhaps the most essential ingredient to a business being successful. Knowing the customer starts with building a sophisticated 360-degree customer view that can capture, process, and present all relevant relationship data in a single role-based 360-degree client view. You will be introduced to a real-life solution of building a comprehensive 360-degree client view from one of the author's partners that he has been working with in many projects and in different countries, which is VeriPark, a very successful CRM company operating globally.

Chapter 3, Conceptualizing the CRM Design from Business Requirements, explores the design elements of a modern CRM solution that are dictated by business requirements, including processes, applications, data, security, integration, and deployment decisions. We will walk through the process of design and will recommend some very simple tools that could help you manage the design process for your new CRM solution.

As CRM provides a good opportunity for your digital transformation, we will explore the five technologies that are the basic ingredients of a digital transformation and essential for a modern CRM solution, including two case studies of successful digital transformation. This chapter will also provide you with a comprehensive overview of the design elements at a high level and set the stage for the next chapter.

Chapter 4, Architecting Your CRM Solution – Preparing for Today and Tomorrow, looks at the work of CRM architects, exploring techniques in architecting a business solution that could solve the business challenges of today and tomorrow. This chapter is not only for architects but also for all technical team members including consultants, project managers, and developers. It could also be relevant to key sponsors in the business departments. We will cover the major elements of solution architecture such as the viewpoints, quality attribute trees, measurement metrics, and architecture trade-off techniques. We will start briefly exploring some of the software engineering techniques— only as much as is relevant to the CRM architecture—including the so-called Agile development methodology, as this methodology is proving to be the most efficient in designing and implementing business solutions in the light of recent technology innovations.

Chapter 5, Utilizing Artificial Intelligence and Machine Learning in Your CRM Strategy, explores how **Artificial Intelligence** (**AI**) and **Machine Learning** (**ML**) could support your CRM processes and enrich traditional business applications to enable higher process automation and better business outcomes. We will bring a few real-life examples of implementations showing how these newer technologies including AI, ML, speech recognition, image recognition, pattern recognition, and cognitive services could be embedded in customer processes to provide self-service and automated customer interactions, and deliver recommendations and personalized customer experiences at an affordable price.

Chapter 6, GDPR and Regulatory Compliance, explores how a CRM platform could be leveraged to support and implement regulatory compliance in general and a real-life **General Data Protection Regulation** (**GDPR**) implementation with Microsoft Dynamics 365 to illustrate the practical use of the CRM platform.

GDPR is a regulation in European Union law on personal data protection and privacy for all individuals within the European Union. All global businesses that are dealing with European Union users and European Union clients are affected by this law. GDPR was adopted by the European Parliament on 27th April, 2016 and has been enforceable throughout the European Union since 25th May, 2018. GDPR regulates the collection, storage, use, and sharing of personal data for all businesses dealing with European Union clients. In this chapter, we will take you through the design proposal for implementing GDPR on your CRM platform.

Chapter 7, *CRM Integration Strategies*, explores most common data integration factors such as business requirements, related technologies, and stakeholders in CRM integration projects because building a 360-degree client view and enabling end-to-end customer processes often requires integration with various legacy applications and different data sources. Many factors such as security, performance, quality, and portability need to be considered in your integration strategies and in your solution design. We will explore various integration techniques, implementation scenarios, initial data load, and some of the performance considerations for your design. A modern CRM platform should integrate with an ever-growing eco-system in the cloud in order to consume data and leverage other services in the cloud, such as AI, social media platforms, and data lakes, to build a comprehensive customer view or to enable social selling and social advertising. We will also set the stage for the last chapter of the book, *Chapter 9*, *CRM Differentiators*, where we will explore the platform capabilities that are essential to integrate with the cloud.

Chapter 8, *Cloud Versus On-Premise Versus Hybrid – The Deployment of a CRM Platform*, explores factors such as the options and services that are available to you, regulatory compliance, security, portability, how and when you can access your data, who is responsible for keeping your solution safe, and obviously the overall cost of the CRM system, including the money you spend to buy, maintain, and operate, as well as any other ongoing costs (Capex/Opex). These are the factors directly influencing your choice of platform and the hosting of your solution since how you choose to host your CRM application can significantly impact the cost and functionalities of the solution. We will also evaluate the pros and cons of cloud, on-premise, and hybrid deployment.

We will explore CRM deployment options and compare them with each other to provide you with some good tools to help your decision-making processes regarding your CRM deployment.

Chapter 9, *CRM Differentiators*, shows that the competition among the market leaders is not going to be about a feature list anymore, as the functionalities of the most available tools in the market are continuously improving and are on par with major vendors such as Microsoft and Salesforce.com. The differentiators between the vendors will be more about how the CRM platform is able to leverage the broader technology innovations that are evolving today with the smart cloud, such as big data, AI, ML, and cognitive services. In this last chapter of this book, we will explore how the CRM platforms available in the market today can provide you with some powerful options and services that are usually ignored or neglected during the platform selection process. We will explore some significant capabilities of the CRM platforms that are needed to enable a sustainable solution for the long run.

We will talk about the elements and characteristics that make a successful CRM implementation in today's market environment. We will not compare CRM products explicitly but will explore the eco-system a new CRM platform should provide in order to solve the business challenges of today and tomorrow.

To get the most out of this book

This book covers all the important aspects of a modern CRM implementation with many real-life examples and also provides the tools and a high-level design and implementation guide for building a sustainable CRM solution for your business.

You will discover the most critical elements of a modern CRM implementation, both in theory and in practice.

We will talk about many great new ideas and technologies such as AI and ML, developments in recent years, state-of-the-art techniques, and finally how these technologies could actually be implemented within your CRM for your business.

This book is not deep technically. If you are a technical expert, you will be able to apply these ideas easily to your CRM implementation. It provides you with guidance for design, architecture, platform-selection, and implementation tools. It does not explain the bits and bytes of CRM; it assumes that you are either familiar with the basics of CRM or you can find the basic information easily on the internet.

This book involves storytelling, experience sharing, and knowledge sharing. It also covers the use of technological innovations in CRM solutions.

Download the color images

We also provide a PDF file that has color images of the screenshots/diagrams used in this book. You can download it here: `https://www.packtpub.com/sites/default/files/downloads/9781789538922_ColorImages.pdf`.

Conventions used

There are a number of text conventions used throughout this book.

Bold: Indicates a new term, an important word, or words that you see on the screen, for example, in menus or dialog boxes, also appear in the text like this. For example: "The bank's **Customer Experience Program (CEP)** is to start simplifying and improving the way in which the bank interacts with their clients."

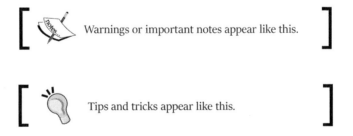

[Warnings or important notes appear like this.]

[Tips and tricks appear like this.]

Get in touch

Feedback from our readers is always welcome.

General feedback: If you have questions about any aspect of this book, mention the book title in the subject of your message and email us at customercare@packtpub.com.

Errata: Although we have taken every care to ensure the accuracy of our content, mistakes do happen. If you have found a mistake in this book we would be grateful if you would report this to us. Please visit, http://www.packt.com/submit-errata, selecting your book, clicking on the Errata Submission Form link, and entering the details.

Piracy: If you come across any illegal copies of our works in any form on the Internet, we would be grateful if you would provide us with the location address or website name. Please contact us at copyright@packt.com with a link to the material.

If you are interested in becoming an author: If there is a topic that you have expertise in and you are interested in either writing or contributing to a book, please visit http://authors.packtpub.com.

Reviews

Please leave a review. Once you have read and used this book, why not leave a review on the site that you purchased it from? Potential readers can then see and use your unbiased opinion to make purchase decisions, we at Packt can understand what you think about our products, and our authors can see your feedback on their book. Thank you!

For more information about Packt, please visit packt.com.

INTRODUCTION

My history with CRM

Some 20 years ago, I started my small **Customer Relationship Management** (**CRM**) business in Vienna. Since then, I have been involved in a number of CRM implementations across the globe and in various roles. My first role was within a small company in Vienna, where I was delivering CRM solutions to banking clients together with Hewlett-Packard. As my career developed, I spent a period of time being a mentor and trainer, teaching CRM classes across Europe.

Before long, I was working with Microsoft International as a CRM senior architect in both a sales and delivery role for the EMEA, APAC, and LATAM regions, which took me across the world, working with people from multiple countries. As a CRM architect, I've participated in a number of CRM implementations, at some 200 companies, in both pre-sales and delivery roles as the lead architect, designing both some very successful solutions and some not-so-successful designs; solutions of each category will be detailed throughout our journey.

Most of the companies I was engaged with were global companies with operations in multiple countries and continents. Within these companies, I've acted primarily as the CRM lead architect, but sometimes the focus has been put more on a dual role as the architect and/or the project manager.

In a nutshell, all these CRM implementations had common elements, including improving process efficiency and reducing operational costs, along with improving customer interactions and experience across the company, and often across different markets. But these engagements also had some differences. As you will learn in this book, every organization has to implement its own unique sales process based on its vertical, products, industry, culture, strategies, and market position. The one key element we need to know before we start is that what works for one company will often totally fail for another, and throughout this book, we will explore a wide range of good examples that reflect this idea.

I have worked with the **Shanghai Pudong Development Bank (SPDB)**, one of the largest banks in China. This bank specializes in commercial banking and operates as an international hub for the Asian region. Likewise, I've been engaged with Barclays, a British-based bank, and its CRM projects in the UK.

My experience also involves the retail sector, and both universal and private banking. This included working with the Société General in France, where I collaborated with both the corporate and investment banking arms on credit cards and wealth management business. My experience is not limited to just Europe or Asia; it also extends to Central America, where I worked with the Banco Industrial Guatemala, one of the largest retail banks in Central America with a network of more than 1,600 service points throughout the region.

This book is all about storytelling and sharing some of the best, and worst, experiences that I've encountered and learned from as an architect throughout my CRM journey.

You'll find that most of the stories are from the financial services industry, as this has been my primary industry focus for the last 10 years and most of my clients have been from the financial services sector. However, don't worry; all of these examples, as you will see, can be applied to other industries.

I will not disclose customer names or any confidential data in this book, for obvious reasons, but all the stories we explore are real, involving real clients, real customers, and real-world impacts.

The key ingredients for a successful CRM design

The work of a CRM architect is very much like the work of an architect that is designing the structures of a conventional building. This is perhaps the best way to describe what successful CRM design looks like. Much like a traditional architect, a CRM architect also needs to address elements such as security, usability, portability, performance, and regulations.

To highlight the similar elements of CRM architecture work and traditional architecture, I would like to compare two very famous historical buildings, both with very different architectural approaches. The purpose here is to evaluate the key design elements and the resulting outcomes for the Sydney Opera House in Australia and the Taj Mahal in India.

The case of the Sydney Opera House

In his biography, the architect of the Sydney Opera House, Jørn Utzon, talks about his Nordic sense of concern for nature, which, in his design, is emphasized in the synthesis of form, material, and function. His fascination with the architectural legacies of the ancient Mayas, the Islamic world, China, and Japan also enhanced his vision.

This developed into what Utzon later referred to as **Additive Architecture**, comparing his approach to the growth patterns of nature. A design can grow like a tree, he explained, saying, "If it grows naturally, then the architecture will look after itself."

The construction of the Sydney Opera House began in 1959 and was formally completed in 1973. In total, it ended up costing $69 million during its 15 years of construction. Much like any enterprise CRM project, it was built in three stages:

- Phase one (1959-1963): Consisted of building the upper podium

- Phase two (1963-1967): The construction of the outer shells

- Phase three (1967-1973): Interior design and completing the construction

Yet, if we go back to the original cost and time plan estimate from 1957, the entire projected cost was AU$7 million, and the completion date was due to be January 1963. In reality, the project was completed with a 10-year delay and ended up coming in at 1,300% over budget.

There were numerous disagreements between the architect and the client, and in February 1966, Utzon resigned from the project. The newly appointed architect found himself with an enormous amount of work ahead of him. His task was huge, with many required aspects of the design, such as capacity, acoustics, and structure, having been completely unresolved by Utzon. There were countless issues that he had to face, such as the unexpected difficulty in diverting stormwater. This one issue resulted from construction work beginning before proper construction drawings and planning had been prepared.

Changes were made to the original contract documents, including one that meant the podium columns were not strong enough to support the roof structure, and thus had to be rebuilt, adding a delay to the completion date and more cost to the overall project. The curved shells of the roof also caused a number of problems because they were so difficult to calculate for.

With this project, it was often found that new architectural territory had to be entered and the problems faced were corrected as they were encountered. Through this approach, the design often had to be adapted to new realities on the fly. Years later, the complex geometry of the roof alone, which was redesigned over 12 times in six years, resulted in extensive renovation and redesign work having to take place after only 50 years, which is now due to take until 2021.

The case of the Taj Mahal

On the other hand, the Taj Mahal, which was commissioned by the Mughal Emperor Shah Jahan to house the tomb of his wife, is a masterpiece of architectural design in regard to security, simplicity, performance, and usability. The tomb is the centerpiece of a 17-hectare (42-acre) complex, which includes a mosque and a guest house. All of this is set in formal gardens bounded on three sides by a fortified wall, such as that of a city or a castle.

The Taj Mahal was commissioned in 1632 and the construction of the mausoleum was essentially completed in 1643, after only 11 years. The entire complex is believed to have been completed in its entirety in 1653, at a cost estimated at the time to be around 32 million rupees. Compared to the Sydney Opera House, this project was delivered on time and on budget.

The Taj Mahal has never had any major architectural deficiencies in the 400 years that it's been around. The complex surrounding the building has, over the years, changed its original purpose several times ever since its construction some 400 years ago. Originally serving as a mausoleum, before serving time as a caravanserais, bazaars, and markets, before now serving as a popular tourist site and mosque. Taj Mahal is today one of the major sources of tourism income in India, with some 10 million paying visitors attending each year.

32 million rupees converted from 400 years ago to the current inflation rate of India's currency is almost impossible to calculate. However, a Taj Mahal copy on a 1:1 scale was built by a wealthy private man in Bangladesh. Located about 16 km east of Dhaka in Sonargaon, the construction took five years (2003-2008) to complete, and the cost was reported to be about 58 million dollars, or over four billion rupees.

Will this replica be as successful as the original one? I highly doubt that, but going back to the topic of this book, the same idea can be applied in the CRM space. You cannot replicate the exact same solution by taking it from one company to another and expect it to be as successful. In some cases, as we will see, you cannot even replicate it in the same company if the company is operating across different markets. Each CRM system is built for a specific company and adapted to its culture, supporting the specific business strategies of that company.

The examples in this book will give you a great range of material to support your CRM design. While I'll be highlighting critical success factors, it's important to remember that, as I've stated, these designs are not universal, and they will not work exactly the same outside of their original design; for example, they will not work in another business context. However, the same ideas can be applied outside of their original design.

Summary

Throughout this book, we will be exploring the key elements of how to build successful CRM solutions that are highly configurable, while being able to satisfy the security, usability, portability, and performance requirements of a business. At the same time, the systems we will be building will still provide a good **total cost of ownership** (**TCO**) and **return on investment** (**ROI**) ratio, very much like the Taj Mahal example we explored in this chapter.

CHAPTER 1

WHAT IS CRM?

Orchestrate your business and get your team on the same page with a central repository of customer data.

I n a nutshell, **customer relationship management (CRM)** is about process efficiency, reducing operational costs, and improving customer interactions and experience. In today's world, building a deeper and closer relationship with customers is critical to any business' success. Harder economic fundamentals, increasing competition, stricter regulations, digital disrupters, demanding customers, mobility, and price sensitivity are shifting the power from companies to customers.

If you are starting your CRM journey and you're an architect, project manager, business owner, or a business analyst, never be shy in asking each and every key stakeholder on your team about their view on CRM. You could ask them:

- Where do they want to go with it?
- How do they view the outcome?
- What do they expect from the system?
- What is the role they play in this journey?

The never-ending CRM journey could be beautiful and exciting; it's something that matters to all the stakeholders in a company. One important idea that I live by is that CRM matters to people in all roles in a company and everyone needs to feel a sense of ownership right from the beginning of the journey.

The sense of ownership in a CRM project, regardless of whether it's a new or even an upgraded project, is important and needs to be nurtured right from the start by all employees at all levels. From the CEO to business leaders, managers, sales, marketing, and service personnel, everyone is affected by a CRM implementation, and they all need to be involved. It's important for stakeholders to have a clear understanding of the vision statement of a CRM project. This can be achieved by maintaining good communication about a project and building a solution that will address individual business pain points.

The three main pillars of CRM

The main role of the architect is to design a solution that can not only satisfy the needs and requirements of all the stakeholders, but at the same time provide agility and structure for a good foundation that supports future business needs and extensions, very much like the Taj Mahal, which has changed its role over the years while remaining robust and with low maintenance costs.

Having understood the drivers and the requirements, you are ready to establish the critical properties that the system will have to exhibit in order to identify scenarios and characterize each one of them. The output of the process is a tree of attributes, which is a quality attribute tree including usability, availability, performance, and evolution, which are all things we will explore in more detail throughout this book.

You always need to consider that a CRM rollout in a company will affect everyone. Above all, it needs to support the business strategies while improving operational efficiencies, enabling business orchestration, and improving customer experience across all channels.

Technically speaking, there are three main pillars for any CRM implementation and they deliver value to the business:

- **Operational CRM**: The operational CRM is all about marketing, sales, and services functionalities. We will cover some case studies later in this chapter from different projects I've personally engaged with across a wide area of applications.

- **Analytical CRM**: The analytical CRM will use the data collected from the operational CRM and provide users and business leaders with individual KPIs, dashboards, and analytical tools to enable them to slice and dice data about business performance as they require. This foundation is for the business orchestration.

- **Collaboration CRM**: The collaboration CRM will provide the technology to integrate all kinds of communication channels and frontends with core CRM for both internal and external users: employees, partners, customers, and so-called bring-your-own devices. This includes support for different types of devices that could integrate with a CRM core platform and be administered with the same tools, leveraging the same infrastructure, including security and maintenance. The focus is on using the same platform, same authentication procedures, and same workflow engine, and fully leveraging the core entities and data.

With these three pillars in place, you'll be able to create a comprehensive view of your business and manage clients' communication over all your channels. Through this, you'll have the ingredients for predictive client insights, business intelligence, marketing, sales, and services automation. Later on in this chapter, we will see examples of these pillars.

Before we move on, *Figure 1.1* is an illustration of the three pillars of a CRM solution and related modules, which should help you to visualize what we've just talked about.

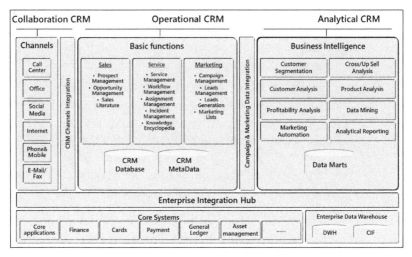

Figure 1.1: The three pillars of CRM

It's also important to remember that any CRM journey always begins with either a business strategy or a business pain point. All of the stakeholders must have a clear understanding of where the company is heading and what the business drivers for a CRM investment are. It's also important for all CRM team members to remember that the potential success or failure of CRM projects remains primarily on the shoulders of business stakeholders and not on those of the IT staff.

Typically, the business decision makers are the ones bringing up the need for and sponsoring a CRM solution. Often, but not always, the IT department is tasked with the selection of the platform and conducting the due diligence with a number of vendors. More importantly, while different business users may have different roles and expectations from the system, everyone needs to have a common understanding of the company's vision.

Team members need to support the same business strategies at the highest level. This means that the team will work together toward the success of a project for the company as a whole, while having individual expectations.

In addition to that, you will notice that the focus and the level of engagement of people involved in a project (the project team) will vary during the life cycle of the project as time goes on. It helps to categorize the characteristics of team members from visionaries and leadership to stakeholders and owners. While key sponsors are more visionary and, usually, the first players to actively support and advocate for a CRM strategy, they will just define the tactics. The end users will ultimately take more ownership during the deployment and operation phases.

In *Figure 1.2*, we see the engagement level of stakeholders, key users, and end users in a CRM implementation project. The visionaries are here to set the company's vision and strategies for a CRM, the key users (department leads) are the key sponsors who promote the solution, and the end users engage in reviews and provide feedback.

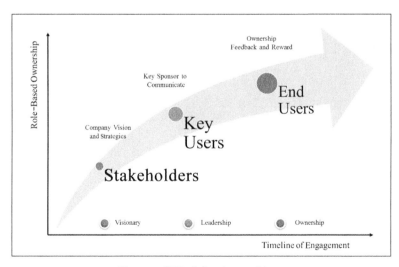

Figure 1.2: CRM role-based ownership

Before we start the development, we must have identified the stakeholders and have a crystal-clear vision of the functional requirements based on the business requirements. Furthermore, we must ensure that we have converted these to a detailed functional specification. All this is done by business analysts, project managers, solution specialists, and architects, with the level of IT engagement being driven by the outcome of this process. We will explore some really great examples and case studies later in this chapter, where we will highlight the importance of aligning team members with business strategies in order to achieve expected benefits from the CRM investment.

This will also help to identify the metrics for the **Key Performance Indicators** (**KPI**) of the business and consequently the metrics that you will need later on to measure the **Total Cost of Ownership and Return on Investment** (**TCO/ROI**) of your project. These metrics are a compass and a measurement tool for the success of your CRM project, and will help to justify your investment but also allow you to measure the improvements you've made.

You will use these metrics as a design guide for an efficient solution that not only provides functionalities supporting the business requirements and justification of your investment, but is something that also delivers data for your CRM dashboards. This data can then help you to fine-tune business processes going forward.

In *Figure 1.3*, you'll see a graphic illustrating the process of defining the TCO/ROI metrics. Right now, don't worry too much about it as we will be looking more at this subject from different angles later on throughout this book.

The following are the steps that are taken toward defining the TCO/ROI metrics:

1. Business strategies and pain points are the main drivers of the investment.
2. A business KPI for the measurement of process improvement is selected.

3. CRM functional requirements address pain points and support business strategies.

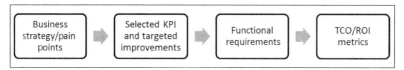

Figure 1.3: Defining CRM KPIs and metrics for success

The TCO/ROI metrics, which are the last definition in *Figure 1.3*, are measurement tools that are used to evaluate the business improvements compared with the investment in a CRM solution. You define these metrics based on business goals and selected processes that are to be improved, versus the cost of implementing the functional requirements.

Throughout this book, we will engage in deeper discussions on this topic of defining CRM KPIs, with a number of real examples that could be applied in your business. Our discussion has so far presented a very simplified way of looking at things, and real life can be a lot more complex; here's an example.

A bank and a new CEO

I was the architect and project manager of a CRM solution for a large bank with eight totally different divisions, all with different types of clients and business models. The bank went through a period of financial difficulties, and the CEO of the company was replaced by a new entrant from another country and another company. This new CEO had to make some tough decisions and therefore cutting costs by canceling some of the ongoing projects and planned investments was a priority for him.

He was commissioned to turn the company back to profit within a three-year time window by reducing operational costs and improving market share in what was a very tough environment.

At the very start of his assignment as the new CEO of this company, he called all the business leaders and board members to a meeting and asked them to provide him with a clear picture of how often they, and their respective staff, were interacting with their customers and what the outcome of all these interactions was.

In some cases, the same customer was connected with different business units for different subjects on various occasions. The new CEO wanted to know what the subjects of interactions were and what was moving customers and the market. He also wanted to know how the staff were capturing this valuable data and how they followed up on interactions and opportunities. In a nutshell, he wanted to know if the bank had a central repository for all customer interactions and the detailed data related to these interactions in order to slice and dice the data.

The new CEO wanted to make decisions based on important business metrics and so he needed this data. You would expect every organization would have this data repository, especially a large, multi-division bank, yet unfortunately, this was not the case, and actually, in many companies today, this is still not the case. We know customer interaction data is highly valuable for any business and you would agree that every company needs to capture this data.

Customers will contact your company on many different occasions and for many different reasons. They are typically asking for your advice on your products. They may submit a complaint, submit a request for support, respond to a marketing campaign, or even give you information about your company and your market.

Your customers will happily provide, at no cost, continuous feedback about your products and your services. They very often tell you what your competitors are doing and they share their sentiment with you on every single connection. You will know whether they are very happy or not so happy with every interaction. Just think about how valuable all this data could be to your business if you had a central repository of structured data about all these interactions. You could slice and dice the data for better business insight and through that, make informed business decisions.

In this bank, the new CEO found out that all these client interactions were not managed and captured systematically by all eight business units. There was no central repository of customer interactions except that of the call center, which collected limited information when capturing a customer complaint or a service request. Each business unit had its own tools and its own way of managing interactions with its clients. Clients were categorized into different segments in several databases, depending on revenue and profitability, and sometimes the same customer was managed by multiple departments. Each business unit was using a different process to manage and collect client interaction data. In some scenarios, a single client interaction was captured with different tools and different databases.

So, in this company, a central repository of the client interactions, their relationship with different business units, and the overall view of customer contacts was missing. There was no data available to the new CEO to make insightful decisions. He wanted to have the data to build data marts and eventually make decisions based on the data.

The CEO wanted to know how often customers were connecting with the company's staff, how they connected, what channel they used, how long they interacted with the employees, and what the subjects of these interactions were, along with outcomes and business opportunities with different departments of the bank. He wanted to use this data to improve processes, products, services, marketing campaigns, and customer satisfaction.

As an example, if a customer has a product or service issue and has opened a case with the customer service center and the very next day, she or he is connecting with your company's relationship manager in private banking or facility management, how is this data collected and connected? Is the information available and considered in all interactions with the customer?

Is the relationship manager informed about the open customer case while interacting about a business opportunity with her or his client? From the CRM point of view, the CEO was asking for a comprehensive 360-degree client view with full data on all the interactions, over all channels, stored as structured data in a single repository. This is often the first step toward any successful CRM implementation and is something we will cover in *Chapter 2, Getting to Know Your Customer.*

In this particular case, the CEO formed a task force to implement an enterprise-wide solution that would capture all interactions between clients with all eight business units, something that would be deployed within three months. The requirement was for a strong interaction management tool to efficiently capture, acknowledge, assign, track, and resolve all the different types of customer requests. The application would provide a facility for inter-department collaboration. He communicated his vision over all available channels with all the staff of the company over and over again, repeatedly explaining what his expectations were and why the company and all the staff needed to support this initiative.

This was a great success, mainly because of strong top-management support. We completed the requirements of gathering workshops with the eight different business units within three weeks. We then spent another three weeks compiling both the **Business Requirement Document** (**BRD**) and detailed specifications.

Next, we got approval from business leaders in three weeks, with another three weeks spent on designing and customizing the solution, based on a standard CRM packet. Parallel to that, we completed the integration work with the **Data Warehouse** (**DWH**) and the initial data load.

User Acceptance Testing (UAT) and **System Integration Testing (SIT)** each took a week, before we started the **Train-the-Trainer (TTT)** sessions in parallel to UAT and end-user training in parallel to SIT. We went live on time and on budget in less than four months!

Jumping on board with CRM

As the preceding example shows, a CRM strategy should be extended to the overall business strategy. A while back, I had a workshop with the business leaders of a company about CRM investment and CRM strategy, and the CEO of the company decided to be there for the first day as well.

The company's strategy was straightforward enough. It wanted to grow the business by 5% each year, increasing its market share by 5% year on year, and improving operational costs by 5% every year. If it should succeed with all these objectives, then the company would become the number one company in its market in five years based on actual data. This was the business strategy at the highest level and it needed to be broken down into business tactics.

I asked the CEO if it would be possible for him to share the business tactics plan with us. I wanted to know what specific steps and actions the company was taking to support the business strategy. Obviously, implementing CRM was not the only factor that could achieve this ambitious goal. There were other factors including people, processes, and infrastructure, but the chances were that CRM would be affecting other pillars as well, and the plan would help us to understand metrics and design solutions.

What follows is the plan the CEO shared with me:

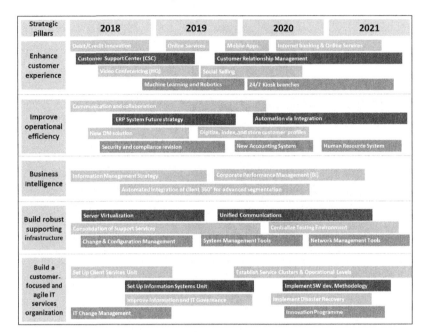

Figure 1.4: The company's business tactics plan

The company was obviously taking a number of steps to innovate both the backend and the frontend applications and processes. It wanted to improve its business intelligence and infrastructure, in order to support the five-year growth plan.

Everyone in that workshop agreed that CRM was needed not only for improving the customer experience and managing the relationship with the clients as the first pillar, as shown in *Figure 1.4*, but also as the backbone of the business strategy to support almost all other pillars of that strategic plan. It would help the company in improving operational efficiency, business intelligence, agile application services, and more. CRM needed to integrate with all processes and include all people involved in the process of innovating the business in order to work.

Introducing case studies

We're now at a point in this chapter where I can share some case studies of CRM implementations that I have been engaged with over the course of my career. Each of these case studies will help us in underlining the processes involved.

For each case study, I will be outlining the business visions, the pain points, and the environment. We will then explore how I mapped this data with the functional requirements needed to create the KPIs and metrics that will help us to build a good TCO/ROI, and justify a CRM investment.

The aim here is to give you an overview of what these cases have in common and how business vision could drive the functional requirements in different scenarios. In addition, we really want to be looking at and understanding why it is so important to align with the business objectives.

These case studies are derived from the BRD, the **Request for Information** (**RFI**) document, and the **Request for Proposals** (**RFP**) document, as well as both the implementation and the delivery of the solution. They include information about the environment, organization, processes, and integration with current and future systems, along with the foundation to enable flexible development, low-cost maintenance, and ongoing operation of the systems.

There are other factors influencing the design of a sustainable CRM solution, such as security, usability, portability, performance, and possibly the regulations, which we will address in more detail across other chapters in this book.

In these case studies, we focus on:

- The business environment
- The pain points (or drivers)
- The business objectives

All of those are factors that are important to the key stakeholders, processes, and functional requirements. Your design will need to consider business strategies/objectives, the business pain points, the existing application environment, the processes, the functional requirements, and the strong buy-in from key users.

In *Figure 1.5*, we see the top three drivers for your solution design, including business objectives, business pain points, and the application environment. All of these will provide functions and processes to enable key users to improve the operational efficiencies:

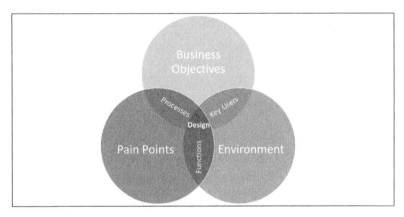

Figure 1.5: Key elements for functional design

For confidentiality reasons, these case studies have been fully anonymized, so if you find some similarities in the stories with your organization, then it is purely accidental.

The reason behind having five case studies here is to demonstrate a rich variety of business objectives, how they resemble or are different to each other, and how factors such as company size, market, and business objectives influence the functional requirements and the design of a solution.

Even though every business is different, I have tried to keep the same format when describing the use cases, to make it easy to compare and draw a conclusion from them.

Case study 1 – A mid-size European retailer selling goods

This is a CRM project from a mid-size company with about 1,000 employees in a small country in Western Europe. The company is selling goods and services into the retail (consumer) segment. The market size is about two million consumers, while the company is selling to about 200 local and foreign commercial customers. It has many local competitors in this small country and is facing even more competition from abroad and digital disruptors.

Pain points

The proliferation of choice in this small country has changed customers' behavior and attitudes, with an increased demand for transparency, and individualized or customized products or services. Most products and services in this segment have become commoditized within a very small market. Customer loyalty, customer retention, and share of the customer wallet have become increasingly challenging for this company.

Channel integration has also emerged as a key requirement to ensure a uniformed customer experience across all the channels, including the Internet when addressing the younger generations. This includes integration with social media for social selling and social advertising. To meet these challenges and business pain points, the company decided to implement a CRM strategy for its consumer sector.

In *Figure 1.6*, we see the top three business pain points for case study 1:

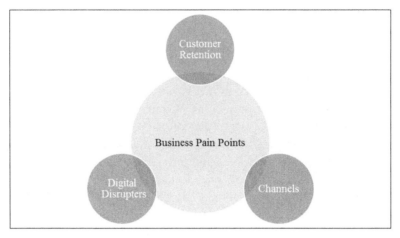

Figure 1.6: Business pain points for case study 1

For this company, the top business pain points were unsatisfied customers, losing market share to digital disrupters, and a lack of social media integration with the sales and marketing channel.

Business objectives

The company's business objectives were to implement a CRM strategy in order to transform its consumer business into a customer-centric business. It aimed to offer more individual products and services with the following tactics:

- Use CRM capabilities to understand existing customers, in addition to providing a single company-wide view of customer interactions. This would allow the company to model current and future value potential to offer effectively individual services and products.

- Launch targeted and effective marketing campaigns based on customer value segments to increase the share of wallet, optimize lifetime value, and reduce marketing costs.

- Gain a competitive advantage from superior customer service through interaction management across channels.

- Provide customers with consistent and uniform experiences across touch points of the contact center, direct sales, outbound sales, and retail stores through channel integration.

- Increase the profitability, revenue, and ROI through directed cross-sell and upsell efforts using *propensity to buy* through the lifecycle stage of the customer.

- Improve sales effectiveness and tracking.

- Implement an appropriate CRM solution(s) that will support the preceding objectives.

Functional requirements

To achieve these business objectives, we then identified a number of key functionalities for CRM application, including:

- **360-degree view**: Provide a single company-wide view of the customer by aggregating the data from multiple systems about the profile, products, interactions, service requests, complaints, campaign history, and so on. CRM is able to display the details from various systems without replicating them in a CRM database, which is sometimes not practicable. There should be an ability to aggregate this data before displaying it on the **user interface** (**UI**), in order to avoid performance issues.

- **Campaign management**: Primarily, there are four types of campaigns that need to be supported first:

    ○ Acquisition of new clients and cross-selling to existing clients.

    ○ Pre-approved offers for existing clients.

    ○ Usage-based offers for existing clients.

    ○ Running of special programs based on predictive modeling.

Over a period of time, the business intelligence unit built a data mart. The data mart extracts data from different source systems, such as **Enterprise Resource Planning** (**ERP**) applications, and loads it into the data mart on a regular basis. The CRM application is able to run various campaigns on this data mart.

The key capabilities are:

- Campaign planning.
- Campaign definition.
- Customer segmentation.
- Event detection.
- List management.
- Campaign delivery (contact center, SMS, email, direct mailer, Internet, and so on) and response management.
- Campaign effectiveness analysis.

The segmentation capabilities of the tools support the building of a logical layer over the existing data mart and provide UI support for developing the target list intuitively without writing any SQL queries. The application allows the scheduling of multi-stage campaigns for recurring programs:

- **Service request management**: The consumer department receives various types of service requests via emails, calls, stores, and so on. The requirement is for a strong case management tool to efficiently capture, acknowledge, assign, track, and resolve the requests. The application provides a facility for inter-department collaboration and workflow management, along with an automation facility to define standard routes for different types of requests. The application is able to talk to multiple systems for data updates and provide a facility for Service Level Agreement (SLA) management.

- **Contact center management**: The company has established a 24/7 contact center as part of its alternate delivery strategy to provide a channel for customer service requests either through a toll-free number, email, or the Internet. The contact center's role is to capture customer requests, feedback, inquiries, complaints, and suggestions. The contact center currently operates on the Avaya platform, and a CRM platform integrates with the **Computer Telephony Integration (CTI)** infrastructure to be able to search the customer data, leverage **Interactive Voice Response (IVR)** functionality, manage call scripts, and log the interactions. This channel can also use other interaction means such as email management, online chat, or co-browsing.

The other functionalities provided by a CRM application are listed here:

- Lead management:
  - Lead acquisition
  - Lead duplication

- ○ Lead qualification
- ○ Lead assignment
- ○ Lead tracking
- ○ Lead source analysis

- Sales management:
  - ○ Sales planning
  - ○ Activity management
  - ○ Pipeline management
  - ○ Calendar and task management

- Customer analytics including customized dashboards and ad hoc reporting.

In *Figure 1.7*, we see the top functional requirements for case study 1:

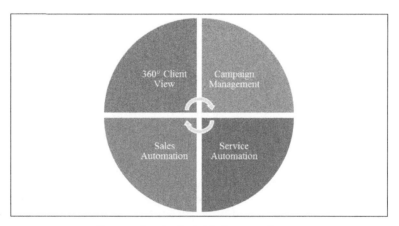

Figure 1.7: Functional priorities for case study 1

The top functional requirements were to create a comprehensive 360-degree client view and provide a single company-wide view of the customers to enable various types of service requests via emails, calls, stores, and so on. It was also required to introduce sales and service automation for better service request handling and improved sales-pipeline management.

Case study 2 – A mid-size Eastern European retailer selling consumer goods

This is a mid-size company in a small Eastern European country, selling high-end service-intensive commodities to consumers. Currently, it is number three in its market, and has the ambitious plan to become number two in just over five years. The company is planning on achieving this by increasing marketing, sales, and services effectively, in order to gain a higher market share.

Pain points

This company had two different CRM applications in place with limited capabilities that were not integrated. One was an in-house CRM, while the second one was from SAP (a German enterprise software company), which was expected to be discontinued. The systems were used mainly for **small and medium-sized enterprises (SME)** and corporate clients, and offered management for the consumer clients in a 360-degree view, campaign management, **Next-Best Offer (NBO)** propositions, sales processes, and reporting.

The company felt the pain of not having the capabilities to support social media sales and marketing initiatives. Likewise, by having two different CRM systems that were not interoperable and not supporting the latest technologies, such as AI, the company was struggling.

In *Figure 1.8*, we see the top three business pain points for case study 2:

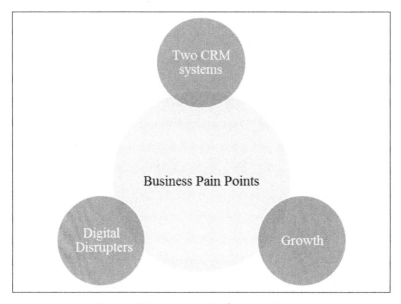

Figure 1.8: Business pain points for case study 2

The top business pain points for this company were two separated CRM systems, and therefore the lack of a single repository of customer data; the growing competition from digital disrupters; and an aggressive growth plan that needed additional management tools.

Business objectives

The company wanted to implement a new enterprise CRM system to replace its two existing CRM applications and to support the company's growth plan by leveraging newer technologies.

The new system would enable improvements in the performance and capabilities of operational CRM in the areas of sales, service, and marketing automation for existing and potential customers across all segments, including consumer, SME, micro, and corporate clients, including but not limited to:

- Generation and distribution of sales leads.

- Increase sales generated through effective marketing campaigns.

- Improve the rate of sales opportunities converted to a product sale.

- Improve knowledge management and leverage machine learning in order to increase the ability for targeted marketing and sales.

- Provide supporting applications and **business intelligence** (**BI**) tools for stores and regional offices to manage and analyze a client's product portfolio.

- Provide operational reports and dashboards for CRM data and sales.

- Provide tools to improve employees' collaboration in order to increase employee engagement, productivity, and satisfaction.

- Give the ability to support and to maintain different sales and product pricing management processes.

- Improve marketing automation with additional BI, AI, and effectiveness measurement tools.

- Increase engagement of the clients through community buildings including Facebook and other social media platforms.

- E-channel and social media integration, including the ability to provide the business logic of a CRM platform to customers via social media platforms, and adding a social media profile of clients into a CRM 360-degree client view.

Functional requirements

The following functional requirements were identified as top priorities for phase one of the project:

- 360-degree client view across all customer segments.

- Event management for sales and marketing events.

- Campaign management, with the ability to set campaign targets, generate target lists, and create campaign performance reports.

- Prospects, offer, and preference management.

- Pricing tool.

- Task and staff management tool.

- Sales processes, showing client needs, referrals, and onboarding, and so on.

- Both reporting and individual role-based dashboards.

- Accounts management and monitoring, including call reports.

- Automated tasks and templates for predefined events.

- Client revenue management.

- Microsoft Office integration, including Outlook.

- Integration with an SMS platform.

- Mass mailing solution.

- Social CRM.

- Integration with both the Cisco system and Altitude for the contact center.

- Real-time integration.

- The interaction between CRM and DWH.

- Integration with all core systems, including **Enterprise Resource Planning (ERP)**.

- Integration with analytical tools and old CRM systems data.

- Integration with Active Directory.

- Provide the ability to use external data solutions.

- Intra-company and intra-group collaboration management.

- Provide clients with business analytics.

- Integration with the company's Advanced Data Analytics system.

- Provide business insights.

In *Figure 1.9*, we see the top functional requirements for case study 2:

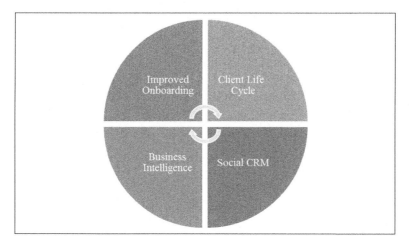

Figure 1.9: Functional priorities for case study 2

The functional priorities for this company were to implement a better customer onboarding process, improve customer lifecycle management, integrate with social media such as social selling and social advertisement, and introduce business intelligence tools for better reporting and dashboards.

Case study 3 – A new entrant in the UK retailer sector

This is a new entrant in a very tough consumer market in the UK, with giant competitors that are already very well established in the same market. The company sells commodity products to the mass market and currently has 100,000 customers. It has the ambitious goal of growing the business fivefold in just five years.

Pain points

There are tough market conditions for a new company, especially while competing with the big market players in a saturated market. In a nutshell, the company decided to implement operational CRM in order to gain process efficiency, reduce operational costs, and improve marketing. The company wanted to build a customer-centric business, and effectively and securely underpin the next five years of growth aspirations.

In *Figure 1.10*, we see the top three business pain points for case study 3:

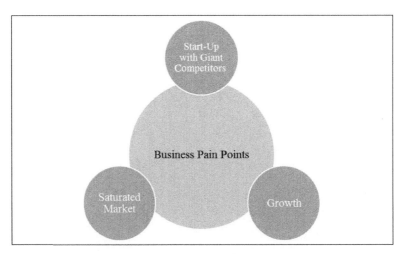

Figure 1.10: Business pain points for case study 3

The top business pain points here were that this was a start-up company in a very saturated market and there was a need to have strong growth in order to survive.

Business objectives

The company aims to exceed the expectations of customers every day and make them "fans." It introduced a number of quirky programs to entice new members, such as dog-friendly environments with free biscuits and a kids' corner, along with a host of other services in stores to make clients feel at home.

With over 2,000 new customers being added each week, the company rapidly needed to update its systems to cope with the demand and deliver better service levels. To accommodate the rapid growth, it decided to go fully into the cloud for all of its customer-facing applications, including CRM.

The business leaders of the company want to achieve higher process efficiency, continuously improve operational costs, and improve marketing operations to support the strategy of growing the business in the high-street market (mass market). They have the vision to grow the business in the next five years from:

- 100,000+ to 500,000 customers.
- 600 to 3,000 employees.
- 15 to 150 stores.

To support its aim of becoming one of the UK's leading players and support its growth, the company is investing heavily in client relationship management to support customer strategies including:

- Supporting and engaging the company's staff and employees in all customer interaction processes and when promoting the company's culture of excellent service delivery.

- Building a trust relationship with customers by letting them feel that the person they are talking to is well informed about who they are and is in a position to provide excellent customer service.

- Helping the client processes within the company to happen efficiently, effectively, and to prescribed SLAs.

- Working with the company's sales forces and sales managers to ensure they are supported with KPIs, tools, and the visibility they need to do their jobs effectively.

- Supporting the company's infrastructure/environment in the processes of growth. This should be reflective of the progressive growth the company is expecting to have.

Functional requirements

The first and most important functionality for the company is to create a comprehensive 360-degree client view. The solution provides integration with Single Customer View and Agile Analytics. The Single Customer View and the related Customer Data Management/ Analytics capability are developed as enterprise capabilities outside of the current client applications and provide both an operational Single Customer View and an analytical view.

The analytical view is based on the company's data warehouse platform. All CRM components and processes are integrated with the Single Customer View including operational and analytic components to support:

- Data management
- Integration
- Analytics using external and internal datasets

This is a multi-year investment in developing the capabilities and key functionalities that the company has identified for a CRM application, in order to achieve its business objectives and bring a lot of automation, such as:

- **Deeper client insight**: For example, role-based Single Client View across the company and business areas.

- **Richer functionality**: A capability that supports the full breadth of client processes, recognizing that these differ by client segment and across businesses.

- **Automation and usability**: Improved front-office efficiency through automation and access to responsive and easy-to-use tools.

- **Enhanced controls**: Provide a robust control framework that can manage role-based access to client data, control client service consumption, and ensure compliance with policy and regulation.

- **Scalable and modular architecture**: Build capabilities iteratively with the ability to scale with evolving requirements and meet the customized needs of particular product areas.

- **Productivity improvements**: This will allow the company to realize business efficiencies that are required to support the ambitious growth plan at lower operational costs.

The system provides a rich marketing functionality for these purposes:

- Create and manage campaigns across events, email campaigns, and online campaigns.

- Use segmentation tools to create dynamic lists.

- Full company view and role-based dashboards of events and campaigns.

- Automate marketing distribution, integration with third-party email blast tools, campaign file and distribution lists determined by client preferences/ subscriptions, and/or bespoke campaign lists. Capture readership/bounce-rate metrics for analysis.

- Target events to specific clients based upon user-defined filters, client preferences, and segmentation rules.

- Attendee management for attendee information, invites, preferences, feedback, and recent attendance.

- Service awards, management surveys, and awards.

- Mail merge and Office compatibility.

- ROI analysis tools and campaign statistics. Measure the effectiveness of campaigns, through tracking the campaign member through the sales cycle from lead, to opportunity, to sale.

A rich call list functionality to provide:

- Default and user-defined call lists based upon user preferences.

- Configuration of dynamic call lists based on market events, trigger points, call-level alerts, and so on.

- Search and filter facilities.

- Single click, intuitive interaction capture, and fully configurable forms.

- CTI capabilities, including click to dial, and the ability to integrate CTI connectors into telephony systems.

- Call logging: single or group (mass action) with fully customizable call reports required.

- Workflow management with bespoke workflow required.

Comprehensive case management to:

- Incorporate email and case handling into customer service, including:
    - ○ Automatic case creation rules from a single email queue.
    - ○ Routing rule sets.
    - ○ SLAs.
    - ○ Queues.
- Enable effective tracking of customer email requests between multiple departments.
- Track SLA and escalations of customer requests received via email.
- Create flexible and extensible workflows, and dialog capabilities that allow you to drive repeatable and predictable service experiences.

Extended reporting and dashboards analytics:

- Standard report types.
- Report customization tools.
- Report-writing template tools to create a template, define formats, and chart types.
- Formulas and conditional highlighting.
- Formatting compatibility; for example, with mobile devices.
- Excel compatibility.
- Customizable dashboards, both through real-time and historical snapshots, allowing the drag-and-drop creation of customizable dashboards; that is, pie charts, bar charts, and line graphs.

Better collaboration, including:

- Chat groups and forums (private and public); for example, clients, contacts, opportunities, documents, and so on.
- Social media integration, through LinkedIn, Twitter, and Facebook.
- Follow topics and make recommendations.
- File sharing and feedback.
- Alerts and notifications.
- Mobile capability.
- History and audit trail.
- Integration with video conferencing tools.
- Workflow approval through collaboration tools.
- Thematic and thread search.

In *Figure 1.11*, we can see the top functional requirements for case study 3:

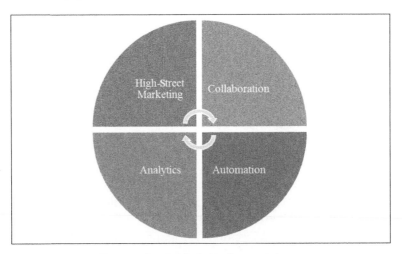

Figure 1.11: Functional priorities for case study 3

The top functional requirements for this company were to introduce mass marketing tools that would enable addressing consumers in the high-street market, be able to create a collaboration platform for employees both in the back office and front office, implement automation in customer processes, and use powerful analytical tools to enable better insight into the business and market.

Case study 4 – A large financial services company in Africa

This is a well-known financial services provider in Africa that is operating in a very competitive market across continental Africa. It is no longer defined by its products or even its brand. Its expectations are not limited to comparing its products and services to its industry competitors, but also to providing the best customer service it can in a time with digital disruption posed by Fintech companies. The Fintech sector will undoubtedly be in a permanent state of disruption within this industry, especially in Africa. The company realized that it could no longer ignore the reality that it needed to focus on keeping up with its clients' expectations rather than competitors.

Pain points

Customers being highly influenced by the Internet and mobile applications was taking the market share of this bank away. As a large and long-time player in the market, it still had many old legacy applications and had fallen behind with the latest technologies.

The challenge was how efficiently the company could leverage its existing investment in applications, data, and skills in order to enable the digital transformation needed. The bank wanted to provide customers with better service and a positive experience in every interaction, using all kinds of channels.

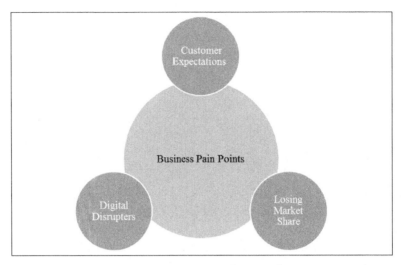

Figure 1.12: Business pain points for case study 4

The top business pain points here were that this company was losing its market share, customers' expectations were increasing, and it was facing challenges from multiple digital disrupters.

Business objectives

The goal was to enable the bank to transition from a predominantly product-centric organization to a more client-centric one. The task for the bank was to differentiate itself in a very competitive marketplace by engaging clients to win new business. It needed to grow its clients in Africa and international markets. In a nutshell, the bank's vision was putting the clients first, creating sustainable shareholder value, striving for excellence, igniting energy in others, making people think and act as an owner, making diversity happen, and building upon the bank's reputation of being a trustworthy partner.

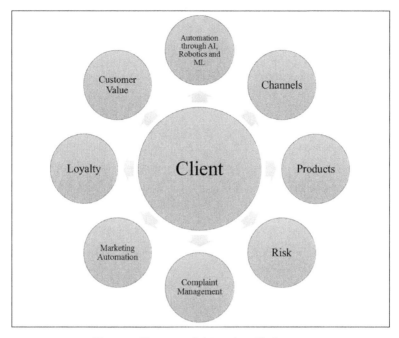

Figure 1.13: The company's interaction with clients

There were two desired outcomes from a fundamental transformation of the bank's client and digital offering:

1. **Client advocacy**: For this brand, its name is synonymous with client centricity, and the value that it adds to clients is recognized and respected by them and the market. Clients are its best ambassadors, with the power to promote excellence to other prospective clients.

2. **Breaking client inertia**: Offering a level of measurable value that is so significant and unique to clients that they are excited about their relationship with the bank, and so they put effort and urgency into pursuing that relationship.

The bank's client-centric strategy is now being driven through two primary approaches:

1. Via cultural messaging and reinforcement through bank executives, bank-wide communication, strategic presentations, and the activation of the lead purpose statement with an emphasis on brand principles.

2. Via the delivery of the **Customer Experience Program (CEP)**, which is a set of projects aimed at building the data, processes, and technology platforms from which the bank's client onboarding and maintenance processes are being designed, with a mindset to be more client centric.

Considering the preceding, the bank is simplifying and improving the way in which it interacts with clients, with the initial focus being establishing a solid foundation on which to build. The CEP's vision is to create a differentiated, seamless, and first-class client experience throughout the bank's client value chain, from prospecting and onboarding, to product sales and maintenance.

Functional requirements

Due to the depth and breadth of the strategy for the bank's business and digital transformation, its CEP was split into two phases. Each phase had one year of implementation time and one year of window in between to let employees adapt to the new changes.

Phase one of the CEP focused on data architecture alignment and data clean up in order to achieve a single view of the client, as well as the establishment of a single client team to assist clients from an onboarding and maintenance perspective:

*   A simplified technical and data architecture for the optimization of processes for end-to-end client onboarding and maintenance functions.

- The creation of a definitive bank Client Master List for client-friendly, simplified, and reusable client forms, legal agreements, and documents.

- Improvements in client data governance and data quality for the implementation of the **Know Your Client** (**KYC**) API utility.

- Implementation of a workflow solution for client onboarding for a reduction in client touchpoints.

In detail, these are the functional requirements for the Client Golden Record system:

- Define which client attributes make up the **Master Data Record** (**MDR**) for clients and hierarchies, as well as the different views required.

- Define which target system will be the master for each attribute as part of the journey to simplify the client architecture (what are the fields and where will they be hosted?).

- Client data store.

- The group has made a decision to make **Customer Information Mainframe System** (**CIS**) a master data source for Proof of Existence (Core Customer Data) purposes as part of the customer strategy. Core customer data is stored and maintained on various systems without automated integration. This has resulted in different versions of customer information existing on various systems.

- The client data store delivered a Client Golden Record and a Master Client List that is comprehensive, accurate, and accessible to everyone who has an impact on the client experience.

Single client team structure:

- Create a single back office team for onboarding and maintenance of clients across corporate investment banking.

The system of record:

- Update the CIS and the bank's client systems with the updated KYC client information.
- De-activate all invalid client records.

Client onboarding workflow:

- Introduction of workflow to enable account management processes and lay the foundation for a streamlined, scalable, and automated client onboarding and maintenance discipline for corporate clients.

Building blocks for phase one:

- Streamline corporate bank onboarding and maintenance forms, as well as introduce the overall **Master Service Agreement (MSA)**.
- To reduce the amount of paperwork and duplicate information requested from clients during the onboarding process, both for new clients as well as for existing clients.
- Create an API that enables the bank system to interface with the outside vendor KYC utility.

Phase two of the CEP aims to deliver several value add-ons that are impossible to deliver without the foundation put in place by phase one; for example, improved and predictive client insights, service management, sales collaboration, customer relationship management tools, and a digital omnichannel experience for the bank's clients as it strives to be a more client-centric business.

Onboarding and maintenance:

- The continuation of the development and implementation of a workflow in the client service teams across the organization.

- Continuation of the simplification of client and product onboarding forms.

- Service optimization and improvements.

Replacing the old CRM:

- Implementation of a new CRM solution and decommissioning the current CRM. The objective is to improve the sales management (leads/ opportunities and client interaction management) as well as cover marketing management (manage and track campaigns and events), plus service management (create and manage client records, related contacts, and service requests).

Client data utility:

- The client data utility project will seek to implement the Golden Source Client and counterparty module. A project will perform a proof of concept undertaking to establish the suitability of the Golden Source platform to meet the bank's client data consolidation requirements, testing its master data management, workflow, onboarding, rules engine, and data integration capabilities.

Omnichannel:

- Implementation of an omnichannel solution for the bank, which facilitates the creation and delivery of inbound and outbound communications and content, including for marketing, new product introductions, notifications, instruction confirmations, and product lifecycle correspondence.

Africa and international:

- To streamline and standardize the onboarding processes for Africa and international subsidiaries, including onboarding, product forms, document storage, server maintenance, and client service requests.

Client analytics:

- Establishing and embedding client analytics, providing client insights to client-facing business units, with the capability to profile clients and accordingly tailor propositions.

Corporate banking service:

- Create a client-centric service model commencing with the Corporate Banking business. The most important element is to have a structured call report.

Social media:

- Providing social media integration such as Twitter, Facebook, LinkedIn, and a similar African (social listening) activity overview in the 360-degree client profile.

- A CRM should be able to monitor social networks under predefined parameters, in order for the bank to be able to better react and respond.

- On social media platforms, if a client asks for advice on credit or discusses issues (advice, complaints, or praise), the bank should be able to respond in real time by communicating with clients. In addition, a change of profile information should initiate changes to the system, including entry to marketing.

In *Figure 1.14*, we see the top functional requirements for case study 4:

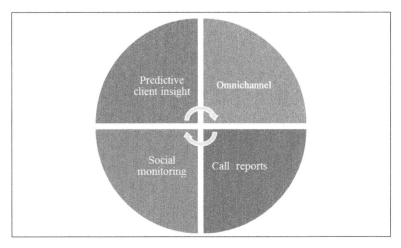

Figure 1.14: Functional priorities for case study 4

The top functional priorities for this company were to enable predictive customer insights by measuring customer sentiment and activities. In addition to this, it also wanted to implement an omnichannel process engine for handling customer requests over all the different channels, integrate with social media for social selling and social advertisement activities, and apply call reports to create better insights for capturing the details of all customer interactions.

Case study 5 – A very large global private bank with international operations

This is a globally successful private banking and investment firm. I would like to extend the case study into details of processes, as private banking and investment is one of the most sophisticated sectors, and there are more comprehensive requirements here than any other CRM project I have ever seen. This firm is one of the largest subsidiaries in Western Europe.

The company wanted to leverage years of investment in developing processes, procedures, and commercial tools to support the business goals of being a global player in private banking in terms of winning, maintaining, and nurturing current and potential clients (leads). While at the same time, it wanted to create superior sales processes, including those processes that would help, in a sustainable manner, to accomplish the vision of the company.

Pain points

The company had a sophisticated CRM application in place, but it was still not doing exactly what the business users and relationship managers would expect from the perspective of having an efficient way of serving high-end customers, such as dealing with the vast amount of data about customers. Business applications have become more complex in the course of the last few years, and relationship managers and investors have become increasingly overloaded in dealing with the many applications and data sources.

In a nutshell, the company had developed a successful sales process that technically could not be managed with the existing CRM tools without heavy investment.

In *Figure 1.15*, we see the top three business pain points for case study 5:

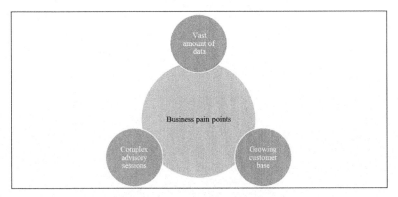

Figure 1.15: Business pain points for case study 5

The top business pain points for this company were the increasing amount of data from business applications, the growing business and customer base, and the very complex sales processes that needed to be better managed.

Business objectives

Currently, the company has a set of applications and processes to support business management and customer care within the private banking and investment business sector. With the new CRM, it intends to improve all the client tools by means of the implementation of an enterprise-wide CRM application, which will serve to support the excellent management of client relationships.

The new system is designed to unify and centralize the diverse tools, and the vast amount of data available to investors and financial advisors in the company across the many different applications and data stores. This is to support the business processes of the whole organization with faster response times, and lower operating costs to improve the business efficiency and elevate customer relationships to the next level.

A CRM application is designed to give a better user experience in order to:

- Improve financial advisory sessions by providing better client services and having the capacity to analyze client conditions accurately, along with offering financial planning that meets their requirements.

- Facilitate the efficient management of the business processes in which the advisory service articulates the unique position of the bank; that is to say:

    ○ The winning of customer trust by providing better customer insight to **Financial Advisors (FA)**.

- ○ Improving customer loyalty by providing faster and more profitable services to investors.

- ○ Managing the abandonment and recapture of client processes in both private and institutional investors.

- ○ Allowing higher productivity across the organization through integration with applications to support collaborative functions across a global team of investors.

- ○ Supporting the daily activities of the FAs, including follow-up with client activities for a faster response to market and client needs.

- ○ Supporting centralized, territorial, and local workforces by means of generating alarms for related events in the market supported by the global workforce.

Functional requirements

This project is framed fundamentally in the scope of the private banking and investment business unit of this global financial services provider. It is based particularly on the requirements of the financial advisors for **Private Banking** (**PB**), but also it covers the requirements of related business entities such as the business development unit, research, and **Corporate Investment Banking** (**CIB**) groups. Last but not least, the project needs to support a digital transformation the company is going through.

There are a few challenges when attempting a successful transformation, starting with the question of costs versus output. Remember how we talked about ROI? How does this company transform and what does it get back from the investment in this transformation? How smoothly and intelligently can it manage the transformation without any major investment and business disruption?

Finally, how does the company leverage the enormous amount of data it is collecting every day and every hour while serving its customers? As the processes and roles in the PB and CIB groups are the most sophisticated when it comes to a CRM solution, we will cover some of them in more detail here.

This is not only related to private banking, but could be applied in any other business where customer relationships are an essential part of the success of the business.

With this new CRM, the company is consolidating all existing business solutions and processes that have helped to successfully grow the business and support the overall strategy of the company. The new CRM should build on the investments of the last few years. This includes integrating the tools that were supporting the daily operations of the business and all 100+ financial advisors.

The new CRM system needs to incorporate both commercial and non-commercial applications, including all the sales tools and processes that were developed with in-house resources.

In the definition of commercial systems, the best practices of a company are obtained through a set of critical processes, information, and business standards, with the main goal of serving each customer or potential lead effectively in terms of advising, relationship management, product offering, and services, in order to win business, develop, grow, and ultimately avoid losing customers.

The company has established a system for each particular segment of clients; for example, the minimum contact annually with a particular client segment (calls and visits (activities)) to guide FAs.

The four main processes that make up the client lifecycle are:

- Winning a client (pick-up process).
- Nurture and development processes.

- Grow customer loyalty.

- Management of abandonment and recapture.

These processes constitute the client lifecycle at a very high level and the processes that follow are the supporting pillars. The new CRM solution will then need to bring all these procedures under the same umbrella and build a central repository of client data with role-based dashboards and control panels to orchestrate business more efficiently.

For the pick-up process, which is how this bank is defining the process of winning a new client, success relies mainly on the principles of teamwork and co-management. The teamwork is guaranteed through the allocation of client teams within the company. Each team has several FAs who will have to deal directly with their assigned clients.

Throughout the process of pick-up, which is a company-developed process that is used to identify and manage those potential leads who are susceptible to becoming clients of the company, you'll also encounter those who are nonqualified references (non-qualified leads), references, and opportunities to manage. A client is managed by the **new client process** when they have spent less than a year with the company. This is reflected in the particular processes, views, and dashboard listings of new clients.

The next step is the **nurturing and development** processes that are carried out on existing clients. Nurturing is mainly those activities in the day-to-day life of the relationship manager or the FA, whereas development process is about increasing the entailment of existing clients; for example, an increase of portfolio or share of wallet. These processes start with the identification of new business opportunities and go up to the closing of deals.

Next is **customer loyalty management**. This includes all of the activities developed with the purpose of maintaining and increasing relationship lifetime with the most profitable clients; for example, through specific campaigns and events that are organized for these clients.

After that stage, there's the process of **abandonment and client recapture**. This is activities developed with the purpose of anticipating (early detection) and managing the loss of customers, as well as recapturing those profitable clients who were lost.

Figure 1.16 illustrates the complex client lifecycle for this company, including the client pick-up stage, the process of onboarding a new client, the nurture and development of a client relationship, improved loyalty management tools, and last but not least, the process of a client leaving and winning them back (recapture):

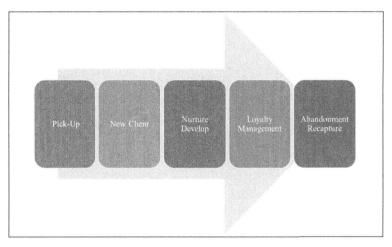

Figure 1.16: The client lifecycle

This company created a very comprehensive customer lifecycle management process for its **High-net-worth Individuals (HNWI)** whose investible assets (such as stocks and bonds) exceed €1 million.

The sales team

The sales team consists of different roles from different business units and the new CRM platform, which needs to fully support the complex organizational structure and processes that play a significant role in the architecture of a CRM solution. This is actually an integral part of the successful CRM solution for the company. Therefore, we have to take a closer look at the roles of the protagonists who deal with clients:

- **Coverage**: These people have a clear focus to activate, develop, and increase business with new clients or increase business with a profitable existing client base of the company in order to increase the share of wallet. They are called hunters internally.

- **Developers**: They focus on the relationship with existing clients, right after customer onboarding and throughout the relationship lifecycle, in order to develop new client opportunities.

- **Research specialists**: They support the FA and the relationship manager in the identification of business opportunities, as well as supporting the preparation for visits with new potential customers or with ex-clients. The research specialist assists the FA in overcoming possible objections, while supporting developers with due diligence research.

- **Middle office**: Its mission is to support the FA in putting together financial proposals for investment and customized information specific to the client (comparative evolution of a portfolio, risks, studies, and so on).

- **Group leaders**: This includes the director of the office/branch (if large enough) and is the central piece of the process of management and collaboration. Group leaders report to the regional directors and are able to delegate certain activities to the team leaders. The group leader has, therefore, a superset of functions of an FA and is also directly involved in the processes with clients through winning, maintaining and development, loyalty, and recapture.

- **Golden Pipe Sales (GPS)**: Throughout the last few years, the company has developed its own sales methodology, which is a unique sales process (`https://blog.hubspot.com/sales/sales-process-`) based on its market and products. GPS is a new in-house business solution that is managing these sales processes consisting of a number of processes for the Gold client segment.

FAs and relationship managers start the day with their sales funnels created in GPS. GPS has been successfully piloted and deployed in most branches of the company, and it supports the commercial network of the company across Europe, managed by locations and territories. 70% of the total business is already managed by GPS and it has been proven to be a successful sales methodology for the company. GPS will be on everyone's home page at the start of the day with the new CRM.

In *Figure 1.17*, we see GPS implemented within a CRM. This starts with lead management, before moving to developing business opportunities, improved customer onboarding processes, and business planning.

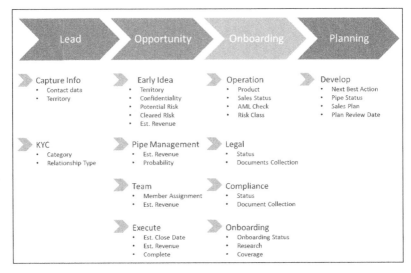

Figure 1.17: The GPS process

All of these processes will be explained in more detail in this book. In summary, the new CRM implementation includes an FA desktop, supporting the definition of roles and organizational structure within the team, supporting GPS processes, presenting related KPIs, supporting commercial workflows, providing role-based control panels/dashboards, and being supported by applications and functions managing the sales pipeline, which is placed on the home page.

The implementation of the system articulates through use cases, which are associated with activities and are monitored by a reporting tool that lists the client activities. GPS was developed with only one goal: to support processes and provide transparency to business leaders by monitoring the activities of clients and FAs. It needs to integrate with an automated agenda of activities and facilitate the change management that is crucial to streamlining the consultation processes. As the processes have been successful, the company decided to extend the GPS both in functionality and territory.

All offices will receive the new CRM system, as well as extended functionalities of GPS, including automated agenda management, individual KPIs, and control panels, so that all FAs of the commercial network can use the new enhanced system based on the success of GPS.

All of this will help to build a centralized repository of all sales activities that are aligned with and supported by a global network of investor relationship specialists. This will enable better business insights and orchestration, which will be a supporting pillar for continuous business improvements and even higher profitability in the coming years. The solution provides a portal enabling the FAs to have a better insight into their clients, sales pipe, activities, and more. The main function is to provide a client 360-degree view.

The portal includes the most critical operations of an FA, including:

- **The control panel, the entry page, or home page**: Mainly for the FAs and investor relationship managers. This page provides a quick view of daily activities, emails, and business-related alerts. It is the starting page to search/look for all related elements. It includes a dashboard for the FAs, which is individually tailored for each member of the team. The page also supports extended GPS processes for users such as FAs, relationship managers, and administrators, along with supporting the consultation process and financial planning.

- **The client card**: Allows FAs to consult and store commercial-related data about their clients. It's also the integration point with other systems; for example, the order entry. This is an extended 360-degree client view, which we will cover extensively in the next chapter.

- **The client flash**: This page gathers and displays the most important information about the client; for example, position holding, transactions, last activities, conversations, and more. It provides a quick snapshot of the business in terms of a particular client.

- **Identification and qualification**: This page contains client information coming from the back office (current addresses, accounts, nationality, and so on). Also, it provides information about the sales team that takes care of this client and opportunities. Also included are qualitative documents (financial planning, assets, and so on), a professional profile of the client, opportunities, objectives, family data, and more.

- **Business actions**: The management of business activities with clients. This data is extended and migrated to the new CRM system to support sales process automation and related data for regulatory authorities, such as the **Markets in Financial Instruments Directive** (**MiFID**).

- **Holding**: This page lists the positions of the client for any member of the client team. It allows for tracking loss and gains, movements of the account, and the composition of the portfolio (distribution of assets).

- **Share of wallet**: On this page, the FA maintains information about the position that the client has with an outside company/competitor. It includes the share of wallet and also serves to highlight the interest that a client can have in other products (NBO).

- **Order entry**: This page is simply a link to the application for order entry. This will be later realized natively in the new CRM system.

- **Notification archive**: Provides the FA with a list of documents and notifications sent to his or her clients, allowing them to search, filter, sort, and print notifications sent to clients.

- **Documentation**: For each client, group of investors, or corporate accounts there are obligatory documents that are scanned and stored in the file system. Under this page, the FA is provided with functions to manage and explore documents scanned for each client. This also supports the MIFID and **General Data Protection Regulation** (**GDPR**) processes.

- **Account planning**: Here the relationship manager will do their account planning, see account-related notifications, see consultation plans, get alerts, and follow up on tasks.

- **100 days**: The company strongly believes that the first 100 days of the client life cycle are the most valuable for building a strong relationship and for cross- and up-selling opportunities. Here the FA will follow the processes for nurturing and building a long-lasting relationship with new clients.

- **Sales management**: The FA will follow and monitor the progress of leads and consider opportunity management. This page keeps information regarding client telephone calls and visits (call reports) and turns a lead to an opportunity, which should turn into a client. This is basically reflecting the GPS processes.

- **Intermediation**: Related to the intermediation of the type of news, analysis, and documents.

- **Learning**: Contains the list of mandatory and recommended training and compliance courses, readings, questionnaires, and the tracking of the completion of mandatory courses.

- **Markets**: Quotations of the different indices and values that have the ability to capture historical data and export it to Excel.

- **Financial planning**: Designed to hold general information regarding the financial planning of the client and the investment objectives. This tool collects data that is duplicated in other systems including a profile of the client, the personal data of the client's contacts, their objectives, and a proposal. This is a mandatory process for regulatory authorities in most countries.

What to take away from the five case studies

As we can see in these five case studies, one of the most common elements of all CRM projects is building a comprehensive 360-degree client view that will be a supporting pillar for sales, marketing, and services processes automation. It is also important to support the company in building long-lasting relationships with clients, while managing the business and resources more efficiently based on insightful decisions, at a reduced cost of operation.

A comparison of these five case studies also reveals that every organization must implement its own unique sales process based on its vertical, products, industry, culture, and market position. What works for one company will often totally flop for another. As a case in point, I remember implementing a CRM solution for a company in Hungary that had the mother company in Norway. It was the same company, the same product, and the same industry, but each location had different sales processes that had to be optimized to the local company's culture and market position.

When you start the daunting task of designing the architecture of your CRM solution, you will find that you have some architectural questions that need to be answered in order to build a solid foundation:

- What information will be managed, stored, and presented?
- What are the main functional entities of your architecture?
- How will these entities interact with each other and with the outside world?
- What are the top processes to be supported by a CRM?
- Will a development, test, support, and training environment be needed?

Then there are a few concepts that you need to think about when you're finding a balance of these viewpoints:

- **Static structures**: Also known as cross-cutting concerns, these will impact all of the other architectural viewpoints.
- **Dynamic structures**: This is where you apply perspectives to your viewpoints in order to build a dynamic structure to better satisfy stakeholders who have different ideas about the key requirements.
- **Quality properties**: These look at performance, security, and availability.

Stakeholders, architectural description, viewpoints, and perspectives will be in your **Solution Blueprint** (**SBP**), along with a process catalog, use cases, and integration points, all of which we will cover in later chapters.

There are many dependencies to be considered; for example, the main users claim to need totally different information from what the staff members at the head office need. This is really connected information that supports a multistep process, which is often built on top of the same data from the central repository of customer data.

The business managers say it's crucial to have real-time summary reporting throughout the day, which may slow the transaction flow significantly, which is not acceptable to the main users of the system. Meanwhile, IT members are worried about adopting new technology, security, and compatibility issues. As you can see in the figure that follows, there are a number of different stakeholders involved in any CRM system.

The design of a sustainable CRM architecture will have to consider many dependencies, such as stakeholders, data centers, functional requirements, business processes, the feedback loop, and review management. In *Figure 1.18*, you can see these dependencies mapped out:

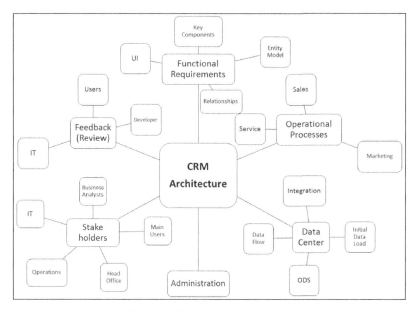

Figure 1.18: The dependencies illustrated

The case studies we've looked at in this chapter also demonstrate the need for an architect to identify and connect with all the key stakeholders. They need to understand stakeholders' objectives, perspectives, and conflicting priorities, and design an architecture that satisfies all the business requirements effectively within a reasonable TCO/ROI.

On top of a great CRM architecture design, there are a few important success factors that I will introduce here and discuss in more detail throughout this book:

- Management and employees must get involved and work together towards the success of a project.

- CRM is primarily a management and business issue, not an IT issue.

- CRM will support all channels, business units, and users.

- Business processes will define CRM processes and not the other way around.

- CRM will enable the measurement of success, customer profitability, share of wallet, and business process automation.

- Change management is crucial for success.

Summary

In this chapter, we've looked at all the important elements of a CRM system, including operational CRM, analytical CRM, and collaboration CRM. We also saw in five different case studies how particular business pain points and strategies will shape functional priorities for your CRM design.

We touched upon the TCO/ROI for CRM projects. These metrics are measurement tools that are used to evaluate the business improvements achieved through CRM compared with the investment in a CRM solution. You define these metrics based on business goals and selected processes that are to be improved versus the cost of implementing the functional requirements.

Throughout the rest of this book, we will engage in deeper discussions on all these topics, with a number of implementation examples that could be applied in your business.

In the next chapter, *Getting to Know Your Customers*, we will explore the most critical element in CRM, before we deep dive into CRM design techniques in *Chapter 3, Conceptualizing the CRM Design from Business Requirements*.

Chapter 2

Getting to Know Your Customer

The end-to-end story of the customer's journey

I n this chapter, we are going to explore how getting to know your customer, otherwise known as KYC, and subsequently storing and representing the relevant customer data in your CRM system, can improve operational efficiency, reduce the cost of operations, and improve customer satisfaction. Understanding your customer through maintaining and managing the relevant customer information is at the heart of any successful business and CRM strategy. In fact, it's safe to say that customer knowledge is the essential ingredient to a business being successful.

Building a single, sophisticated, role-based, 360-degree customer view that can capture, process, and present all the relevant relationship data is at the heart of understanding and knowing your customer. This is a central repository and, in this case, data access is based on the role and power that a user has in the organization.

This data could cover anything from a history of interactions with the customer to a list of products and services that the customer has with the company.

But beyond that, it could also include the customer's satisfaction level, a list of open and closed complaints, and general information about the customer interactions, and channels, which in turn could lead to a better understanding of the customer from a business perspective.

With this knowledge, the company will be able to better analyze, target, and personalize future client interactions; create an accurate pipeline to automate the processes in sales, marketing, services; and, as a result, better orchestrate its business.

A common definition of a single customer view is an aggregated and holistic presentation of client data that's being held by a company or by its business units. This data could come from multiple sources, and it may be stored and viewed in one place, often as a single page. In larger companies, where multiple business units operate, this may occur with multiple views that represent the same data in different contexts, depending on business needs and the role a user has within the company. In this case, we call it a role-based 360-degree client view.

Throughout this book, I may use different terms for the single customer view, including:

- 360-degree client view
- **Client single view (CSV)**
- **Single customer view (SCV)**
- Single customer repository

However, I will always refer to the preceding definition in terms of a CRM solution.

In almost all CRM projects that I have been involved in throughout the last 15+ years, a single customer view, or 360-degree client view, has been the central element of any CRM system. Without a doubt, it has almost always been the function used in order to build the foundation for all the other requirements. However, as we will explore later, in some scenarios this may not be the case.

Likewise, CSV remains the most popular and useful feature at the start of any CRM journey. However, this approach requires that you undertake it correctly from the start in order to avoid running into issues that could hinder your progress. This topic is the focus of this chapter and will be covered extensively.

Almost every CRM implementation today, regardless of the company's size, market segment, and the functional areas it needs to provide to the business (customer service, sales, or marketing), is involved in the 360-degree client view, at some point. Indeed, the 360-degree client view is the central repository of your customer knowledge. For your company, it acts as the foundation of your communication and business relationship with your customers.

This is indeed the most important element in your CRM implementation, regardless of the type of your business or market segment you are operating in. Therefore, in this chapter, we are going to take a deep dive into building a comprehensive 360-degree client view.

The 360-degree client view

At the start of each CRM implementation, which should occur at the latest by the time you conduct the first Fit/Gap workshops with business users, a 360-degree client view will be one of the most popular subjects.

Once started, you will soon discover that most, if not all, business units and representative stakeholders will become passionately involved in these discussions. These discussions, and consequently, the design of your 360-degree client view, will provide you with a great opportunity to create a solid foundation for your CRM solution. The 360-degree client view will not only be the tool that your company uses to record and assist the customer across all your channels with the best possible customer experience, but it will be the strategic approach for your business to streamline processes and reduce operational costs.

A 360-degree client view often initiates a big debate between all the key players and business stakeholders. The discussions taking place are mostly about the type of client data needed in order for the business unit to be more efficient. Additionally, it's important to define who should be entitled to see what type of data (entitlement) from customers (role-based). A discussion about how much information is enough information to be on a client page will also need to occur. What absolutely needs to be there at the minimum and what is considered too much, to the point that it could make the system expensive?

This is the type of information that the architects, together with the application manager, of which there is typically only one per application, will need. These people will need to make design decisions about where this information comes from, where it should be placed, how it should be imported to the 360-degree client view, how to keep it updated, and how often to synchronize the data.

In an average company, there are many different types of users. They have different roles, different business needs, and are in a different capacity when interacting with the client and using the system. All these users will be using the same system and the same data repository, but where they differ is that they'll all be using the systems in very different scenarios, needing a role-based and scenario-based single view.

As you can see in *Figure 2.1*, a 360-degree client view is a single, end-to-end story of the customer's journey with your company:

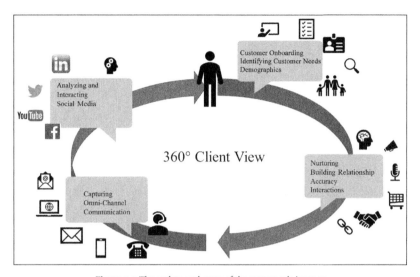

Figure 2.1: The end-to-end story of the customer's journey

Designing a sophisticated 360-degree client view that satisfies the variety of different requirements presented by all the different business units in a single company could indeed be a very complex task. It's going to require a lot of experience and a flexible design that's going to need to satisfy all the expectations of the parties involved, while improving all of the customer processes.

In a badly designed system, we may end up with too much data, or too many views, to name just two examples. Therefore, if you do not have a good and healthy comprehensive discussion at the beginning of your journey, where you can identify all the requirements, processes, and opportunities you'll need, then you'll almost certainly fail. To underline this, these discussions could indeed be very fruitful and could be the beginning of creating a great team and more importantly, they could be the start of getting everyone on board to work toward the same goal: the success of the operation at hand.

I remember working with a large international bank in London. It spent years of development time on building a 360-degree client view for its private banking and investment unit. This bank had a team of business analysts, software developers, and system engineers who spent three years, with a 100-man stark team, building this 360-degree client view. After all that time and money, they failed miserably, mainly because they ended up putting too much data on too many forms, and even too much data on one single form. There was a jungle of views and a lot of confusion among the users, coupled with the fact that there were big issues with the system performance.

A great way to grasp the concept we're talking about is to compare the idea of a single customer view with that of a Rubik's Cube. Your single customer view will not only need to be adaptable, agile, and as magical as the Rubik's Cube is, but it will need to do much more. A Rubik's Cube only has three dimensions and six faces that are covered by nine stickers. Each face is one of six solid colors: white, red, blue, orange, green, and yellow. Yet, for us, our single customer view will have more dimensions and more faces.

Building a 360-degree client view could have many more faces, such as the size of the organization, the role of the user, the processes involved, the business unit requirements, the nature of the industry, and the client segment, to name a few.

So, as a result, the system needs to be flexible, and through that, it must be designed in a way that satisfies the requirements of all the users, in all the processes, over the many channels and in the different capacities that you're dealing with clients.

We can visualize the building blocks of a 360-degree client view with the aid of *Figure 2.2*:

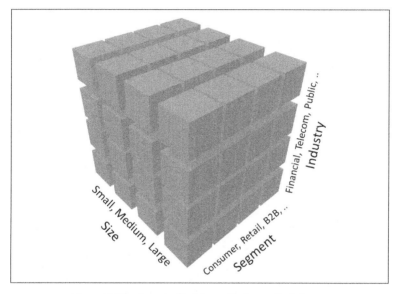

Figure 2.2: The elements of building a 360-degree client view

In *Figure 2.2*, you can see a comparison of the faces and dimensions. With that, you can see how different the business settings might be when it comes to building a single customer view for different industries, segments, sizes, or even in the same company when you are dealing with different types of customers.

As we begin to look into the business units of a single company, often each business unit will have a unique business requirement that differs from other business units within the same company.

For example, in the financial services industry, a multinational bank can have several business units, which could include a retail unit, a corporate unit, a private banking unit, an investment banking unit, and much more. While they are all under the same company umbrella, these business units can have common customers who operate in completely different scenarios.

What is also important to highlight here is that in a comprehensive CRM system, a 360-degree client view can easily be extended to include sales, marketing, and service data. This could be sales opportunities, including both cross-selling and upselling, or the list of open cases, such as complaints and service requests for customer service, and even for marketing, where it could include current campaigns related to the client.

In summary, there are multiple parameters to be considered when creating your 360-degree client view, including your industry, volume, segment, size, and the nature of your business. To expand on them, think about this:

- In a simple but large-volume business, such as the consumer industry sector, let's say a telecom company, the focus of SCV is on storing the customer profile and limiting the use of demographic data to mainly billing purposes, but also for cross-selling and upselling purposes, and customer service.

- In a more sophisticated industry, where an extensive 360-degree client view is used, the view and knowledge should primarily enhance both the sales and marketing, but also customer satisfaction, through retail or online stores, resulting in improved customer loyalty.

- In a high-end customer services industry, such as private banking, where KYC is mandatory, extended customer knowledge is present, with a comprehensive understanding of the sales and marketing data related to the client and to the business, such as products she or he owns, share of wallet, satisfaction level, and so on.

- In this business, the CSV is the most comprehensive variation. It's used for building a trust relationship with the clients when it comes to the most sensitive matters, such as managing the wealth of clients and advising them on future financial planning, and **Customer Life cycle Management** (**CLM**).

There are some more aspects to consider when you are designing the 360-degree client view for your company. These include the **Customer Health Index** (**CHI**), a sophisticated graphical illustration of the overall customer relationship, such as the business volume, customer satisfaction level, loyalty level, profitability level, age, and segment, which can be used to empower your employees with the information they need when interacting with customers and collecting business information, with an example being shown in the screenshot that follows:

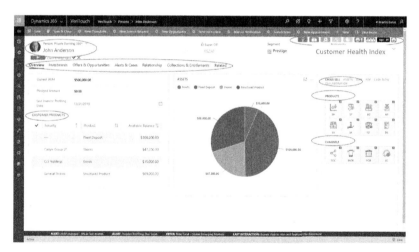

Figure 2.3: CHI in a 360-degree role-based view

Your employees need this information when doing their jobs and dealing with customers, including all the different types of operations and interactions with the customers of your company.

This is where the role-based 360-degree client view can benefit all of your employees. We will be exploring the elements of the CHI later on in this chapter.

As we have explored, the complexity of both the SCV and the 360-degree client view is role-based and industry-specific, where the size and nature of the business are important for the solution design, and above all else, company vision and strategies will ultimately need to be supported by the solution. As we have previously discussed, the most common strategies in CRM deployment are to improve the operational efficiency, reduce the cost of operations, improve customer service, improve profitability, increase client satisfaction, and subsequently increase the market share of your company.

The defining parameters are universal and the approach to building a 360-degree client view has applications in any industry, but early examples have been seen in the financial services, healthcare, government, retail, and telecommunications industries. As time goes on, every industry will benefit from it and as we have highlighted, CRM will use different terminology for the same meaning; for example, 360-degree client view and the term KYC are often used to mean the same thing in the banking industry.

Across the many implementations that I have been involved in, probably the most comprehensive 360-degree client view that I have ever seen was in the private banking sector. Here, there was in-depth customer knowledge from both the business point of view, as well as per regulatory authority requirements, which made the 360-degree client view in this industry the most complex, comprehensive, and challenging for everyone involved.

In our journey, we want to deep dive into building not only a good but a sophisticated 360-degree client view. However, we're going to be creating one that's been designed from my own experience in private banking.

This shows the best practices behind building a customer knowledge and 360-degree client view for private banking. However, take note that what we're going to build can be applied to any industry, so if you're not a bank, then don't worry!

Case study — VeriPark

Before we go any further, I would like to take a real-life example from one of my partners I have been working with. The company is called VeriPark and it is a very successful CRM company that is operating across all the continents of the world. With its permission, we're going to explore its base (out-of-the-box) solution for a 360-degree client view and see how it has built a sophisticated role-based solution. We're going to share its experience, along with some of the best practices it committed to, and let you extract some of the knowledge that you'll be able to apply to your own journey.

After conducting business workshops with stakeholders and business analysts, VeriPark typically configures and integrates the base module for role-based solutions to each individual company's requirements and pain points. As we've highlighted in this chapter already, building a role-based, comprehensive, 360-degree client view is not, as it might look as a first impression, a walk in the park.

I remember working on a **request for proposal** (**RFP**) from another large multinational bank in the UK, where I was working on an operational company-wide CRM implementation. This bank decided to deploy a standard CRM solution and make in-house adaptions to it with its own in-house developers and business analysts in order to build the base system it wanted. This bank spent almost three years, and likely millions of pounds, in building the solution that was supposed to satisfy the requirements of the bank's business units. Yet, the experiment failed and in turn, the bank approached VeriPark for help, as it saw VeriPark's solution at an occasion with other vendors.

Building a single client view in private banking

In a nutshell, the objective of a private banking business is to provide financial services and investment products to **high-net-worth individuals (HNWIs)** who have a sizable asset, or even sometimes to institutional investors, depending on the business model of the company. Understandably, this business model is highly sensitive and personalized and therefore, a deep knowledge of the client is essential to the success of the business.

As I mentioned earlier, the SCV in the finance industry is the most comprehensive approach when compared to any other type of industry. Here, SCV is used for business orchestration, such as sales, the marketing processes, the sales pipeline, marketing campaigns, and customer services. In all of these cases, SCV is used as a measurement tool for managing the client life cycle and share of wallet.

CLM is the idea of using both processes and metrics to enable the company to better manage, measure, and analyze the performance of the business with the client over a longer period of time. The business supports the processes and data from all the business units related to the same client over the client's lifecycle. In the best-case scenario, this will be through all the stages of the lifecycle. The share of wallet is the analysis of the business a client has with your company compared to the business he or she has with your competitors. Through this, you can get a good picture for both cross-selling and upselling with the client.

The lifecycle of your customer starts with their acquisition, before you move on to profiling the customer, selling products, managing retention, loyalty, the growth of the business, both cross-selling and upselling, termination of the customer relationship, and customer win-back.

With the following chart, we can visualize the typical customer lifecycle:

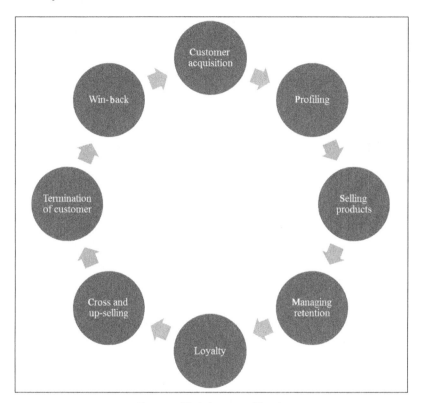

Figure 2.4: Typical customer lifecycle

This process will be supported by the business processes a company uses to move its customer through the customer life stages. It is best managed within a CRM system, with related data in a single, efficient customer data repository. As you can see in the lifecycle chart featured in *Figure 2.4*, collecting, storing, managing, and viewing the data for a comprehensive 360-degree client view could become very complex if it's not designed in a very flexible way and managed by a comprehensive CRM system.

Client profiling

Client profiling is done in the process of onboarding for new clients. Don't worry, we will talk about onboarding through the remaining chapters of this book. The profiling will be enriched and updated continuously with every client interaction during the customer lifecycle, and as part of the CLM. Client profiling is also the initial data gathering stage for building the 360-degree client view. For client profiling, the system will provide the ability to carry out questionnaires in order to both start this process and to assess a client's overall background and potential.

This data will be enhanced and aggregated by each and every interaction the client has across all the business units in the company. In part, this will be automated through the CRM processes and extended with customer lifecycle management processes. It may even include social media activities, if there is consent and it's approved in the boundary of regulations; for example, when a customer tweets and then calls your support center.

Besides the demographic data, the KYC elements, as mentioned earlier in this chapter, will need to be added to the process by regulations in banking. These types of data include:

1. Suitability

2. Lifestyle

3. Objectives

4. Risk tolerance

5. Return expectation

6. Time horizon

Figure 2.5: Additional KYC elements

All of these additional KYC elements related to the client data are to be gathered and assessed during the onboarding stage. In our example of banking, this is required by regulatory authorities in most countries when dealing with investment products. This would lead to questions like, is the client's situation suitable for financial products? The lifestyle, the client's objectives regarding the investment, the risk appetite, and tolerance, along with the expectation and the time horizon are all elements of the information that will be used to assess the client's financial situation and associated risks.

To standardize the quality of the data collected, as well as to reduce the workload in collecting the data in a proper and correct manner, the onboarding questionnaire enables the **Relationship Manager** (**RM**) to design questions and possible answers of various types using a survey module. As explained earlier, going forward, this data will be aggregated not only with every client interaction, but also through a set of periodical procedures and automated processes such as financial planning, or a **Financial Health Check** (**FHC**), which is mandated by regulatory authorities in most countries, and/or by automated pipeline management.

On top of that, there are other regulatory compliance procedures, such as the **Markets in Financial Instruments Directive** (**MiFID**) that applies only to financial products. Another compliance is the European Union's **General Data Protection Regulation** (**GDPR**), which applies to all industries across the globe who are dealing with clients in the European Union. In the case of GDPR, it needs to be considered and incorporated across every single interaction with the client, as well as in product and pipeline management that leverages a CRM process engine to manage and to orchestrate all these complex procedures.

As part of KYC and 360-degree client view, the relationship manager will need to capture the details of a customer's investment background knowledge, along with a list of the customer's preferences to be included in their profile, including:

1. Their knowledge of investments.

2. The objective of their investments.

3. Their investment experience with various instruments.

This information is not only required by the regulatory authorities, but it will also provide the company with the data needed to not only better understand the client's needs and manage the customer relationship in regards to marketing, sales, and services processes, but also for managing the CLM with the company.

In *Figure 2.6*, you'll see a great example of a questionnaire that has been designed to collect that very information in order to build the extended 360-degree client view, including the KYC aspects:

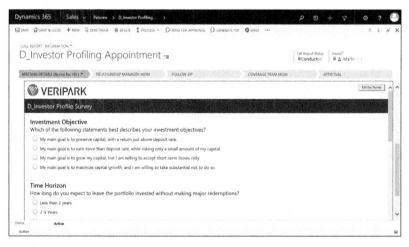

Figure 2.6: Profiling questionnaire (1/2)

In this case, you could scroll the screen, collecting more information as needed. This is better done in the same single process flow. You'll find that typically users are more comfortable with this process of scrolling the screen and answering all related questions regarding KYC.

In *Figure 2.7*, you'll see the latter half of the questionnaire:

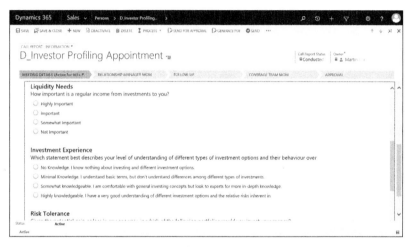

Figure 2.7: Profiling questionnaire (2/2)

As you can see in the preceding profiling screenshots, these questionnaires help the relationship manager and the sales representative to collect a set of data that is needed by the system in order to start building both the general investment profile, as well as the data required for the initial 360-degree client view.

That very idea can be seen in *Figure 2.8*:

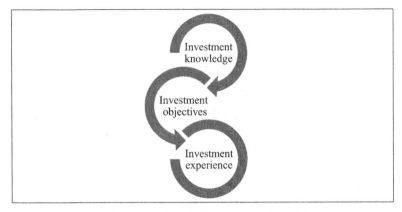

Figure 2.8: Assessing the clients' background and knowledge

The screenshot that follows is a snapshot of the results of the questionnaire and the data collected through the KYC process:

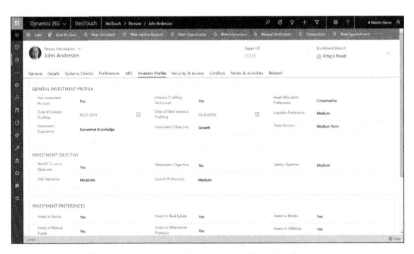

Figure 2.9: A customer's investment profile and preferences

The system now has enough of the basic data to start building the intelligence needed for managing the customer relationship tasks and through that, the overall business processes. In finance, as part of the client lifecycle management process, it's often necessary to nurture a relationship with the client and support building the relationship with other business units based on a client's profile, wealth status, investment objectives, and personal preferences. CRM is the best place for automating these types of processes, building dashboards, delegating tasks, and monitoring the follow-up progress. For example:

- The system will create cold leads (low probability) and assign them to respective business units.

- Automated tasks may be assigned to responsible people and managers.

- The sales pipeline starts to build up.

- Customer interaction history will show relevant data.

In addition, some relationship management offers support alerts and reminders for the employees and relationship managers when dealing with the client. For example, the system should display an alert for a certain type of event, such as the birthday indicator for the client:

- If the birthday is within five days, display a special birthday icon on the single customer.

- When the system user hovers over the indicator, the birthday date is displayed.

- On the actual birthday, a pop-up alert will remind the RM.

- For certain types of client, it will remind you to send a "Happy Birthday" message.

- Create an automated marketing campaign 30 days ahead of the birthday.

As mentioned earlier, the 360-degree client view will be the place to put the essential customer information for orchestrating the business processes around the customer interactions. This will support the employees' specific roles by giving them additional information when dealing with the customer, and act as a central repository for CLM processes.

In *Figure 2.10*, you'll see a sophisticated 360-degree client view. Here the system will provide a comprehensive view of all related customer information gathered so far, and reflect the related, role-based interactions. The following sections will be displayed on SCV:

- Demographic profile.

- Products and opportunities.

- Business-related summary, such as asset under management (AUM).

- Alerts and cases.

- Cross-selling and upselling.

Within Microsoft Dynamics 365, this would appear to you as it has for us in *Figure 2.10*:

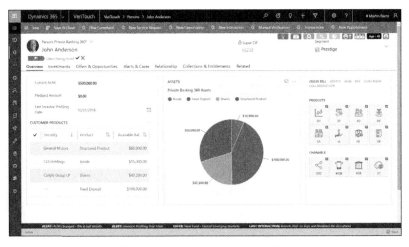

Figure 2.10: A 360-degree client view (1/3)

This is a very good example of what type of information could be useful for the relationship manager in the company. It's also essential for building a powerful single customer repository. This information is also valuable for sales, marketing, product development, and for orchestrating the business.

On the top of the screen, you can see which type of view (role-based) you are currently using and which page of the 360-degree client view is currently on display based on your role in the company. You can then click on each menu option in order to obtain detail information and drill down to the data based on your entitlement and role within the organization:

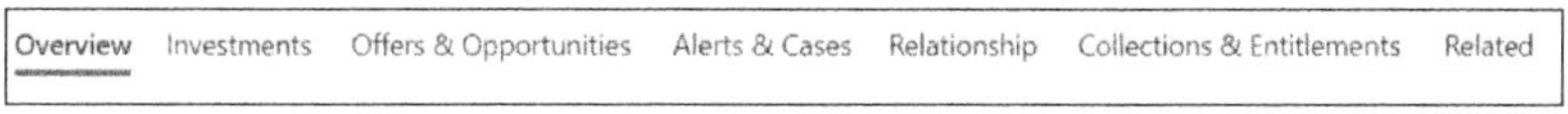

Overview	Investments	Offers & Opportunities	Alerts & Cases	Relationship	Collections & Entitlements	Related

Figure 2.11: What page of the 360-degree client view is currently being displayed

For example, the call center agent will be provided with the following information when she or he is handling a service request for a customer and is visiting the service tab (**Alerts & Cases**):

- Cases
- Alerts
- Enrolled services

Then, on the left half of the screen in the following screenshot, you'll see the list of the products the customer owns with your company, along with some level of detail, including:

- Current AUM
- Pledged AUM (the amount that the client has pledged for investments)

Current AUM	$500,000.00
Pledged Amount	$0.00
Last Investor Profiling Date	10/31/2018

CUSTOMER PRODUCTS

✓	Security ↑	Product ↑↓	Available Balance ↑↓
	---	Fixed Deposit	$100,000.00
	Carlyle Group LP	Shares	$47,200.00
	CLS Holdings	Bonds	$15,000.00
	General Motors	Structured Product	$69,000.00

Figure 2.12: Customer products holding

AUM, also called **funds under management (FUM)**, is the market value of all the financial assets that the financial institutions, such as the private bank, venture capital firm, or the brokerage firm manages on behalf of this particular client. This is not only a measure of the size and success of this particular client, but it's also important for the firm's success, and in most cases, the firm charges its clients fees as a proportion of assets, and consequently, this is the basis for the firm's top-line revenue and the relationship manager's commission and bonuses.

This section also displays a pie chart, seen in *Figure 2.13*, which is representing the customer's investment amount in different asset classes. Obviously, this information is very valuable for analysis of the diversified portfolio, and by being on the 360-degree client view, it will present a quick snapshot of the customer:

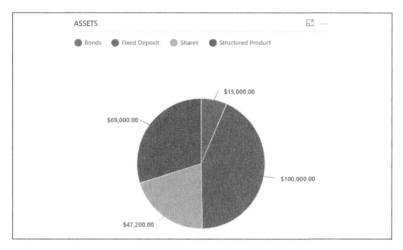

Figure 2.13: Diversified portfolio

The visual representation here enables the RM to get a quick view of the client's preferences and a distribution of the client's assets, but more importantly, the underlying data will help both the marketing and product team to better manage marketing campaigns and product development. The system will also display all the details of the investment products when the user double-clicks on any of the available products.

The next important element of building a sophisticated CSV is the use of visual indicators and icons to reduce the complexity of the 360-degree client view. However, this will still give us a holistic understanding of the client relationship spectrum whenever needed, such as can be seen in *Figure 3.14*:

Figure 2.14: Use of visual indicators on the 360-degree client view

As you see on the top right of the 360-degree client view, the system displays several icons with different colors: green, yellow, orange, red, and black. This helps the RM to very quickly get a sense or view of how the overall relationship with the client is doing in all relevant areas (role-based). For example, the profitability of the entire portfolio of investments held by the customer is presented to the RM or sales rep by a small icon colored in green, yellow, or red, as seen here with .

The value of these icons and indicators is coming from the backend system, such as the **Data Warehouse** (**DWH**), to the CRM as a daily batch feed. The color of the icons is then configured in the CRM to be based on the range of values that have been defined by the company. For example, the color of the icon for profitability will be green if the profitability value exceeds 25%. For lesser values, the color of the icon will be yellow or red.

By clicking on the icon, more detailed information will appear on the screen. For instance, the customer satisfaction level is presented through a face, the icon on the very right. A happy face in the color green, for example, obviously represents the customer being currently very satisfied with the company overall.

Below the icons is a range of additional information, such as the **customer information file** (**CIF**) number (customer number in the core system), client segment, the nationality, and the name of the RM. This information could be very valuable in many situations, such as if further research or data from backend systems is needed to see who ultimately owns the relationship with this given client.

Another important element to be supported by CRM and integrated on the 360-degree client view is managing client communication over omnichannel. Omnichannel is a cross-channel communication technique that will support CRM data and processes over multiple communication channels with the client. A CRM platform will ideally support the orchestration of business processes across all these channels and obviously provides better service to the client compared to if we were using single channels in isolation.

Omnichannel includes channels supported by the business to communicate with the client, such as the Internet, portals, mobile applications, social media, and physical locations, as he or she might be visiting the branch or shops. You'll see on the right side of the 360-degree client view the channels that this customer is using:

Figure 2.15: Customer channels (social media, mobile, branch, and contact center)

In this example, the customer is only using the branch. Therefore, the company may plan dedicated marketing campaigns providing sales incentives if the customer uses other channels, say the mobile application. By doing this, you increase the footprint, improve loyalty, and reduce the cost of sales and operations in the branches.

We will cover social media integration in *Chapter 9, CRM Differentiators*.

We are also able to scroll the view a bit to see the next section of the 360-degree client view. This is to provide supporting data for cross-selling and upselling processes. These processes are based on analysis of the wallet share and product holding a client has with the company. This will, therefore, offer him or her additional products or services in the individualized campaigns, very much like Amazon.com does with its "you bought this, so you may be interested in this" campaign.

With this section, we offer four sections, including:

- **Offers**: Pending offers that have been generated by a campaign for which the customer has been targeted.

- **Opportunities**: Sales opportunities that are in progress with the customer.

- **Eligible products**: Eligible products that are generated by the system based on eligibility criteria.

- **Customer 720**: The list of all individuals and corporates that are related to this customer.

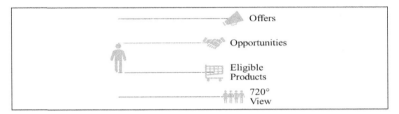

Figure 2.16: Cross-selling and upselling steps

In fact, the cross-selling and upselling process is an important element of the 360-degree client view. It enables the sales representative, or others, within in the company to easily leverage the eligible products list, which is generated by the system, based on product eligibility criteria, before starting a sales conversation with the client.

This data, seen in *Figure 2.17*, is an expanded 360-degree client view that we discussed earlier. It has been provided by the data mart and business intelligence capabilities of a CRM system. It shows the history of interactions, the open opportunities, pre-approved products, and the customer 720-degree view (relationship with your other clients):

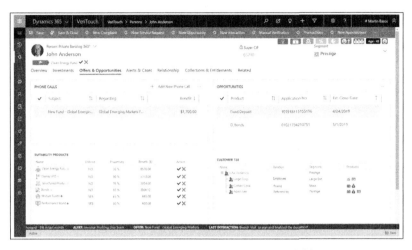

Figure 2.17: An expanded 360-degree client view (2/3)

It is also intended to assist the RM in the preparation, for example, of deciding what offers should be presented to the client when they are visiting the branch. All the RM would have to do is select the eligible products, with the respective discounts to be merged in one personalized offer for the customer. This can all be done with one mouse-click by the sales representative, while the RM is consulting face-to-face, or on the phone, with the customer. If the customer has a positive response to the respective contract or documents with the eligible product, and is ready, then the offer can be printed out and sent out to the customer.

What follows is a snapshot of a perfect 360-degree client view, taken for private banking from VeriPark. You can see all relevant information about this customer in one screen, including the customer health index (top right), cross and up-selling opportunities, eligible products, channels, products owned, role-based information, customer name, and the name of the current view:

Figure 2.18: A sophisticated 360-degree client view

Let's see what the ingredients and the best practices are in building such a sophisticated 360-degree client view. Starting with this example, we'll be looking at the requirements of a private banking institute. However, as I stated earlier, this is due to this being one of the best 360-degree client view interactions that I've encountered. All of these ingredients can be transferred to your own CRM requirements, as this is what you will do for every other business and/or industry before starting to build this solution.

At the highest level, the business requirements of private banking for a CRM solution are to enable the following:

- Client profiling for HNWIs:
  - Detailed demographics and personal data.
  - Portfolio holding and products, both current and potential.

- ○ Investment objectives in order to understand the customers' needs and future plans.
- ○ Household structure and extended demographics.

- CLM, FHC, and advisory:
  - ○ Savings snapshot.
  - ○ Monthly commitments, better known as the customers' fixed expenses.
  - ○ Debt snapshot and planning in a short-term view.
  - ○ Retirement planning, a long-term view.
  - ○ Financial planning and understanding customers' objectives.
  - ○ Advice and report printings through both a trusted advisor and reporting.

These all give the basic ingredients for building a comprehensive customer knowledge base and basic CSV. Let's see how to do that.

Interaction history

More often than not, the difference between an efficient and an inefficient 360-degree client view is how congested the screen is. Users can often be overwhelmed by the quantity of data available on the page. Therefore, using techniques to reduce the amount of information on the 360-degree client view is an important element to consider.

You may consider displaying only the most relevant information. This might be only displaying information with meaning or a reason to be displayed. This could reduce the amount of information on the screen and give the user the opportunity to focus on what really matters to them in this particular scenario.

As an example, a system should display the VIP indicator only if this client is a VIP. Otherwise, if the customer is not a VIP, this icon should not even be visible on the screen.

Figure 2.19 is the third part of the 360-degree client view. As you scroll down the display, you'll see the interaction history timeline, listing when and which channels the customer has been using to connect with you, including the call report and sales activities (coverage):

Figure 2.19: 360-degree client view (3/3)

Summary

In the connected world of today, most companies will have access to plenty of client data. This is data that could be used, as we've explored in this chapter, to build a strong 360-degree client view, which in turn increases the company's understanding of both its actual and potential customers. The ultimate design goal of a sophisticated client view is to enable the company to better serve the needs of its clients, while continuously improving the business processes, the product offering, and the services offered to clients, ultimately improving operational costs and revenue.

A comprehensive 360-degree client view will lead to higher efficiencies of both sales and marketing processes in the company. By creating a customer-centric business, this will lead to an increase in the share of wallet with every single individual customer. It will reduce the cost of operations by unifying the data and processes around the customer, while also providing better insight into business intelligence, something that we will explore throughout the remaining chapters of this book.

In *Chapter 9, CRM Differentiators*, we will explore how a 360-degree client view could leverage new technologies and support social channels to provide self-service and automated customer interactions, deliver recommendations and personalized customer experiences, and implement social selling and social advertising that is enabled by AI, big data, and cognitive services. No doubt, such a client view will be expanding your business abilities and accelerating your company's digital transformation.

CHAPTER 3

CONCEPTUALIZING THE CRM DESIGN FROM BUSINESS REQUIREMENTS

With most CRM solutions, you get what you get, but with the right design, you will get what you need. Design is the intentional creation of a plan or specification for the construction of an object or system, or for the implementation of an activity or process. Design can refer to a drawing or other document, or to a created object and the features of it, whether they are aesthetic, functional, economic, or sociopolitical.

In this chapter, we're going to cover the CRM design elements that are driven by business requirements, including:

- Processes
- Applications
- Data
- Security
- Integration
- Deployment decisions

We will walk through the process of design and along the way, I'll recommend some straightforward tools that could help you to manage the process. This chapter will provide you with a comprehensive overview of the high-level design elements that I will make reference to throughout the rest of the book.

My experience

Over the years, I have been fortunate enough to work with so many talented people: business analysts, architects, peers, partners, and customers from across the globe. From Argentina, Brazil, and Guatemala in Latin America, to Australia, Indonesia, and China in Asia, and multiple European and African countries, my experience has taken me around the world. Therefore, everything mentioned in this chapter is based on my own experiences and I will share with you some of the best practices.

In most CRM projects that I have been involved in, I've found myself working alongside a large team of experts. Within those teams, there are people with specialized expertise, namely so-called **Subject Matter Experts** (**SMEs**). These teams typically get engaged in the very early stages, when responding to a **Request for Proposal** (**RFP**), and work together with the stakeholders in setting up a **Proof of Concept** (**PoC**).

If these teams are successful at that stage, then their co-working nature will continue all the way down through diagnostics, project initiation, execution, stabilization, deployment, and operation. Sometimes, in the very early stages of a project, depending on the maturity level of the business, this involves working with a team of business analysts to collect and compile business requirements and assist with crafting the RFP or **Request for Information** (**RFI**) for collecting proposals from vendors.

I remember some 15 years ago I had my own small CRM consulting company. I was traveling across Europe and delivering CRM projects, but at the same time, I was also a CRM training partner. Through that, I was meeting Microsoft employees in most European countries. This was one of the first general questions from both the partners and attendees at my classes: "What are the most common pain points and requirements for CRM investment that are driving your design?"

My answer was twofold. Firstly, the drive to invest in CRM comes from top management. A company's top management has a CRM vision that is, usually, followed by a number of CRM strategies designed to improve the customer's experience, processes, information, and reporting tools. That being said, there are a number of other components to every CRM project, such as people, efficiency, culture, and ecosystem, all of which will come into play once the CRM journey has started. This can be seen in *Figure 3.1*, which shows us the high-level CRM components needed:

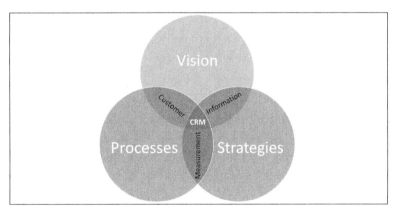

Figure 3.1: High-level CRM components

Secondly, once you have the high-level strategies outlined and approved by the top stakeholders, then you need to start with identifying business pain points. These pain points (business requirements) will typically drive the conceptual design of your solution. But you also need to keep in mind that pain points are always different from business to business, and from industry to industry. Even for the same company and the same industry in two different countries, the requirements can and will be different. You are designing a solution to resolve the specific business pain points for a company.

Top 10 common business pain points

One thing I always give my students is a list of the top 10 most common business pain points that are often driving CRM projects. We have covered most of these points throughout the previous chapters, as seen through the case studies, and we will touch on them again and again throughout this book, but as a reminder, they are:

1. **Market and price transparency**: Markets are changing; prices are comparable as never before.

2. **Increased competition**: Both from local and global competitors in your market.

3. **Increased market complexity and dynamics**: Digitalization and digital disrupters, such as big tech companies.

4. **Interchangeable products and conditions**: Innovation and changes in customer behaviors or habits.

5. **Increased customer claims and individualization of customer claims**: Increasing customer expectations.

6. **Shrinking margins**: Tough market conditions through digital disrupters. I cover examples in *Chapter 5, Utilizing Artificial Intelligence and Machine Learning in Your CRM Strategy*, in more detail.

7. **Declining customer loyalty**: Younger generations are not loyal to vendors and businesses.

8. **Rising acquisition costs**: Sales and marketing spending.

9. **Customer contact through different channels**: Internet and mobile.

10. **Information silos**: Growing number of legacy applications used by companies over the years.

Compared to 15 years ago, these pain points have not changed much, but the driving forces behind them have changed dramatically in so many ways. While CRM visions and strategies at the highest level are still the same as they were years ago, the pain points and the market dynamics have changed, especially over the last few years, and they'll likely continue to change for the next few years to come. I believe we are just at the start of an entirely new era of doing business with customers.

Business pain points have shifted mainly in two major areas compared to 15 years ago. Firstly, there has been a significant paradigm shift in regards to the competitors that are entering the market. These are mostly high-tech companies, or what I call big tech companies such as Amazon and Google. Secondly, competing strategies and tactics have changed a lot. It's no longer about the three competitive elements (price, quality, and delivery); it's about competing with high-tech companies that are very different from the traditional companies. Sometimes, these companies are coming out of the blue and from some far-out location, with the latest technologies that are attracting customers, coupled with extended business models that seem to be convenient for the newer generations.

The millennials, generations X and Y, and your new competitors are entering your market dynamics. These high-tech companies are leveraging new technologies that make them different and allow them to stand out from traditional businesses. It's difficult to identify an industry whose business operations have not been profoundly altered by new technologies, and we will cover this topic throughout this book.

With the massive adoption of the Internet, the World Wide Web, and mobile devices, the scale, speed, and scope of innovation in technologies, such as artificial intelligence and machine learning, continues to grow. We are currently in the midst of the so-called fourth industrial revolution, which you can see visualized in the following chart, which is mainly being driven by artificial intelligence. This is posing a challenge to most traditional businesses, which are now facing competition from these big tech companies leveraging the latest technologies to enter new markets and gain more market share.

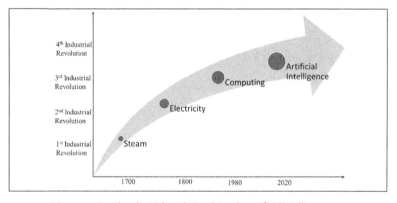

Figure 3.2: Fourth industrial revolution driven by artificial intelligence

We are in an age of digital disruption. Some of the innovations that are driving this revolution are customer-driven by millennials and generation X, as well as the upcoming generation Z. These groups are understandably more attracted by innovations in technology, as they grew up alongside a very different set of tools than previous generations. But most of the innovation is coming from a whole new set of companies: so-called high-tech start-ups across the world.

We are witnessing high-tech companies, such as Amazon and Uber, entering new markets and geographies with no footprint in the business and the location they are going to operate in.

These high-tech companies enter one market first, then they keep growing and expanding their footprint in all other geographies; this is digital disruption. For instance, Uber first started in San Francisco by offering taxi services there. Several years later, it now operates worldwide and offers many other services, such as food and entertainment, with, as of 2018, a user base of 100 million customers.

The change we are witnessing is not necessarily about digital technologies but about the fact that new technologies allow people to solve their problems differently. People prefer these digital solutions to the old solutions, and that's what we call **Digital Transformation (DX)**. This is something that you may agree is affecting every company across the globe.

DX

Two decades of digitalization has changed business. Traditional businesses are facing digital disruption across the globe and this will undoubtedly be a permanent state for all industries in the years to come.

Digital disruption posed by high-tech companies is forcing traditional businesses to go through DX by adopting new technologies and redesigning the way they do business with their customers in order to stay competitive. Otherwise, if they failed to implement digital transformation, they would go out of business and have to start all over again.

This DX is not going to be an easy task, but CRM offers a lifeline and can help to resolve some of the pain. It achieves this in two different ways by utilizing these points:

1. Traditional companies have a customer base and market knowledge.
2. Traditional businesses have a vast amount of data and information they could leverage.

Many of the customers that I have met and been engaged with in recent years are facing competition from digital disrupters, and many have started to realize the full potential of the digitalization of their existing application landscape. Through that, they have begun adjusting their business model accordingly. We will explore this in greater detail later on in this chapter; we will discuss how to overcome the challenge posed by high-tech start-ups and big-tech companies.

What we are observing right now is that most of the disruption is coming from faraway places and mostly from outside a given industry. As mentioned earlier, a good example is Uber, a tech company headquartered in San Francisco, California. The company is now operating in some 800 areas worldwide, from the U.S. to India, and from Finland to South Africa. Uber is competing with traditionally well-established local transport businesses. It does so by leveraging the latest technological developments, such as artificial intelligence and machine learning; two topics that we will cover in *Chapter 5, Utilizing Artificial Intelligence and Machine Learning in Your CRM Strategy.*

Uber's customers are offered a fare before taking a ride, which the system generates by using a dynamic pricing engine. Quotes are based not only on the distance but the time of day, the supply and demand of services, and the projected duration of the ride. The payment is not conventional with a physical credit card or cash, but instead is taken through a number of payment services based on the customer's preference, such as Apple Pay, Google Pay, or in some geographic regions, such as India, a mobile wallet or **Unified Payments Interface** (**UPI**).

With this approach, it's all about customer convenience. On the screenshot of the Uber app that follows, you can see several examples of how the convenience expands beyond just the payment feature and into features such as customer service:

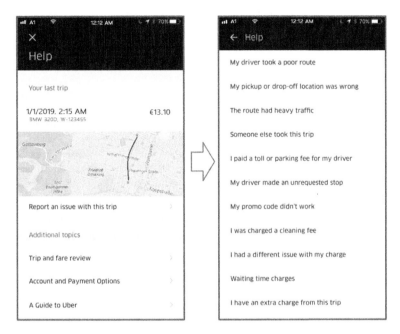

Figure 3.3: Example of customer convenience with Uber

But why is a successful DX important? Of the top 10 most valuable companies in the world, at the time of writing, five are in the technology domain: Apple, Alphabet, Facebook, Microsoft, and Amazon. Just recently, Alibaba, China's biggest e-commerce platform, announced record sales of $30 billion over a 24-hour period during "Singles' Day," soaring 25% over last year's record of about $24 billion. With those figures, it's clear to see how the big tech companies are pushing other businesses out of their markets.

The impact of digital disruption is most dramatic in sectors such as financial services, industry, and retail. Traditional banks and insurers are no longer competing with firms and financial institutions in the same market, or even the same industry, country, or continent.

They're actually competing against an entirely new set of competitors, so-called FinTech companies, in almost all areas of their business, but mainly in only profitable areas, leaving the non-profitable business elements to the traditional banks.

Digital disrupters

As we've just explored, high-tech start-ups are going to be your next competitors, no matter what industry you are operating in. They will come up with new ideas and business models leveraging all those new technologies, giving them the ability to cross international borders, across all industries and markets.

We've discussed how the FinTech industry is a great example. It competes with traditional financial institutions in the delivery of financial services with a whole new approach and customer experience. Smartphones are used for mobile banking, investment, and payment services, while cryptocurrency is used for transactions. Those are just a few examples of the technologies aiming to replace traditional financial service companies. While FinTech is revolutionizing the banking industry and giving millions of people access to financial services for the first time, new business models are emerging with FinTech start-ups and tech firms, potentially disrupting the status quo.

All other industries are also going to be affected by this new trend; it is truly an industrial revolution taking place! The use of technology to innovate and sometimes even to replace traditional resources and businesses is becoming a highly profitable business in itself. These new start-ups aim to become an essential player within your marketplace. They don't want to only be a market player; they want to be the market itself.

An excellent example of this is Amazon. It is taking market shares away from traditional companies and intermediaries in the delivery of goods and services, while still expanding into the consumer sector, which is highly scalable with all other types of services.

So, what are the options traditional businesses have in order to deal with digital disrupters and stay competitive? Some larger companies are acquiring high-tech start-ups, some are partnering with and investing in start-ups, and some have started to digitize their existing application infrastructure. They've taken this approach in order to come up with competing solutions that fit future needs and can leverage (build upon) their assets, market share, and the knowledge they already have about their market and their customers.

The latter is probably the best approach for smaller or mid-size companies, but they still need to undertake the process correctly, step by step. I call these companies digital heroes because they manage to digitize their business while leveraging their know-how from customers at a reasonable cost.

Digital heroes succeed in digitizing their business by leveraging the vast knowledge and data they already have, while innovating their business applications by the so-called DX process. We will look at some examples of this later on in the chapter. But for now, let us look at some of these high-tech start-up companies, along with their business models and the markets they are operating in. Note, this is from my own post a year ago on LinkedIn:

- Klarna allows shoppers (mostly in Europe) to check out 65,000 merchants with just an email address, with the option to pay after delivery, or within a grace period. It's also interest free. 45 million people across the globe have shopped with Klarna. About 40% of all e-commerce sales in Sweden go through Klarna. The company has more than 2,000 employees, most of them working at the headquarters in Stockholm, Sweden. It is present in Finland, Norway, Denmark, Germany, Austria, the Netherlands, Switzerland, Belgium, the UK, Italy, Spain, Poland, and the U.S.

- M-Pesa is not really new anymore. I saw it some eight years ago in Kenya for the first time. M-Pesa (M for mobile and Pesa is Swahili for "money") is a mobile phone-based money transfer, financing, and microfinancing service. It was launched in 2007 by Vodafone for Safaricom and Vodacom, the largest mobile network operators in Kenya and Tanzania. It has since expanded to Afghanistan, South Africa, India, Romania, and Albania. M-Pesa allows users to deposit, withdraw, transfer money, and pay for goods and services easily with a mobile device. In Kenya alone, it processes more transactions than Western Union does globally.

- FutureAdvisor is a digital investment manager registered with the U.S. Securities and Exchange Commission. Founded in 2010, it was acquired by BlackRock in 2015. FutureAdvisor leverages robo-advisors to automate the asset allocation of investments via a computer algorithm. FutureAdvisor was founded by two former Microsoft engineers, Bo Lu and Jon Xu, in Seattle, U.S.

As highlighted earlier in this chapter, the challenge for traditional companies in improving customer experience and competing with high-tech firms is not only the old-fashioned business model they have cultivated over their years in business, but the way that they have set up their application landscape, which is, at best, a mess of legacy applications and data silos.

The illustration that follows is an example that visualizes a bank I was engaged with a few years ago. Many businesses are still organized this way with multiple user interfaces, multiple silos, and multiple process engines. On purpose, you will not be able to read this graph; it only shows how messy a traditional application landscape looks.

Sometimes even the application managers (or the responsible team) have difficulties in gaining a clear picture of where every component is and how they all interoperate with each other.

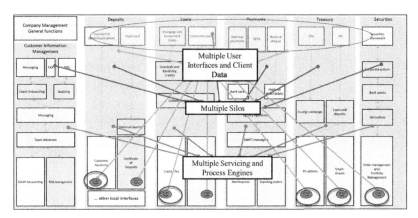

Figure 3.4: A messy application landscape with multiple silos

There are multiple user interfaces, multiple application silos, multiple workflow engines, and multiple amounts of customer data in a traditional company. The question is, how do you digitize a business in a smart way and become a digital hero?

To do this, companies need to put all of their focus onto using to their advantage the vast amount of information they already hold about their customers. Most companies agree that they already hold a considerable amount of personal customer information. Some companies are in knowledge-intensive sectors that are highly digitized across most dimensions, but even those companies do not necessarily use this to provide the best possible advice and customer experience.

In light of this, maximizing the use of customer intelligence and advice for superior results, along with focusing on the key issues and challenges in developing a new customer relationship model, is more suited to today's digital environment. It's been mentioned before, but it's vital to remember that DX is the next industrial revolution, and it's something that's already underway today.

Digital heroes digitize the business at a lower total cost of ownership (TCO) by applying a few simple steps with a customer-centric approach. At the same time, they are also providing better customer engagement, advanced analytics, and faster data monetization. These heroes manage to re-design and automate business processes into new digital experiences for customers.

We will have some examples of this throughout the rest of the book, so don't worry if you don't understand it now. It may sound harsh, but in reality, DX is no longer considered a luxury or as something nice to have; it has become a modern necessity that for most businesses is required to survive. It's now defensive and not offensive, as it was initially.

The only question now is how to go through the DX and be ready for new challenges posed by high-tech and big tech companies. Many of the traditional companies have already started with DX one way or the other, but only a few of those companies have been successful.

In a nutshell, what we are observing right now is that some of this digital disruption is coming from the high-tech industry, and some of it is customer-driven, as I highlighted earlier, by such factors as millennials and generation X. It's here that we start to see some fundamental shift towards customer behavior. For example, it has been reported that millennials will pick out their holiday destinations based on their social media exploitability. This is something that the tourism industry could take advantage of if it has successfully adopted and is ready for the change. These are the kind of factors we need to consider in the design of any CRM solution today. The bottom line is that it's about customer experience, customer expectations, and customer channels.

It's about customer experience

Like Steve Jobs, one of the founders of Apple, said, we must start with customer experience and go back to technology, and not the other way around.

I was recently conducting a workshop on DX for the business leaders of a mid-size company. They were telling me, very proudly, that they are now a truly digital company, having gone through DX over the last few years. Right now, the company has Internet shops, automated kiosks, video conferencing with sellers advising clients remotely, and it can set up accounts at the click of a mouse. The company is also able to identify clients by video trust, it has a mobile app, and it is using advanced analytics to slice and dice customer and market data.

I asked the leaders whether they had applied at least three of the following five technologies. If they had, then there is evidence that they started the journey of digital transformation. The five technologies are:

- Machine learning
- Robotics
- Mobility
- Internet of Things
- The cloud

Those five technologies are the essential ingredients for DX that provide the kind of customer experience that is expected by customers today. These technologies help with connecting with the next generation of clients in order to stay competitive and not let outsiders (big tech firms) take the market.

As an example, by 2020 it's predicted that 75% of chat and messaging services, such as Facebook, Skype, Amazon, and Google, will provide members with easy and low-cost payment services, just as the M-Pesa service is doing in Kenya.

Most businesses are traditionally in the knowledge-intensive sector, which is a sector that is highly digitized across most dimensions (IT-driven). However, what they are missing is the new and powerful technologies that can connect with the new generations of clients, such as millennials.

Once these businesses both realize and leverage the new technologies, and they successfully create new business ideas or new business processes that provide that digital convenience for their customers, they will be able to call themselves a digitalized company and stay in business.

I created the illustration that follows to showcase the ingredients of DX, along with the core components of the digital business. With the tools in the chart, you can build a solution to provide a customer experience in today's business world:

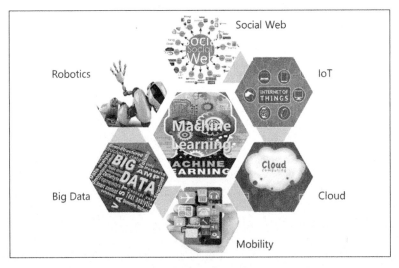

Figure 3.5: The ingredients of DX

Most of these technologies are only in the cloud. The first step is to adopt an interface with the cloud one way or another. Like all other related components, such as machine learning and artificial intelligence, robotics can be had at a low cost if the cloud is integrated. These are services that are offered in the cloud by the so-called pay-as-you-go method. This is something that is easy to do and will be the focus, in a more technical sense, of *Chapter 5, Utilizing Artificial Intelligence and Machine Learning in Your CRM Strategy, Chapter 7, CRM Integration Strategies,* and *Chapter 9, CRM Differentiators.* But, in this chapter, we're going to stay focused on the design concepts.

Customers are highly influenced by the Internet and mobile applications that they use every day. They want better service and digital experiences in every interaction and across all possible channels. Companies are working smarter than ever before in order to gain confidence and trust, and to ultimately develop that personal relationship with their customers.

While some companies are highly digitized across most dimensions, most do not necessarily use the latest technologies to connect with their clients and provide the best digital experience to their clients at a lower price. Digital heroes are maximizing the use of client information and serving (connecting with) customers over their preferred channels; for example, the kind of experience Uber or Amazon are providing to their clients. This way, the companies are able to overcome the challenges they are facing from digital disrupters and using their customer knowledge to their advantage in developing a new customer model that is suitable in today's digital market.

A tale of two case studies

Let's explore two examples and compare a successful high-tech start-up, in this case, Uber, with an old-fashioned traditional company, the Guardian newspaper.

Both of these companies are in very old industries, namely transport and media. Thus, both of these companies will provide us with a unique opportunity to explore how competition with high-tech digital disrupters can be successful.

Case study 1 – Uber

As highlighted earlier in this chapter, CRM design is all about providing a digital experience for your customers. Let's analyze the customer experience with Uber first, in order to see how it leverages the five technologies we explored earlier as ingredients of its digital business.

Uber customers are mainly millennials and mobile users, so by using the mobile app, they are offered a fare before taking the ride, as mentioned earlier. This method creates the first level of trust and comfort for the customer experience. The payment system uses a dynamic pricing engine that is a convenient commodity in the cloud. The system is leveraging machine learning and analytics in order to provide a dynamic price, which will create a level of transparency that the new generation of customers is expecting from any business.

Payment is not conventional or traditional but through a number of payment services based on customer preferences. Uber, like many other high-tech companies, is using the cloud and leveraging the so-called cloud **Infrastructure as a Service (IaaS)** by using software applications (cloud services) that are only available in the cloud (the tracking of the taxi, for example).

Traditional companies could use these cloud services very conveniently. This is known as **Software as a Service (SaaS)**, which is also called software-on-demand, and is licensed on a subscription model, in that you pay as you use, or **Pay As You Go (PAYG)**. That method is as convenient and cost-effective as any other utility billing system and thousands of these services are available in the cloud today.

We will deep dive in the technical design, the deployment options, and integration in *Chapter 7, CRM Integration Strategies* and *Chapter 8, Cloud Versus On-Premise Versus Hybrid – The Deployment of a CRM Platform*.

These cloud applications, which are offered by multiple vendors today, are affordable and accessible to every business. Companies such as Microsoft and subscription models such as PAYG allow companies and businesses to customize, scale, and provision those ingredients and resources, including the development platforms, with a very low cost of ownership and faster time-to-market rate.

SaaS is becoming a common platform for many business applications, including:

- Office-based software
- Database analytics
- Messaging software
- Enterprise Resource Planning (ERP)
- CRM
- Gamification
- Virtualization
- Collaboration
- Human Resource Management (HRM)
- Artificial intelligence
- Machine learning

SaaS has been incorporated into the strategy of nearly all of the leading enterprise software vendors, while artificial intelligence, analytics, and the Internet of Things are being incorporated into start-up spaces and as a result, these enterprises are becoming mainstream.

Gartner, among others, has reported that cloud adoption strategies will influence more than 50 percent of **IT Operation (ITO)** spending through 2020. According to Gartner, the worldwide public cloud services market grew 18 percent in 2017, and by 2020 will be worth an estimated $383.4 billion.

Case study 2 – The Guardian

Now let us explore how a traditional company succeeded in defeating the digital disruptor. This example looks at the Guardian newspaper and provides a great example of a successful digital transformation.

The Guardian is a British daily newspaper that was founded in Manchester in 1821. The Guardian is editorially independent, meaning its journalism is free from commercial bias and is not influenced by the owners, politicians, or shareholders. Three and a half years ago, in 2015, the situation looked bleak across the media sector. Print advertising was in steep decline and digital advertising growth was going almost entirely to Google and Facebook, along with other high-tech companies. During this time, news organizations across the globe were searching for answers to the challenges they were facing from digital disruptions.

While the Guardian was being read by more people than ever before, it had fewer ways to cover the costs. As the months went past, more and more news outlets were going behind a paywall. The revenues from the newspaper had diminished and the technologies that connected it with a global audience had moved the advertising money away to the big tech companies. The Guardian knew it needed to find a way to keep its journalism open, accessible, and convenient to everyone. This was the same strategy as the big tech companies were taking.

The management team came up with the vision to make the Guardian sustainable by deepening its relationship with its readers, who in the case of this newspaper are real clients. It decided to embrace new technologies and adapt its business to support new strategies in order to improve customer experience, processes, information, and measurement tools, as the other tech companies were doing. The Guardian moved its efforts to providing news on the internet, including portable devices such as tablets and mobile, while using artificial intelligence and business intelligence to analyze customer behavior.

Some of the changes included the Guardian publishing all its news online across mobile devices, with free access both to current news and an archive of three million stories, which is important as a third of the site's hits are for items over a month old. The company expanded the business by competing with high-tech giants, such as Amazon and YouTube, by providing books, videos, music, podcasts, and entertainment to its customer base.

The story goes on. The Guardian successfully managed to go through a DX, both communicating and achieving its vision of an independent, investigative journalism editorial approach. By collecting voluntary contributions, membership, or subscriptions, the company managed to overcome the urgent financial situation it was faced with. Today, it is being supported by more than a million readers, who are voluntarily paying clients around the world. The Guardian provides readers with media products over all channels and social media. It is the most popular UK media and newspaper website, with over 10 million unique visitors per month, and in 2018, the newspaper announced that its apps and the mobile website would be redesigned to coincide with its relaunch as a tabloid.

Design elements of a CRM solution

The customers of today are not particularly more demanding than before, but they have a changing lifestyle. They expect personalized information and expert advice that is delivered at the right time (almost immediately), preferably over mobile channels, and an overall better experience when connecting with staff and employees. Marketing, sales, and services organizations are redesigning their processes and applications to comply with these new customer behaviors and fulfill customer preferences, while competing with big tech firms more effectively.

Sales reps are guided and equipped with qualified leads and the appropriate customer knowledge when connecting with their clients. These are the same tools and procedures as I described in the case studies in previous chapters. Business leaders have market and competitor insights, allowing them to take faster decisions with instant access to expertise and knowledge throughout the organization, which helps them to make better decisions.

Marketing executives must continuously find ways to grow their market share, using insights from a variety of sources, both traditional and social, with advanced analytics. They also need to monitor performance, take corrective action that is data-driven, proactively coach their teams, ensure that marketing campaigns are effective, and ensure that they can justify the spending with campaign measurement tools that prove the **Return on Investment (ROI)** at the end of the campaign lifetime. Through all these design elements, both service managers and reps are able to deliver faster and better customer service across all the communication channels and devices regularly, at a lower cost of operation.

For a successful CRM implementation, CRM experts and business leaders often consider a mix of both cloud and on-premises applications and technologies in order to leverage the latest technologies, such as machine learning and artificial intelligence, when combined with the existing application and business environment.

In *Figure 3.6*, you can see a mixture of cloud and on-premises applications:

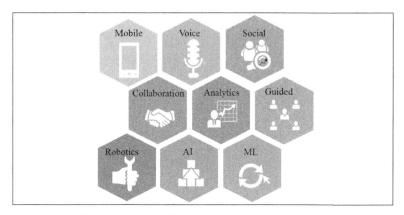

Figure 3.6: A mixture of cloud and on-premises applications

So, elements such as bots combined with artificial intelligence and cognitive services are able to play a substantial role in your design of a CRM solution, and will help you to provide a digital customer experience at a lower operational cost. What's more important is that it gives you tools to assist in competing with big tech companies.

We will cover tools and integration strategies in *Chapter 5, Utilizing Artificial Intelligence and Machine Learning in Your CRM Strategy*, and *Chapter 7, CRM Integration Strategies*.

Where to start?

Conceptualizing a CRM design from the needed requirements, while at the same time delivering a reasonable TCO, starts with the business requirements analysis workshops, and interviews with both the **Business Development Managers** (**BDMs**) and the **Technical Decision Makers** (**TDMs**), followed by compiling the list of use cases, scoring, and fit/gap, all of which results in the creation of a Solution Blueprint.

You can see a visualization of this entire process in the flowchart that follows:

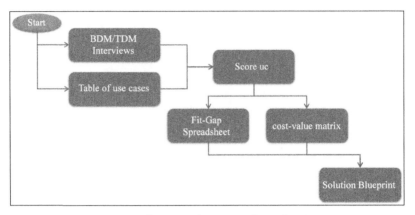

Figure 3.7: The process of creating a Solution Blueprint

The solution architect, together with the business analysts, will apply advanced analytical skills and their experience in project implementations to compile a list of business requirements. They'll score the priority of each business use case, along with its cost of implementation, after conducting the fit-gap workshops, as we can see in the preceding chart.

As we have explored, we have a list of use cases with priorities that are scored by business stakeholders and users participating in business units. You have identified each item, with the ID number for later reference, both in the cost-value matrix and in the Solution Blueprint. You will refer to this ID number later; for example, in the processes catalog, which we will cover later in this chapter.

From here, you could set a cost range, as well as applying a value to the business with a score from 1 to 100, and from there compile the table as I've done here:

#	Use Case	Cost	Value
A9	Measure Data Quality	10	85
A8	Manage Offer	9	88
A5	Log Metrics	10	86
C2	Manage Accounts	11	90
C6	Manage Quick Campaign	12	81
Y1	Measure Cost of Offer	14	86
F2	Import Leads	16	76
F1	Manage Activities	18	69
C7	Activity History	20	90
...			
B7		95	11

Figure 3.8: Example of a use case catalog

In the preceding table, you'll see that case studies **A9**, **A8**, and **A5** have a high value for the business, with a relatively low cost of implementation. Compare this to **B7**, with the high cost of implementation and low business value. Those with a higher priority will go first to the backlog to be implemented. However, don't worry if you don't understand this now, as we will cover this through the book in later chapters.

The cost-value matrix, seen in *Figure 3.9*, helps to identify the low-hanging fruit; these are the least expensive use cases that have the most positive impact on your business' success. This is a good starting point for your CRM design and implementation, as it helps to deliver a good TCO and ROI while still satisfying most user requirements.

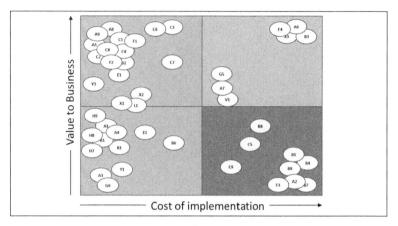

Figure 3.9: Example of a cost-value matrix

Those in the green quadrant, in the top left, are low-hanging fruit because they have significant value to the business with a low implementation cost. Those requirements in the red quadrant, in the bottom right, are of low value to the business and have a relatively high cost of implementation, so you would likely keep them for the next phase, as they could possibly change or disappear over time.

Solution Blueprint

A Solution Blueprint contains both the scope and design of the solution through a series of architecture patterns. Each architecture presents the solution and its core design assertions through a unique perspective, as we will now explore.

A blueprint is used as either an architectural plan or technical drawing. The concept was first introduced by Sir John Herschel in 1842, using a contact print process on light-sensitive sheets. It was a drawing of white lines on a blue background, thus its name. Traditional blueprints became obsolete as less expensive printing methods and computer technology became widely available.

The term has been used since then for many other purposes, including within the software industry, where it's taken on the role of the Solution Blueprint. It's best suited for CRM solutions, as well as solution architectural plans for other types of business applications where there are many stakeholders and different views are required to break down the complexity of the architectural plan.

A Solution Blueprint is a living document and is updated throughout the entire lifetime of a CRM solution. It's intended to catalog the design of the solution and the processes, as well as the architecturally significant requirements and constraints that drive the solution design. Given that the Solution Blueprint is forward-looking, it also documents the current open issues and risks within each architecture design.

At the very highest level, it includes:

- **The process catalog**: Defines the operational processes that will be implemented within the solution. This architecture forms the basis of the solution's scope and all remaining architectures are mainly supporting the implementation of the process architecture.

- **The application architecture**: Defines the application components that will be involved in the solution. This includes those that are implemented explicitly by the solution, as well as those that are integrated either through automated or manual processes.

- **The data architecture**: Defines the data entities involved in the solution and describes how they relate to one another and to external entities.

- **The security architecture**: Defines the means by which access control and permissions will be implemented for those components with the solution. This includes how the solution is enabled and or constrained by the security of components external to the solution.

- **The integration architecture**: Defines the relationships between and interactions of the various components involved in the solution, as well as the components of the solution that are explicitly implemented to facilitate those interactions.

- **The deployment architecture**: Driven by all the other architectures within the blueprint as it represents the physical architecture on which all other aspects of the solution will be based. This typically includes such things as hardware and networks. However, it's not the **Technical Design Document** (**TDD**).

The relationship between all of these elements is shown in *Figure 3.10* in a graphical visualization of the Solution Blueprint:

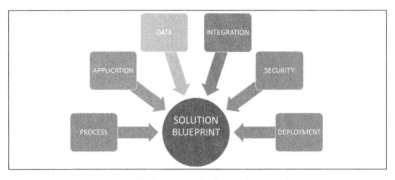

Figure 3.10: A simple illustration of Solution Blueprint elements

You may agree that this is a handy document for all the parties involved in a CRM project throughout its lifetime. This document could be referenced throughout the whole life cycle of the project and afterward throughout the lifespan of the solution. Creating, maintaining, and updating such a document could be a daunting task, and **Solution Architects** (**SAs**), whose job it is to do that task, must be competent in fostering executive-level sponsorships for developing and maintaining the Solution Blueprint, whether the product is still in development, or has been deployed for a number of months or years.

Solution Blueprints also play a crucial role in engaging business stakeholders, partners, and the development team as part of the overall process. Almost everyone involved in the project will have ownership for creating and maintaining at least one part of the Solution Blueprint.

A Solution Blueprint is the master document for conceptualizing the design of a CRM solution. It could be in either a Word or PowerPoint format, and it is not replacing other related documents, such as a detail specification, functional design document, or TDD.

A Solution Blueprint is a short, combined version of all the architecture decisions, along with design assertions and open issues. It's not only a comprehensive and brief solution description, but it also helps to enable all the parties, including the users, project managers, trainers, architects, partners, and everybody else involved, to get a quick view of all related elements of a CRM solution.

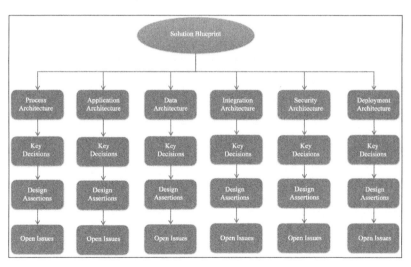

Figure 3.11: Key architectures in a Solution Blueprint

Processing catalog

The key artifact of a Solution Blueprint is the processing catalog, and it's the basis of all solution-related artifacts. The framework of the processing catalog is composed of base processes that represent a general flow of a business operation. Each base process has one or more specific execution paths referred to as scenarios, use cases, or user stories.

This framework is formed of processes and scenarios used to catalog the requirements of the solution, which in turn relate to either fits or gaps. Let's take a look at each one of them:

- Fits are requirements that are supported by the standard application. Fit requirements eventually drive application configurations.

- Gaps are requirements that require application modifications. Gap requirements are related to the functional and technical designs that describe how the gap will be addressed through code modifications or code extensions.

The statistics about the total workstreams, the total processes, and the requirements are listed in a Microsoft Excel sheet.

Here are some examples of statistics:

- Total workstreams: 5
- Total processes: 331
- Total requirements: 1,355

Let's have a look at both the workstreams and the processes catalog:

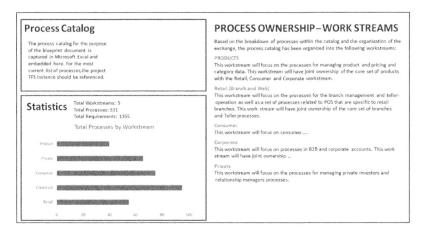

Figure 3.12: Workstreams and processes catalog

Application architecture

Application architecture that comes from Microsoft Excel references the software components of the solution and their relationships to one another. It also includes critical elements of the application architecture, such as:

- **New standard components**: These are the new application components that will be implemented as they come out of the box, meaning that they will not be custom-developed for this implementation.

- **Newly developed or customized components**: These are the new application components that have a basis in the out-of-the-box code, but they will be enhanced to meet specific requirements, or they will be entirely new components that will be developed to specifications.

- **Legacy components**: These are the existing system components that will be leveraged in the new implementation to support the required functionality. These components may either be fully integrated or integrated via a manually executed process.

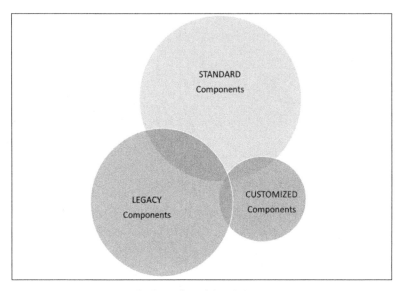

Figure 3.13: The three pillars of the solution components

Data architecture

Data architecture describes how the data will be structured and managed within the system. Example branches will be identified using a 10-digit code. Data architecture will include topics such as:

- Data mastered within the solution boundaries.
- Data mastered outside of the solution boundaries.
- Key data structure designs within the solution.
- Database instance designs.
- Data distribution designs.

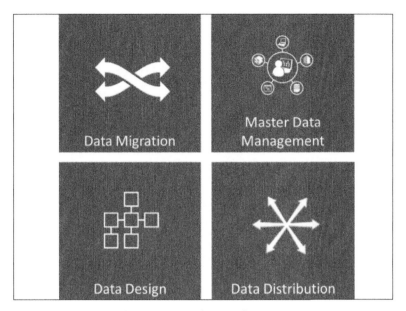

Figure 3.14: Data architecture elements

Integration architecture

The integration architecture defines the relationships between and interactions of the various components involved in the solution, as well as the components of the solution that are explicitly implemented to facilitate those interactions.

In the following graph, you'll see an example of a high-level integration architecture. The contents will depend on the deployment architecture in your design. Deployment architecture and integration are something we will cover in both *Chapter 7, CRM Integration Strategies* and *Chapter 8, Cloud Versus On-Premise Versus Hybrid – The Deployment of a CRM Platform.*

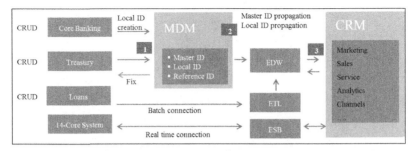

Figure 3.15: Example of a high-level data integration architecture

Architecture Trade-off Analysis Method (ATAM)

Last, but by no means least, is the fact that once you have laid out all relevant architectures in your Solution Blueprint, you need to re-evaluate the design and minimize the risk. One of the best practices is to apply ATAM.

ATAM was developed by the **Software Engineering Institute** (**SEI**) at the Carnegie Mellon University. Its purpose is to help with choosing alternative architecture for a software system by discovering trade-offs and sensitivity points. The method is a risk-mitigation process used early in the software development lifecycle and is most beneficial here because the cost of changing architectures is minimal.

Tools for the Solution Blueprint

You have the freedom to use whatever tool you are familiar with for the design and the format of the Solution Blueprint. I recommend a combination of Microsoft Excel and Microsoft PowerPoint because, for example, you can list the processing catalog or cost-value matrix in the Excel file, slice and dice the information, and link it (or paste the chart) to a page in the PowerPoint document for a better and richer view.

You can see in *Figure 3.16* the process catalog page in a PowerPoint document that will provide an overview of statistics and the workstreams, which are based on the breakdown of processes within the catalog and the business units in the organization. A workstream can represent a business unit, such as customer service; a team, such as the product team; or a person, such as the **solution architect** (**SA**). It could be also based on a process that is a cross-business unit, such as payment or channel management, or managing a product and pricing catalog.

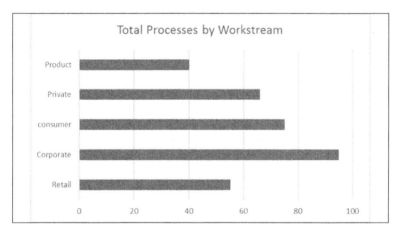

Figure 3.16: Example of process statistics in a Solution Blueprint

Another example was the cost-value matrix that we explored earlier on in this chapter. The business requirements are in a table, with the cost and value captured in Excel and embedded in a PowerPoint document. This will enable a quick overview of the most current list of processes, higher-priority functionalities, and use cases, and could be connected with the project's **Team Foundation Server** (**TFS**) instance.

TFS is a Microsoft tool that provides requirements management, project management, source code management, lab management, reporting, automated builds, testing, and release management capabilities.

Another beneficial outcome of the Solution Blueprint is that requirements and process scenarios are related to requirement tests and process tests, which are further aggregated into the end-to-end **User Acceptance Testing** (**UAT**). Furthermore, scenarios typically define the standard operating procedures that are documented and could be leveraged for training and system operation support, such as a **Train-the-Trainer** (**TTT**) document.

In a nutshell, the Solution Blueprint can be seen as a communication vehicle for all the stakeholders, both from business and IT. It will help everyone involved in a project to effectively collaborate and participate in the design process through the project lifetime.

Trade-off analysis will help to achieve the following:

- **Confirm optimal solution design**: Be confident that the outcome of the project will effectively meet the business requirements.

- **Minimize risk**: Architectural and technical reviews of the Solution Blueprint will help the project and its outcomes to meet expectations.

- **Enhance the ROI**: With the recommendations that are provided as part of ATAM, you will have additional proof that the solution will deliver lasting value to your business and enhance the ROI.

Summary

In summary, your CRM design reflects both the present and future architectural approach you are taking regarding processes, applications, data, security, integration, and deployment decisions that are mainly driven by business requirements. The scope and the design of the solution are determined through a series of workstreams as shown in figure 3.17.

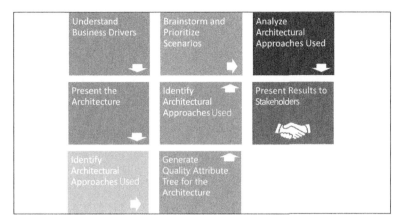

Figure 3.17: Design workstreams

Each workstream represents its core design assertions and the solution. You document the design overview, key decisions, and outstanding issues in your Solution Blueprint. You leverage the Solution Blueprint as a documentation and collaboration tool for all the stakeholders, including:

- Architects
- Business analysts
- Business users
- Business leads
- Developers
- Testers
- Trainers
- The end users

This is what we will be covering in more detail in the next chapter, *Chapter 4, Architecting Your CRM Solution – Preparing for Today and Tomorrow*, where we will be looking at how to design a CRM platform that will work today but also has the necessary elements to be prepared for the future adaptions.

ARCHITECTING YOUR CRM SOLUTION – PREPARING FOR TODAY AND TOMORROW

The best architectures, requirements, and designs emerge from self-organizing teams.

In this chapter, we want to look at the work involved in a CRM architecture and explore the techniques for designing a software solution that could solve the challenges that businesses are facing both today and tomorrow.

This chapter is not only for architects; it has been written in a way that all team members, including technical and business members, will benefit from.

We will cover the major elements of solution architecture design, including:

- Viewpoints

- Quality attribute trees

- Measurement metrics

- Architecture trade-off techniques

In recent years, the dynamics and the business parameters of markets have been changing rapidly, and we can expect to see a profound innovation in CRM technologies. Therefore, we will see even more fundamental changes in the ways that we design and consume CRM solutions for today and tomorrow. We will cover CRM innovations extensively in *Chapter 9, CRM Differentiators*.

We'll start by briefly exploring some software engineering techniques, specifically the ones that are relevant to CRM architecture design. These include the so-called Agile development methodology, as this methodology has proven itself to be the most efficient for designing and implementing business solutions that consider recent technology innovations.

Agile software development is a methodology in software engineering. Under this, the requirements and solutions that a company requires evolve through the collaborative effort of self-organizing and cross-functional project teams and business users. This methodology requires empirical knowledge, adaptive and flexible planning, an iterative and evolutionary development of functional areas, and continual improvement. It encourages rapid and flexible response to change.

All these elements make this methodology best suited for CRM implementations. We do not expect a lot of new software development in modern CRM implementations, rather more of an approach focusing on the configuration and modeling of functional areas, which is called low-code development.

The Agile methodology, as we'll discover throughout this chapter, proves to be more and more valuable in developing today's business solutions, which include both CRM and Enterprise Resource Planning (ERP).

The history of the Agile methodology

Back in 2001, 17 software developers met at a resort in Utah, U.S., to discuss lightweight development methods, which they called Agile. Since then, it has become the most popular methodology in the history of software development.

 Note: The Wikipedia page for Agile, `https://en.wikipedia.org/wiki/Agile_software_development`, is a great resource for understanding its history.

Nowadays, a bigger gathering of organizational anarchists would be hard to find, and so what emerged from this meeting was a symbolic manifesto for Agile software development, which was signed by all 17 participants. Together, they published the *Manifesto for Agile Software Development*, which you can read fully on their site: `http://agilemanifesto.org/principles.html`. However, for ease, you can also read the 12 principles here:

1. The highest priority is to satisfy the customer's requirements through early and continuous delivery of valuable software.

2. Welcome changing requirements, even if it's later in the development cycle. Embrace change for the customer's competitive advantage.

3. Deliver working software frequently, at best in a couple of weeks and at the latest in a couple of months, with a preference for the shorter timescale.

4. Business people and developers work together daily or weekly throughout the project.

5. Build projects around motivated individuals. Give them the environment and support they need, including trusting them to get the job done.

6. The most efficient and effective method of conveying information to and within a development team is a face-to-face conversation.

7. Working software is the primary measure of progress.

8. Agile processes promote sustainable development. The sponsors, developers, and users should be able to maintain a constant pace indefinitely.

9. Continuous attention to technical excellence and good design enhances agility.

10. Simplicity, being the art of maximizing the amount of work not done, is essential.

11. The best architectures, requirements, and designs emerge from self-organizing teams.

12. At regular intervals, the team reflects on how to become more effective, then tunes and adjusts its behavior accordingly.

These basic arguments and previous industry experiences, learned from years of successes and failures, have helped to shape Agile development's favor of adaptive, iterative, and evolutionary development. The software industry is uncovering better ways of developing software by applying Agile methodology and helping others to do it. Some very interesting findings of Agile methodology are:

- Individuals and interactions over processes and tools

- Working software over comprehensive documentation

- Customer collaboration over contract negotiation

- Responding to change over following a plan

One of the statements of the Agile Manifesto is that "the best architectures, requirements, and designs emerge from self-organizing teams." From my own experience in CRM projects, I would add to this "experienced teams with industry knowledge."

Agile development is breaking a project into small functional areas consisting of user and business requirements, which are then stacked in the backlog. These requirements are often formed as user stories or even use cases. We covered the process of collecting and prioritizing use cases in *Chapter 3, Conceptualizing the CRM Design from Business Requirements*.

These user stories and use cases are typically collected during requirement analysis workshops with business analysts. The backlog is continuously updated, and new requirements or use cases are added to the stack.

Iterations are short time frames of one to four weeks of development work done by a cross-functional team, which does the planning, analysis, design, coding, unit testing, and **User Acceptance Testing** (**UAT**) of these use cases and the deployment. In the following chart, you can see how this is visualized:

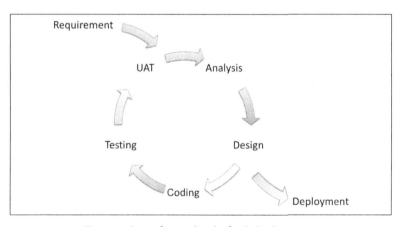

Figure 4.1: One-to-four-week cycle of Agile development

By undertaking this task, you'll minimize the amount of planning needed, while still designing the project, lowering the overall risk, and enabling change requests. All of this will bring down the overall costs of the project, while increasing user acceptance.

Backlog

The backlog plays a very important role in keeping the project time plan and project costs under control. It also reduces the project's risks, improves the value of the solution for the business (user acceptance), and reduces the complexity of the solution by re-ordering and prioritizing user requirements.

A backlog enables step-by-step and business-priority-based delivery. From my own experience, I have observed that business users demand a functionality that often is not used later in the production system. This mostly happens because of the lack of experience that a "normal" business user has when it comes to implementing a CRM solution. Agile iterative methodology will provide the opportunity for the users to get to know the system, while more effectively gaining insight about the solution through an evolutionary and adaptive design.

The cost-value matrix, as we discovered in *Chapter 3, Conceptualizing the CRM Design from Business Requirements*, is an excellent tool for managing and organizing the backlog in Agile methodology. In *Figure 4.2*, you can see a graphical visualization of the Agile iterative methodology:

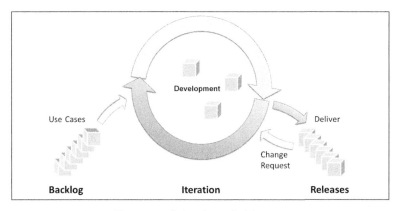

Figure 4.2: Agile iterative methodology

In recent years, Agile software development has been gaining more and more ground. The main argument, or benefit, of this methodology is the approach by which solutions and requirements evolve through the collaboration of cross-functional teams and business users (end users), as I explained before.

As a point of reference, the main characteristics of Agile software development are:

- Adaptive planning
- Evolutionary development
- Early delivery
- Continual improvement
- Flexibility for change

This makes the Agile iterative methodology best suited for CRM implementations, as it allows the CRM to resolve immediate business pain points, while supporting the long-term business vision and strategies.

The long list of benefits associated with Agile software development, and the success of iterative methodology in the software industry, speaks for itself. Responding to change, being flexible, and delivering business requirements in a shorter time, rather than following a strict long-term plan that will change over the course of the project development cycle, is one of the key factors and benefits of the Agile iterative methodology for the CRM projects of today and tomorrow.

The recent developments in the market, coupled with the fundamental and constant changes in the way our customers do business today, mean that CRM design criteria are very different from two or three years ago. Companies need to be Agile through CRM solutions.

We will dive deeper into CRM selection criteria in *Chapter 9, CRM Differentiators*, and explore in detail the changing market and technology environment.

Before we move on to looking at why you need a modern CRM platform, take a minute to look at the graph that follows, which shows the evolution of software development methodologies, which we are going to look at in the next section:

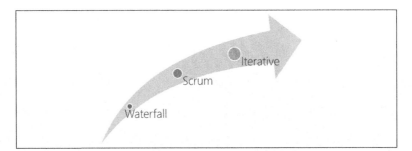

Figure 4.3: The evolution of software development methodologies

You need a modern CRM platform to start with

You may ask what the relationship between the software development methodology and the CRM architecture is. You may, or may not, agree that the methodology you use will have some impact on the design and delivery of your CRM solution. Most CRM implementations today are based on a comprehensive and modern platform, such as Dynamics 365 from Microsoft.

These platforms are based on entity models and the logic of the application is described in a metadata technique that is portable, easily configurable, and allows on-the-fly configurations that are best suited to the Agile project methodology.

In the early days of CRM projects, often the Waterfall methodology was applied as the implementation methodology, as the older platforms were complex and had limited configuration capabilities in a time where more customization and coding was needed. As a lot of coding was required, Waterfall was best suited for development.

Waterfall is a delivery execution methodology based on a sequential, steadily flowing series of implementation phases: conception, initiation, analysis, design, construction, testing, production or implementation, rollout, and maintenance. This is sometimes a multi-year development that is done prior to you delivering any working software to the business. However, with most CRM projects, by the time that the solution is ready to be delivered, the business requirements will have changed, and the project stakeholders and the market requirements will have changed, too.

Iterative is an Agile delivery methodology where requirements are defined and analyzed prior to the beginning of the CRM journey. While you have a holistic CRM and a design based on a solid modern architecture, you are also able to deliver faster business value through iterations.

The iterative methodology utilizes proven best practices developed from thousands of solution deployments. The use of the backlog, which is a stack of business items (use cases or user stories) with priorities associated with them, will continuously improve the TCO/ROI during the implementation, while also reducing project risks.

The priorities are defined by the business users and a cost-value matrix, as I explained in *Chapter 3, Conceptualizing the CRM Design from Business Requirements*, and they could (and very often do) change during the project implementation.

CRM architecture is often a complex undertaking with many dependencies. From my personal experience, CRM touches several different areas and subjects within a company, where both processes and employees are affected. Therefore, both current and future business strategies will need to be considered and supported by the new system.

All the business units should, and will in time, leverage the CRM platform. After all, the sections of a modern business include marketing, sales, and services processes, all of which are automated through the CRM system. Often, these are not considered to be part of the CRM design.

Last, but by no means least, this is about change management; I will give some examples later in this chapter. More importantly, we must consider that the business continues to change or evolve while you are developing and deploying your CRM system. So, by leveraging an iterative methodology, you will have a roadmap to success associated with lower costs and lower risks.

Let's look at some solid advice for project stakeholders to take on board:

- **Plan ahead**: Make sure you have all the right people, tools, and checklists for the trip before you start your journey.

- **Know the road**: Set clear expectations around the start and end dates, and project milestones, so that people know the plan and what to expect, and what is expected from them.

- **Avoid pitfalls**: Utilize proven best practices, developed by an Agile iterative methodology, that minimize the risks and costs, and deliver faster business value.

- **Get there faster, but be open to change**: Think out of the box, be open to change, and take advantage of shortcuts and other strategies that help you save time and money.

- **No surprises**: Delight executives and users by delivering the right results on time and on budget.

Having discussed software development methodologies here, it is also important to notice that in today's world, you don't want to create or build your CRM system from scratch with in-house or outside resources; not even one small module, such as case management. A TCO/ROI analysis before starting any CRM implementation with in-house resources will help you to get a better picture on this.

In today's world, companies are building their business requirements on top of a standard and available CRM platform, such as Dynamics 365 from Microsoft. Depending on several different factors, which we will cover later in *Chapter 8, Cloud Versus On-Premise Versus Hybrid – The Deployment of a CRM Platform,* and *Chapter 9, CRM Differentiators*, you may decide to go for an online, hybrid, or on-premise CRM solution.

A Baltic bank and its business pain point

Several years ago, I was delivering a workshop to a large bank in the Baltic region. The company was telling me that it had a 200-strong team of smart developers that had spent the last 10-15 years developing CRM modules for the bank.

This started with a call center app, before expanding to marketing campaign apps, sales automation, customer onboarding, customer loyalty, service request management, pipeline management, incentive management, and territory management.

But the big business pain point at this bank was applications that had been developed in silos, based on different technologies that are mostly not well connected and not integrated. Maintenance and enhancements had become a costly nightmare. Above all, any change that had been requested by business users was taking up a lot of time and was not only expensive, but often not fully possible.

The activities entity model in the Microsoft Dynamics CRM

This leads to a simple fact: an enterprise-based CRM solution is very complex to build from scratch. Just to demonstrate the technical complexity of a CRM system, what follows is a small snapshot of the relationships within Microsoft Dynamics 365. This screenshot only shows a high-level view of the activities within the Microsoft CRM and the relationships between these entities; it is not meant to be readable by you but to show the complexity of relationships between one entity (activity) and other entities:

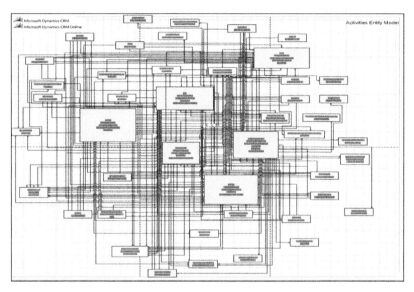

Figure 4.4: Activities entity model in the Microsoft Dynamics CRM

In *Figure 4.5*, we can zoom in to show just how complex things can become:

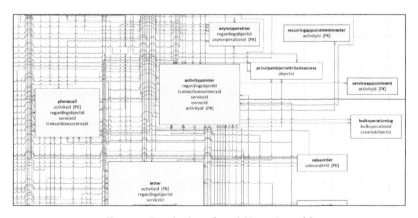

Figure 4.5: Zooming in on the activities entity model

Another important design consideration is that you want to configure and not customize the CRM platform. This is because customization requires code modifications that are often expensive and not portable from one version to the next, versus the configuration option, which is both less expensive and enables better portability.

Another important design consideration is that you need to keep in mind that CRM is connected to other applications and to most other planned projects in the company, such as digital transformation, which we will explore in *Chapter 9, CRM Differentiators*. Crucially, they might have an impact on your design and the scope of the solution. In this chapter, we will discuss the impact of unrelated initiatives in your company on your CRM design.

When you start the architectural design of your application, you will find that you have some tough architectural decisions to make. You will need to consider the viewpoints of people involved in the project; finding a balance of viewpoints is vital. This is represented in *Figure 4.6*:

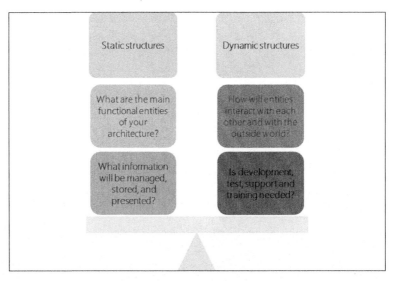

Figure 4.6: Viewpoints and balance

So, before doing a deep dive into the art of design, let's see what traditional elements can be considered when you design your CRM solution.

In general, there are two sets of architectural considerations:

- One set of technical factors, such as your current or future IT infrastructure

- One set of business-related factors, such as your high-level business strategies, the current business requirements, and the long- and short-term requirements

These two architectural considerations will influence the decision-making processes for the selection of the CRM platform, as well as the design of the solution in every enterprise CRM project.

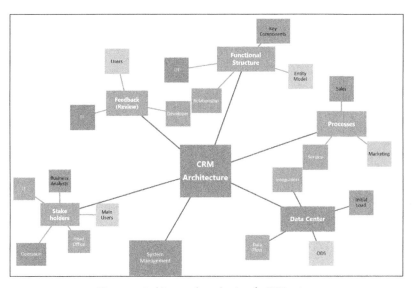

Figure 4.7: Architecture dependencies of a CRM system

Figure 4.7 is a simplified illustration of elements that are traditionally relevant to the CRM platform and the design of an enterprise CRM solution. There are many more components to consider in an architecture design that is platform-independent. These include the stakeholders, the users, the functional structures, processes, and other seemingly unrelated items of CRM, as I explained in *Chapter 3, Conceptualizing the CRM Design from Business Requirements*. Therefore, a standard and powerful CRM platform can bring many benefits to your business. But rather than me just telling you, let's go through a real-world example that I was involved in.

The broken ATM

I was visiting a bank a few years ago and as I stood in the office of the **Chief Information Officer** (**CIO**), I was looking from his office window at a larger room next to his office. I could see people sitting behind control desks and observing a very large screen in front of them like a movie; see in *Figure 4.8*.

I asked the CIO what this room was and what these people were doing there. He told me this room was the management center of all the ATMs in the country. Problems with these machines can be very different, as ATMs have several components, such as paper, cash, sensors, and a camera, that can go wrong. The CIO told me that there is a service level agreement with all the banks in the country to monitor, fix problems, and keep thousands of these machines up and running 24/7 with minimum downtime.

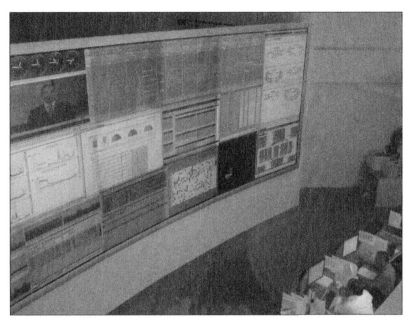

Figure 4.8: The "cinema" used to monitor the ATM operations across a country

I asked whether he knew that you can bring a lot of efficiency and automation to managing ATMs with a CRM solution. He was very surprised, as he had never heard about a CRM system managing ATMs.

Indeed, just a few weeks earlier, I was running another workshop, with another customer. It had leveraged a CRM solution for its ATM management. The idea was very simple but very effective.

ATMs generate log files for almost every event they encounter, including events that occur in the devices of the ATM, such as:

- Cash bin
- Card reader
- Dispenser
- Hardware
- Printer
- Sensors
- Services
- Consumables
- Paper
- Cash
- Camera

These events, if they occur, can be sent to a CRM system to be captured, analyzed, filtered, reported, and fixed if needed. This way, the bank can bring automation to detecting, reporting, and fixing all kinds of problems with the service engine of the CRM system. Then the closest technician will be informed on their mobile of the exact cause of the problem and the severity level, before being sent to fix the problem. This can happen before customers even realize there is a problem with the ATM.

In the next figure, you can see the high-level design of the solution. Here, the ATM will send a log to **Microsoft Operation Manager** (**MOM**), which is then filtered and passed to the CRM system, before being sent to the technicians.

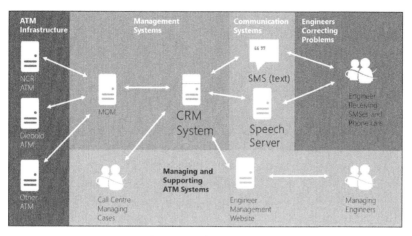

Figure 4.9: CRM solution design for automated ATM management

The preceding solution design brings almost a full automation into effect for managing the ATMs in a country. Being integrated into your CRM platform also brings several additional benefits. It's very cost effective and provides additional benefits when compared to traditional management solutions, such as faster problem resolution, preventive monitoring, better reporting, or much lower cost of maintenance due to location-based service automation.

What most people don't know is that ATMs are mostly Microsoft-Windows-based operating systems. They generate thousands of events every day and the CRM system will receive these events through MOM. It will then analyze events from an ATM, classify them, and open a case. Depending on the type and location of the event, which is analyzed through a service engine, a message and/or voicemail will be sent to the relevant technicians.

Through this, you can see the power of this solution and the benefits it provides to both the business and clients. This way, you are not only saving customer time by increasing the uptime of the ATMs, but you're also able to detect and fix problems prior to an ATM user complaining, and a long time before an ultimate system failure is caused.

I was in France a short time after these workshops were held. In a busy shopping mall, I intended to get some cash from an ATM. There was this **National Cash Register** (**NCR**) machine that was continually rebooting. Eventually, someone behind me told me that it was useless for me to wait for it to recover, as it would crash again; it had been this way for the last few hours. I took a picture, as you can see in *Figure 4.10*. As you read the error message, you can see that it has some hardware errors when a driver starts to load.

Typically, these drivers will fail to start when there is a sever hardware problem, but more importantly, these are problems that don't appear out of the blue. What normally happens is that before the hardware starts failing, it sends warning messages about some minor errors, until it fully stops functioning.

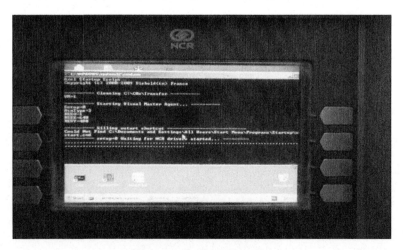

Figure 4.10: A broken ATM machine

This is a good example of thinking out of the box when designing your CRM system. You should expand your discussions to include both short- and long-term strategies, and a development plan (innovation plan), so that you can start your design with a holistic view of the business requirements, no matter whether they are directly correlating with traditional CRM requirements or not.

There are always many more capabilities in a CRM platform than most people would consider. The next personal story is a good example of how to make these discoveries prior to designing your new CRM system.

Business strategies and future CRM

The preceding example could show that there are countless areas that a CRM system could touch upon to improve the business outcome, even if it's not directly a customer-related process. In my experience with so many CRM projects, I suggest you always need to have a holistic view of future strategies for the company. You should at least consider the next four to five years of the business plan and strategies.

To use another case study, I was conducting a pre-sales workshop with the business decision makers of a large bank and the CEO of the company was attending the first hour of the workshop. As I explained how important it is to reveal the short- and long-term business strategies at the beginning of each CRM journey, he decided to stay in the workshop and shared with me the bank's strategies for the next four years.

He explained to me how the bank plans to become number one in the country in five years by improving operational efficiency by 5% per year, reducing the cost of operations by 5% per year, and improving market share by 5% year-on-year. The bank had already engaged with a business consulting firm and through that, built a clear picture of how it will improve the business outcomes through improving its overall business processes.

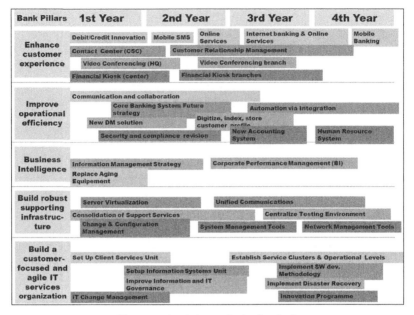

Figure 4.11: A typical strategic plan for a bank

As you can see in the preceding plan, the company has a four-year development and an innovation plan with five pillars, which goes beyond just CRM. The company is looking at CRM in the traditional manner, as can be seen in the first pillar: customer experience. There are also many other areas in other pillars that correlate with CRM either directly or indirectly.

CRM architecture is about designing a solution that integrates all the relevant business areas and processes for today and tomorrow, while supporting the overall business strategies. It will consider the properties of processes and how they interact with each other. Sometimes, this may even include processes that are not directly regarded as traditionally CRM-related, such as sales, marketing, and customer service.

I was engaged in another CRM implementation where we had identified eight different business areas, including card management, property management, and facility management.

They were easily integrated into the CRM processes. The CRM architect is responsible for designing and leading the construction of a system that meets both the needs of the company today and also tomorrow.

Remember some of the learning experiences from the Agile methodology?

- Individuals and interactions over processes and tools.
- Working software over comprehensive documentation.
- Customer collaboration over contract terms.
- Responding to change over following a plan.

The architect is responsible for sharing his or her knowledge, know-how, best practices, and ideas with the customer. They're also there to collaborate with the customer to identify all relevant processes and work with the stakeholders in building a solution that benefits the overall business strategies and brings in process efficiencies that help to reduce operational costs.

One very interesting observation I have made in my career is that often there are other projects and investments in the company that may be even better off when included in CRM discussions. There are actually other areas that are well served by the CRM system, even if not directly touching the customer processes.

In the banking example we discussed, the company discovered that many projects in its four-year plan can be covered fully or partly by the new CRM system, or at least need to be considered in the design phase of the CRM platform.

As you saw in *Figure 4.11*, the bank used the five pillars to find out which one of them could be better served by an enterprise CRM system and maybe even included in the 360-degree client view, as we discussed in *Chapter 2, Getting to Know Your Customer*.

As we have seen, the CRM architect could easily expand the scope and engagement level of a project depending on the strategic plan of the customer. In another project I was recently engaged with, in parallel to the CRM project, the customer was implementing a business innovation project together with one of the big three management consultancies, which are McKinsey, Bain, and **Boston Consulting Group (BCG)**. There are also the big four: PwC, Deloitte, KPMG, and E&Y.

I found out about this other innovation project after starting the CRM design. Luckily, I could manage to incorporate some of the recommendations from the consulting company into the CRM platform on time, including them in the design going forward.

Let's take a minute to look at a graph showing the engagement level for a CRM architect over the time it takes to develop a CRM platform:

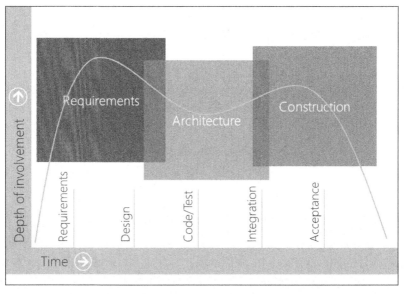

Figure 4.12: Engagement level for a CRM architect

The preceding example shows that the level of an architect's engagement in a CRM project varies throughout the lifecycle of the project. As we can see, there is deeper engagement in the requirement analysis with the business analysts and CRM stakeholders. This means discovering all the business areas that could be easily integrated into the CRM processes, rather than through code/testing. Later, there's higher engagement toward the end, which accompanies the UAT, deployment, and operation phases of development.

TCO/ROI

I always like to reiterate how important TCO/ROI is and remind stakeholders about that. I talked a lot about TCO/ROI and the cost-value matrix in *Chapter 3, Conceptualizing the CRM Design from Business Requirements*.

In this chapter, we're going to focus on designing a solution for the future. To do this, you will need to have some basic measurement metrics that have been agreed on by your business leaders in order to improve processes and outcomes. This is a key success factor for the design and the justification of the investment. All stakeholders need to be on board with the CRM metrics before starting with the design.

The metrics are driven by requirements analyses and are instrumental not only for a TCO/ROI measurement but for the design of the solution, and more importantly, for user acceptance by business departments.

Typically, CRM metrics define the sales, marketing, and customer service process improvements at the very highest levels of a company. You'll define them at the start of the process, and you'll keep measuring them every six or 12 months. They are an indication of success for your solution design and a sign of recognition for the stakeholders because they provide justification for the investment.

The following table is a list of some of the metrics found in a typical company. Though, in this case, we are focused on a bank. You and all the other stakeholders will create such a table of the use cases with both the current and future metrics, which could easily be used as a measurement of TCO/ROI of the project. This could give the architect enough data to design a better solution or at least to measure the overall health of your CRM solution.

Marketing	Sales	Service	Financial	Channels
Campaign Creation	Sales Quantity	Resolution Time	Cost of Operation	Branch visits wait time ratio
Campaign Distribution	Sales Margin	SLA Metrics	Profitabilty	ATM use and uptime
Response Rate	Cross/Up-Sell	Customer Satisfaction	Revenue Growth	Mobile banking growth
Conversion Rate	Lead Conversion Rate	Loyalty Metrics		Length of advisory sessions
Campaign Costs	Portfolio Growth	Escalation Resolution Ratio		Email requests and resolution Ratio
Campaign ROI	Share of Wallet			
	Growth Rate			
	Lead Conversion Rate			

Figure 4.13: TCO/ROI measurement metrics

Keep this exercise as simple as you can. Take the user stories, derive the measurable values from these metrics, measure today's process efficiencies, and set goals for three or six months after the deployment. You should aim to repeat this process periodically every six or 12 months.

This is very much like fitness training, where you use regular measurements to track whether you are improving. You measure, you train, and you measure again. From that, you keep improving your training plan.

You assess your level of physical fitness first with a fitness check. Then, depending on how physically fit you are, or what your fitness goals are, you set a plan for your training. Improving your fitness level may be as simple as starting an exercise program to achieve some specific fitness goals. Over time, you keep measuring and improving, and that is exactly what you will do in CRM implementation.

Following is a good example of measuring and improving data quality in a bank, reflecting one of your measurement metrics in your CRM design. You will have data-quality improvement as a measurement metric in your CRM concept, as shown in *Figure 4.13*. From there, you can create a dashboard that directly measures the data quality going forward. Not only does this help you to justify your design, but it will also help the business to measure the improvement of data quality constantly in the future.

Figure 4.14: Data quality dashboard

In this case, the data quality dashboard is the homepage of the branch manager. After entering the office in the morning, this is the first page on their computer or laptop. It displays the data quality dashboard for all branch customers by customer segment and the type of the bad or missing data.

The entire process allows the branch manager to take actions and delegate tasks to the business leader or responsible staff in order to improve the data quality. Since this is a constant process, in that the data is updated regularly, it will lead to improving the data quality continuously at a very low cost.

In addition, this process is supported by the CRM system and embedded procedures. As for every single customer view, the system will remind customer-facing staff about the missing or bad data in the system. It guides the employees to take action to improve the data every day. It's very efficient, comes in at a low cost, and provides high value to the business.

Non-Functional Requirements (NFRs) and Quality Attribute Tree (QAT)

So far, in this and across the previous chapters, we've covered the functional requirements elements, but as an architect, you probably will need to also consider the NFRs in your design.

These are attributes affecting the system behavior and the development or support of the system. NFR attributes, as suggested by the International Organization for Standardization (ISO) (ISO/ IEC FCD 25010 diagram), are:

- Performance
- Efficiency
- Compatibility
- Usability
- Reliability
- Security
- Maintainability
- Portability

In the best-case scenarios, all this is addressed throughout the RFP/RFI and platform selection process. However, often some of the attributes of the NFRs are either untouched or unknown, and remain to be addressed after the Fit/Gap analyses and business requirements workshops.

These attributes need to be addressed prior to the solution design. This is the time where you are ready to establish or verify the critical quality properties that the system will have to exhibit, and you are ready to identify scenarios to characterize each one. The output of the process will go to the quality attribute tree, which you can see in your Solution Blueprint, as described in *Chapter 3, Conceptualizing the CRM Design from Business Requirements*.

I remember in one of my projects we had a 360-degree client view. It had a response time of 15-45 seconds, in which it loaded the data. In this case, there were some data fields that were collected on the fly from other applications and data sources. Some users were complaining about the response time, and so the business leader requested tuning the time to below five seconds at any cost.

The staff and relationship managers of this business unit, within private banking, were all highly paid and the customers were too important to wait even 10 seconds for a response. On top of all that, this view was one of the most used views in the unit's daily routines. With 100 relationship managers per branch opening this view about 10 times on average per day, there was a total waiting time of 40,000 seconds (100x10x40) or 11 hours a day for both the customer and the employee, totaling about 2,500 hours a year. A relationship manager, on average, has a cost of $100 per hour for the company, which we calculated would result in a $250,000 optimization per year and per branch if the response time was reduced to five seconds. We did this by loading most of the data overnight and in batch.

The typical NFR attributes to be addressed in your CRM system are security, availability, performance, and evolution. These are the non-functional attributes that are driven indirectly by business and by user requirements. However, they may also be influenced by other factors, such as regulatory compliance; for example, GDPR, which we will cover in *Chapter 6, GDPR and Regulatory Compliance*. You may decide to simplify the process with a chart, as follows:

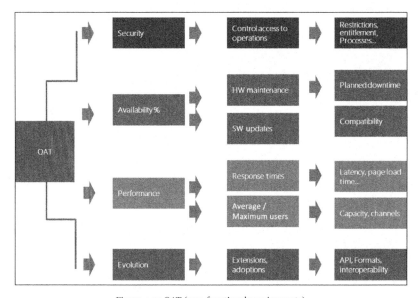

Figure 4.15: QAT (non-functional requirements)

As an example, the **Security** attribute, in the top row, explains how you will need to provide a security model that protects data integrity and privacy, and at the same time supports efficient data access and collaboration between business units and team members. The goals of the model are to:

- Provide users with access only to the appropriate levels of information that are required to do their jobs.

- Categorize users by role and restrict access based on those roles.

- Support data sharing, so that users and teams can be granted access to records that they do not own for a specified collaborative effort; as an example, account teams.

- Prevent a user's access to records that the user does not own or need to know about.

This idea can be seen reflected in *Figure 4.16*, showing the architectural viewpoint:

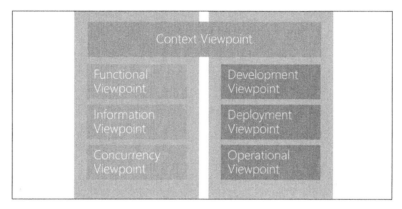

Figure 4.16: Architecture viewpoint

I was working with a bank in the UK and it had a very complex security model that was not provided by any standard CRM platform. It was way more complex than standard security features such as record-level security or field-level security; therefore, it was not fully addressed during the request for proposal (RFP) and platform selection.

In this case, we had to customize the platform to provide a unique entitlement procedure for the bank that was a role-based security model. It could not only group a set of privileges together that described the responsibilities or tasks that could be performed but also, depending on the processes and dynamic events that took place, these security attributes would come into effect.

These are the types of attributes (shown in *Figure 4.17)* that you will address in your design. Before the customization of the system, you will document all that information in the Solution Blueprint.

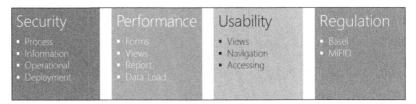

Figure 4.17: Most common non-functional attributes

You'll often have to make some trade-offs for cost and feasibility reasons. You will apply the **Architecture Trade-off Analysis Method (ATAM)**. This is a risk-mitigation process that could be used in the solution development life cycle to help reduce implementation costs and to provide a quicker solution for the business, even if it's not 100% satisfying the business requirements.

ATAM

Applying ATAM was first suggested by the **Software Engineering Institute (SEI)** at Carnegie Mellon University. Originally designed for non-mission-critical applications, it then evolved to more mission-critical applications as it proved to be cost effective and even sometimes a better way to manage the overall development cycle, as I suggested earlier in this chapter with the backlog and Agile methodology.

Leveraging the ATAM reduces both costs and risks, while providing a solution to the business requirements that with time may prove to be a better solution than the one that was initially requested by the business.

The process is simple and the benefits are soon recognized, as you can see in *Figure 4.18*:

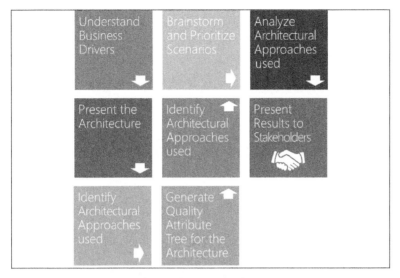

Figure 4.18: ATAM example

But let's take a minute to look at some of the key ATAM benefits:

- Identifying feasibility and risk factors early and continuously in the solution life cycle.

- Increased and transparent communication among stakeholders to engage both in functional and non-functional attributes.

- Exploring quality attribute requirements and coming to an agreement on trade-offs with business stakeholders.

- Improved architecture documentation with justification of architectural decisions.

- Lower costs and faster time to market.

User experience (**UX**) and user acceptance are both very good examples of where you need to apply the ATAM. UX is often neglected in CRM implementations. You will find many definitions of UX on the Internet, but the most common is that UX involves a person's behaviors, attitudes, and emotions about using a particular product, system, or service.

For a CRM system, this is indeed a very critical element and often a very emotive one. A CRM system often fails because of bad user acceptance, but failures are also partly based on emotional reasons. The users often complain that things are more complex and take more time with an enterprise CRM system when compared to the old in-house solution or the Excel solution that was used before, which was efficiently adapted to the business. This is a good place to apply the ATAM to reduce the risks associated early in the project.

Use case – Building an enterprise CRM system

In a recent project, I was involved with a larger team of experts in deploying an enterprise CRM system. This was to be deployed in the back office, in regional offices, and for front office staff at a mid-sized bank. The product design team in the back office was resisting the change, as people were very happy with the current solution they had. The solution was developed for them and adapted fully to their complex requirements, and sometimes lengthy processes.

On the other hand, the bank and all the other business units were complaining about this same solution. Every other business unit had quite a challenge with this legacy application. Basic products, such as saving or checking accounts, were managed in the core banking system. All the other products, which were mostly loans, property, and personal, were managed in this application. It was a silo application, which was the core of the problem for other business units in the bank.

The solution was built by a local software vendor exclusively for the product team. It was a silo application because integration and automation were not considered in the design. For example, a product modification request made by a branch was half automated and had a tracking process that required a lot of manual data entry and intervention.

While the application had a very nice and sophisticated user interface, and an efficient product design interface, it had many dependencies on other tools; most of the other tools were going to be integrated or replaced by the new CRM solution. These dependencies were somehow blurry and often managed manually by means of email notifications, Microsoft Excel sheets, or phone calls. For example, if a product was modified in this tool by request from a branch, there would be a manual email notification sent back to the branch and front-office personnel to confirm the change. Or if an exception was approved in a tariff or in a rate, there would be another email notification sent to the product group, for example.

In *Figure 4.19*, you can see a display of the dependencies of the solution, along with other applications:

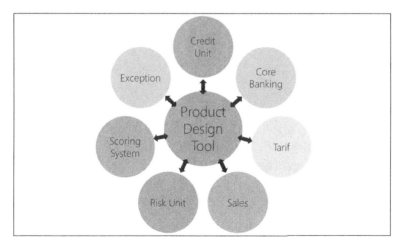

Figure 4.19: Blurry interaction with related entities in legacy systems

In this case, the users of the application were mainly mortgage loan specialists, in addition to personal loan experts within the product group. The requirements or needs for these two main user groups differed a bit, but at a high level, they were very similar.

The application was well designed for the requirements of both groups; it was satisfactory for their business needs. The business pain point was the whole process of handling requests and approvals from and to other business units. It was not part of a comprehensive and relational platform, as I described in the CRM platform and implementation methods. The handling of exceptions during the negotiation process with clients was managed with or within other tools, such as risk management and scoring.

Top business leaders and other business units were complaining about the product group team that operated in a silo and the collaboration defects in many processes. This was a very good example of the ATAM process being applied. You had a fantastic tool that had a beautiful user interface, without considering the other related processes in the supply chain.

For better user acceptance, you may want to engage a subject matter expert in the design of the UX. In most standard CRM systems, the overall the solution usability has good and solid user interface design. The navigation, menu bars, process flow, and forms and views reflect a very modern and state-of-the-art user interface. Having said that, there are a few areas for improvement, and some of them need quick and achievable resolutions prior to the CRM system going live.

Improvements in the user interface of a CRM solution

In this section, I would like to list some of the best improvements. This is not a complete list, and we will explore these in more detail over the next few chapters.

Regarding the user interface in a CRM system, you always must be ready to make some compromises. You follow a new process to collect, maintain, and manipulate data, and overall, you need to follow the processes that help the company and not a particular business unit in a silo:

1. **Automation**: The most important and easy-to-resolve issue is reducing the number of fields on the main forms and views, such as on the customer main form. The number of fields per form or view needs to be reduced to a minimum. This is often expressed by the UAT users before the go-live date.

2. **Simplicity**: User guidance through the automated user interface flow will help efficiency and reduce complexity in the business process. CRM offers rich and easy-to-implement functionalities for automated user interfaces, such as with Portable Business Logic (PBL), to introduce a high degree of automation in the user input or output flow. This will enable the limitation of unnecessary fields on a form.

3. **Help**: User support and context-sensitive help in forms and views will increase the speed of user adoption, which is a critical element in any CRM. Most CRM systems provide simple-to-implement context-sensitive help or support to users. Tooltips in CRMs enable you to change and define tips that users will be able to see when hovering with the mouse over a field. This will increase user adoption and the user acceptance rate in the first place. It will also reduce the training effort required.

4. **Usability**: The UX both for internal users and external users continuously needs improving. Make a good and extended UAT prior to going live, but also ensure you set a roadmap for some longer-term improvements listed in your backlog.

Summary

In this chapter, I outlined that the Agile methodology has proved to be best suited for CRM projects. Modern CRM platforms, such as Dynamics 365 from Microsoft, will provide you with configuration capabilities that require little or no coding.

One thing is for sure: the markets of today, coupled with the environmental and technological advances such as artificial intelligence, big data, and machine learning, will require an open and standard architecture that enables the easy and quick adoption of business change. This will include supporting change management through a step-by-step adoption of these technologies.

While you need to have a holistic view of your company's business strategies for the next five years, you will need to deliver the changes and new functionalities in small steps by applying the Agile methodology. The design and the architecture of your solution will provide a foundation for a comprehensive and extendible solution that will easily adapt to future challenges, both known and unknown.

The last 10 years were undoubtedly remarkable years for technology innovations, but I expect even more changes in the coming years that will affect the way we manage our customer relationships. Therefore, a flexible and configurable CRM platform is essential to the success of your company. A flexible design is even more essential because you can adapt it to the challenges your business will face tomorrow.

In this chapter, we have learned about the Agile methodology, backlogs, and iterations, all of which provide some level of flexibility in the design and delivery of a CRM platform.

We've also learned about some of the essential architects' tools, including the ATAM and the QAT. Again, we touched on the importance of the TCO/ROI aspects of design in your architecture.

We will be exploring the significant elements of the fourth industrial revolution in regards to CRM strategies, including artificial intelligence, big data, and machine learning, in *Chapter 5, Utilizing Artificial Intelligence and Machine Learning in Your CRM Strategy.*

Utilizing Artificial Intelligence and Machine Learning in Your CRM Strategy

Why and how is the emergence of artificial intelligence and big data solutions important to CRM design?

In this chapter, we will be exploring how **Artificial Intelligence (AI)** and **Machine Learning (ML)** can support your CRM processes and, in turn, enrich traditional business applications. This will enable higher process automation and, as a result, better business orchestration.

We will be looking at examples of how these newer technologies could be embedded into customer processes in order to provide self-service and automated customer interactions, while delivering recommendations and personalized customer experiences at an affordable price. We will talk about the development of AI in recent years, its current state, and finally, how AI could actually be implemented into every business' CRM usage.

We are in an amazing period of human development; technological innovations, which are already fast, are accelerating at a faster rate day by day. In this chapter, we will bring in examples of how to leverage these newer technologies for your daily CRM processes.

I remember only a few years ago, everyone in the industry was talking about technology innovations in the Internet era moving seven times faster than they were previously. Something that continues to increase worldwide is people's access to technology and to the Internet. With the **fifth generation** (**5G**) of mobile communication beginning to appear, the world's ability to access the Internet continues to become ever faster and more affordable. From improved user experiences to faster innovations in the high-tech industry, this access to the Internet, and its associated technologies, has led to the empowerment of ordinary people, allowing them to access and use innovative software, hardware products, and services.

With the democratization of both AI and ML, combined with the mass adoption of the Internet, **Internet of Things** (**IoT**), and social media, we are witnessing a fundamental change in the way we do business and communicate with both our clients and partners. This is directly affecting our CRM processes.

In this chapter, we are going to cover the use of AI, cognitive services, and ML in CRM processes. In *Chapter 8, Cloud Versus On-Premise Versus Hybrid – The Deployment of a CRM Platform*, we will discuss the implementation and integration techniques that allow smart client integration.

Then, in *Chapter 9, CRM Differentiators*, we will extend this discussion with the fourth industrial revolution, discussing the importance of CRM platforms for enabling your business to leverage these technologies at a reasonable price, such as what is offered by Dynamics 365 from Microsoft.

When I talk about AI in the context of how we will be using it, I mean the science of training computer systems to complete intelligent human tasks through learning and automation, and, in turn, making bots better at supporting customer interactions.

The purpose of this chapter is to raise awareness about the impact of AI in your CRM solution. I've written this chapter to show you how applying AI, and the technologies around it, can help you to implement higher-level automation, providing better customer service at a lower cost, while staying competitive in a very tough and dynamic market.

We will start by exploring the terminologies and capabilities of these new technologies, before taking a dive into how both AI and ML, combined with CRM processes, will help businesses in all industries to improve their operational efficiencies.

By the end of this chapter, you will have a good overview of these technologies, how they are functioning, how they are related to each other, and how to leverage them in your CRM processes through the use of a real-world example.

Digital business

Recently, I was conducting a workshop for the top executives of a mid-size bank in a Nordic country. These executives were telling me that back in 2013, just 5% of customers emailed or used electronic forms of communication when wanting to connect with the bank. In the present, that figure has gone up to 85%.

For the bank, eight out of 10 customers from across all the customer segments, and nine out of 10 from the younger age groups, are now using a digital communication platform as their method of communication with the bank. This top executive was telling me, very proudly, that the company is now a genuinely digital bank. The bank went through digital transformation and now has 24/7 kiosks and video conferencing with financial advisors, and offers the ability to set up accounts by e-banking or video trust.

I asked the executive whether the bank applied at least any three of the following technologies: AI, **Social Web** (**SW**), IoT, big data, robotics, mobility, or cloud services. This would mean that the bank could genuinely claim that it had started its digital transformation. Why these technologies? These are the ingredients of the fourth industrial revolution that we've discussed in previous chapters, and they provide the platform or foundation for digital transformation, which we will cover extensively in *Chapter 9, CRM Differentiators*.

With the democratization of technologies through cloud service providers, such as Microsoft, these technologies are now affordable for many. More importantly, they are not exclusively for big tech companies, such as Google and Facebook.

In this workshop, this executive was very disappointed when he looked at those technologies and realized that the bank is not ready to compete with digital disrupters. This company is actually just using better communication techniques and faster computers to re-build its existing customer processes, without making any real change to the processes and business operations. The bank does not have any of the technologies for digital transformation implemented into its daily operations.

A successful digital transformation is a necessity nowadays in order to stay competitive and not let outside vendors and big tech companies take your market share away. For example, the "chat and pay" service from Facebook shows how social media is beating the banks in providing an easy money transfer service to millions of consumers around the globe.

The chat could take place on Facebook's Messenger service and finish with a simple click to transfer the cash between friends. It's very similar to M-Pesa, which provides payment services to millions of customers in Africa and Eastern Europe, as discussed in *Chapter 3, Conceptualizing the CRM Design from Business Requirements*.

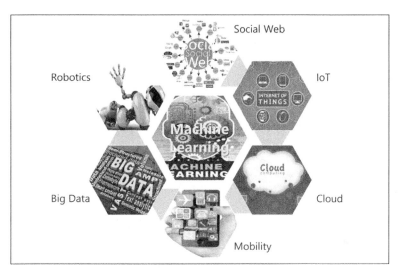

Figure 5.1: Ingredients of today's digital business

Figure 5.1 shows the ingredients of a digital business and where AI or ML is placed. In the example of the bank, while it thought it had completed a digital transformation, the fact that it had not incorporated at least three of these elements meant that it had not.

Evolution of AI

AI is not a new idea. It has been around since the 1940s, when it was a key component in science fiction films as a story-telling device. The algorithms and theories that underpin the modern AI systems that we're used to using in our daily lives have their roots as far back as the 1950s.

The first computer programs in the 1960s and 1970s were followed with LISP, a high-level programming language. Then, as far back as 30 years ago, in the 1980s, the first machines with real AI systems, as we know them today, were developed.

By 1985, the market for AI had reached over a billion dollars in value, which in today's money is over $2.3 billion. For new technology, that's very impressive. By the late 1990s, we began to see AI being used for logistics, data mining, medical diagnosis, and in countless other areas.

In 2019, what's new is access to huge data, which we have gained through the Internet and cloud usage, as well as through business applications on-premise. Through the use of the Internet and cloud services, combined with the ever-increasing power of CPUs and memory space, both of which are now affordable to almost every business, AI is democratized and not exclusive to big tech companies. This makes AI more compelling than ever before and the number of technologies evolving around it is increasing every day.

AI's potential is now starting to be realized by many organizations and early adopters. Its very name is becoming as ubiquitous as electricity. It's taking a fundamental role in the functioning of our day-to-day activities, from shopping to traveling, doing research, making decisions, and filtering emails, and it is driving innovation in both the automotive and aviation industries.

We will have unlimited opportunities to leverage the technologies around AI, such as robotics, cognitive services, and deep learning, which can be combined with big data in almost all kinds of CRM processes. We will cover all of this in Chapter 9, *CRM Differentiators*, where we will look at a CRM platform, specifically Microsoft's Dynamics 365, to see how you can leverage all these technologies with a reasonable amount of implementation effort.

A subset of AI is ML. In the 1990s, ML was reorganized as a separate field from AI and from there it began to flourish. It certainly benefited from the increasing availability of digitized information, and the adoption of the internet in order to exchange information and data.

The development of ML shifted away from the traditional approaches it had inherited from AI and more toward methods and models borrowed from statistics and probability theory. ML changed its desire of achieving comprehensive AI to tackling solvable problems of a practical nature using data.

The algorithms of ML can leverage mathematical models from sample data and, in turn, make predictions or decisions without being explicitly programmed to do so.

The challenge of AI is the fact that the statistical learning theory (algorithms of AI) demands that complex models are trained with massive data, yet labeled data is a scarce resource. Here ML can actually help. A very good example of ML is AlphaGo Zero.

Go, which you can see in *Figure 5.2*, is an abstract strategy board game for two players that was invented in China some 2,500 years ago. Today, the game is played by some 50 million players worldwide. DeepMind successfully trained AlphaGo Zero, without using data from human games (big data), by playing games against itself.

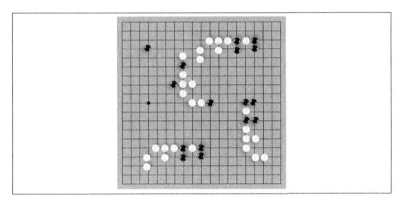

Figure 5.2: The game Go

AlphaGo Zero was able to surpass the performance of all previous AI-based Go players, including AlphaGo Master, which won 60 straight online games against human professional Go players.

The current state of AI

AI today is used in almost all fields and industries, including consumer, healthcare, finance, government, and automotive.

Examples of modern AI use include:

- **Search engines**: Such as Microsoft Bing or Google search.

- **Autonomous vehicles**: Such as airplanes and self-driving cars.

- **Medical diagnosis**: Such as predicting the chances of you having cancer.

- **Playing games**: Such as chess or Go.

- **Online assistants**: Such as Apple's Siri or Amazon's Alexa.

- **Creating art**: Such as poetry.

- **Speech recognition**: Such as speech-to-text software.

- **Image and pattern recognition**: Such as spam filtering and targeting online advertisements.

One of the first mass AI-driven business applications ever was the AutoCorrect feature in Microsoft Office, which was first introduced by Microsoft in 1993. Everyone is using it today in Microsoft Office without even noticing it.

What matters most is the business outcome. Often, when an AI application reaches mainstream adoption, it is no longer considered AI.

Today, 50+ countries are researching and investing in the AI field. China greatly accelerated its government AI funding; given its large supply of data and its rapidly increasing research output, some experts believe it may be on track to becoming an AI superpower. China is aiming to achieve a $150 billion AI business by 2030, while the U.S. government launched the American AI Initiative in 2019 to compete with the ever-growing Chinese technological advances and to secure its global market share in this field.

In the near future, the combination of affordable **High-Performance Computing** (**HPC**), deep neural networks, and big data is going to speed up AI development. Effectively, the future evolution of AI is driven by HPC, big data, and deep neural networks. The formula is simple and effective:

Big Data + Affordable HPC + Deep Neural Networks = Progress in AI

So, where is AI today and what are the technologies around AI? The most advanced technologies driven by AI and available today include:

- Text analysis and understanding
- Image understanding
- Speech recognition
- Robotics
- Deep learning (ML)
- IoT

Figure 5.3 illustrates the ever-growing AI business applications landscape.

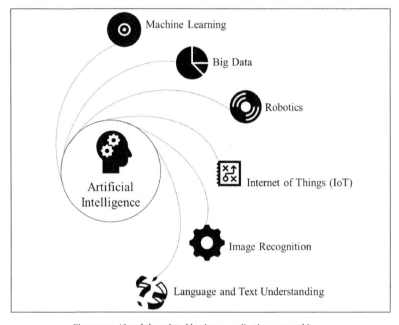

Figure 5.3: AI and the related business applications around it

There are a number of business developments in the market that are driving rapid AI progress. These include shorter innovation cycles, more complex products, greater data volume, individualized production, volatile markets, social networks, and increased competition, especially from digital big tech companies and digital disrupters, as we have talked about in the earlier chapters of this book.

But what are the benefits of all these new technologies in CRM processes, and how could we best benefit from AI and related technologies? As we touched upon earlier, there are already a number of applications out there for AI and ML in finance, insurance, medical diagnostics, and the automotive sector, to name just a few industries.

Both AI and ML will change many things in our lives. Automation is just the beginning, and new business models are yet to be fully discovered and implemented, but in time, our society will (have to) change through AI.

Teaming up AI with people

For businesses that may have been sitting on the sidelines of AI, waiting to learn from other successes or failures before taking their own first steps toward AI and leveraging the technologies around it, there has never been a better time than now.

It's clear that AI is here to stay and will expand functional areas of our daily lives. In terms of CRM, the opportunities AI presents are endless: from operational efficiencies to improved customer satisfaction and increased productivity and revenue. This statement not only stands for large businesses but also for small and mid-size companies, as most of these technologies are available and affordable in the cloud today.

From my personal observations, with customers across the globe, there are a few high priorities in regards to leveraging AI in business:

- Marketing
- Social media
- Chatbots
- Operational efficiency
- Logistics
- Supply chain

To have AI systems function well in the real world with people, we also need to address issues around accountability and responsibility. These can include asking how business leaders prepare for all this change.

Processes need to be changed, the cultural changes in a company need to be managed, and the first steps need to be small. It is not about AI acting alone or even replacing people; it is about ways to leverage AI in business to enable collaboration between people and AI.

In my experience, companies that have deployed AI in operations also have people in place to review the output who can augment and override questionable results. Indeed, one point to note is that AI requires rigorous oversight.

As an industry, we are in the early stages of understanding a number of key topics, including how we can build collaboration into AI, and how we can get AI to understand the goals, intentions, and actions of people and provide support accordingly. For example, Microsoft's Skype translator technology can assist an office worker in becoming more productive by removing language barriers when communicating with business partners and customers; this is a skill that could be very useful in a CRM platform.

To have AI systems function well in the real world with people, we also need to address issues around bias and fairness. In general, more work is going to be needed in order to make AI systems transparent, which, as a result, will enable richer communication and traction between people and AI systems.

AI algorithms are good for repetitive tasks that are well defined, such as those related to customer service, as well as when they are used for processing a large amount of data, finding patterns within that data, and statistical reasoning for decision making, such as in business intelligence, reporting, and forecasting. On the other hand, people are good with negotiation, creativity, and solving problems that have never been encountered before.

I would suggest teaming up AI with real people in order to allow them to collaborate and work together, using their abilities and their strengths to achieve the maximum return for businesses.

A very good example of this taking place is in the version of chess called freestyle. In this game, people and AI software team up to play together. Through this method, superior results can be achieved when compared to the best AI solution acting alone.

Applying AI to your CRM solution

Let's see how we could apply all these technologies into our CRM design. More importantly, let's focus on how we could set the stage for collaboration between people and AI systems in order to achieve more. How can we leverage these technologies for improving processes in sales, marketing, and customer service?

Before we look at a simple solution example for both AI and CRM, I would like to point out that CRM vendors are already infusing AI into their cloud applications. For example, Microsoft Dynamics 365 delivers AI-driven insights based on CRM data coupled with a selection of other data available in your enterprise.

By mixing AI and CRM, you will gain key performance analytics, coupled with easy, natural language queries, in order to respond quickly with the uncovered information and trends in data. The system here is using AI techniques to analyze the sales pipeline in order to discover gaps in data and through that, propose ways to close deals based on revenue, closing date, customer sentiment, and deal probability.

By proactively analyzing data using ML models, you can gain insights into your performance and KPIs. These are elements that you might not be initially aware of that can provide better visibility into your business forecast, actuals, pipeline, leads, and activities.

The ethical aspects of AI

I earlier referred to the risk of bias. Having discovered all the capabilities of AI, we should not forget one important aspect of AI development: the ethical questions around it.

A key principle here is that AI will partly be used to augment human intelligence, but this is not always the case, nor should this be done in an uncontrolled way.

Augmenting humans is not the sole problem for the field of AI, as we must also understand the impact of this space. We have to make thoughtful and transparent decisions to mitigate the potential risks from leveraging AI. We need to engage both employees and customers in the early stages of the processes and create transparency in all these discussions.

We have already witnessed the widespread misuse of data in the 2018 Facebook/Cambridge Analytica scandal, where it was revealed that millions of records of user data had been misused in the run-up to the U.S. election and the UK's Brexit referendum with social marketing techniques that were based on AI.

The ethical design and human control factor have to be a part of every AI and big data project today. There's no doubt across the industry today that AI, ML, and data modeling have to be transparent for all the people involved, whether that is the company or the customer.

From my own experience, most of the clients that I've been engaged with have relatively strong ethical processes in place and ethics committees that review the use of AI, so you may want to consider that as an option when designing your CRM solution.

An example of AI in CRM processes

Looking at what we've just discussed, the benefits of using AI technologies in your business are endless: helping you to achieve improved customer operations, achieve higher productivity, reduce the operational costs, increase company innovation, improve both product and service quality, provide better insights with data, improve forecasting, and ensure better business planning.

Today, AI has been applied in sales, marketing, and services operation, with more and more organizations starting to realize the power of AI when combined in a CRM platform. We will cover platform discussions in *Chapter 9, CRM Differentiators*.

In this part of the chapter, I would like to share with you an example of a prototype that I presented to some clients a while ago. This design is based on several technologies from Microsoft, though they are available from other vendors too. I should also mention here that Microsoft itself is already leveraging all these technologies today on its customer service portals, serving millions of customers globally.

Let's take a look at the four design technologies:

- **Bot Framework (or conversation agents)**: Bots are rapidly becoming an integral part of the digital experience. You can build and connect intelligent bots that naturally interact with users and customers, in addition to multiple channels ranging from text or SMS to Skype, mail, and other popular services. Microsoft's Bot Framework is a comprehensive framework for building enterprise-grade conversational AI experiences.

- **Language Understanding Intelligent Service (LUIS)**: LUIS draws on technology for interactive ML and language understanding from Microsoft Research and Bing. The technology is part of a project called Microsoft Cognitive Service. LUIS is an ML-based service designed to build natural language understanding into apps, bots, IoT devices, and to quickly create enterprise-ready, custom models that continuously improve.

- **Cognitive Services**: Microsoft Cognitive Services let you build apps with powerful algorithms using just a few lines of code. They work across devices and platforms such as iOS, Android, and Windows. They're constantly improving and are easy to set up. With Cognitive Services, you can infuse your apps, websites, and bots with intelligent algorithms to see, hear, speak, understand, and interpret your customer needs through natural methods of communication.

- **Translation Services**: Machine translation makes the most sense when it is available where you need it; in our case, right within the workflow of your tool, application, or solution.

In the next section, we will look at an example that uses elements of these four design technologies.

The insurance use case

In this example, we'll see how the collaboration between machine, users, and customers can take shape, where the combined power will bring better service at a lower price to customers and improve process efficiency, along with both customer and employee satisfaction.

This use case showcases what machines are good for: repetitive tasks that are well defined and often boring for users. In this example, we bring humans into the process when creativity and sensitivity are required.

In the beginning, our visitor will be talking to a bot. The lead here is cold, as there are many repetitive tasks and conversations that could easily be handled by a bot.

However, later on in the process, when the deal is getting warmer, and things start to become more complicated, that's when a sales rep, who is a real human, is going to take over the negotiation and continue with the sales process, integrated and guided by a CRM (in this case, Dynamics 365 from Microsoft).

In the scenario, the customer is searching for both good and low-cost insurance coverage for his new car. He has ended up on the website of the First-City insurance company, where he is now going to get an insurance quote for his new car.

In our case, the preliminary Q&A is completed fully by the bot and the data is stored as a cold lead in the CRM system for future use. When the lead is warm, and an opportunity to complete the process is identified, a sales rep will take over the process from AI.

To simplify and visualize the process here, let's look at some screenshots, along with a brief description of the process. This is to illustrate that the same process and technologies could be applied to other CRM processes and functional areas, such as marketing, sales, customer service, or maintenance.

1. The customer starts the chat window with the bot and can select any language for this conversation.

2. Once the language is selected, the bot will offer to help in that given language.

3. The customer then may ask any question they want. For most questions, they'll receive a reasonable (human-like) answer.

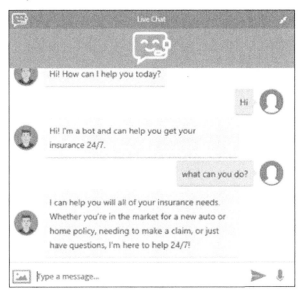

4. In our example, the customer is searching for insurance coverage. Therefore, the machine will guide him through the product selection with supporting text and images.

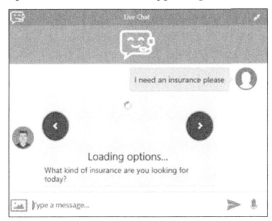

5. The options presented by the bot can be scrolled by the user to the left or to the right. This enables quick selection, even on tablets or mobile devices.

6. Once the selection is confirmed, the bot will be able to check within the CRM data to see if this is an existing customer.

7. The bot will now ask for the name, and possibly other personal identifying information, in order to retrieve the customer data or make other decisions.

8. The bot will then search the customer repository. Note that in this case, I am not a customer, but I pretend to be one.

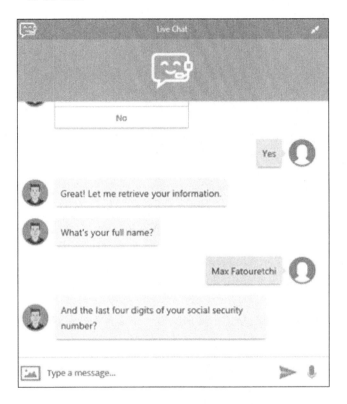

9. Since I'm not a customer, the machine will suggest to me that I connect with the customer center, along with providing me with the details to do so.

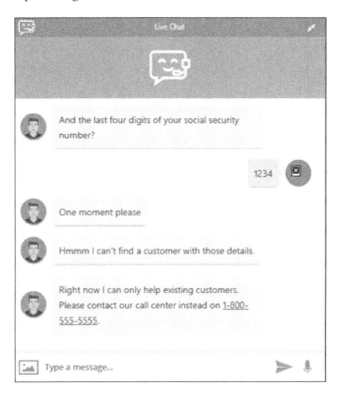

10. However, if I am a customer, then the system will be able to check my data and provide me with an individual offer.

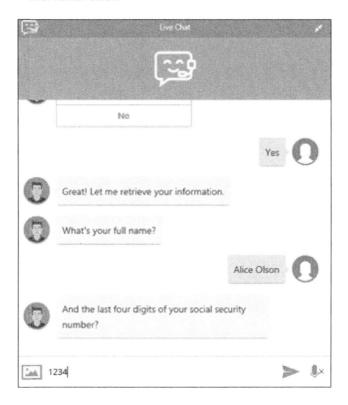

11. Now the system has found the customer and successfully retrieved the data. At the same time, it's also able to check for any event or pre-approved conditions for the client quote. Upselling is an option if certain conditions have been met.

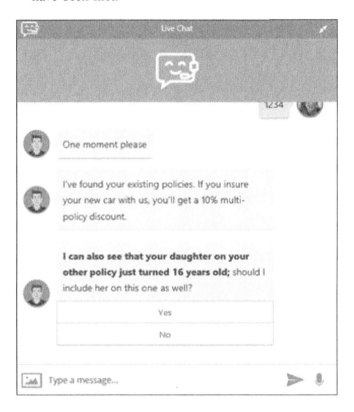

12. The upsell could be accepted and processed if
    satisfactory. Now the details for a binding quote are
    requested by the system.

13. After that's been accepted, the bot quickly completes the information gathering process for the quote.

14. Now the bot will use image recognition software to support the process.

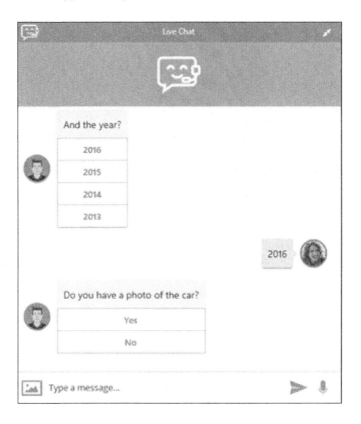

15. For the sake of this scenario, we're going to upload the wrong image to see if the system really cares about the image and can recognize that the image is not a car but a person.

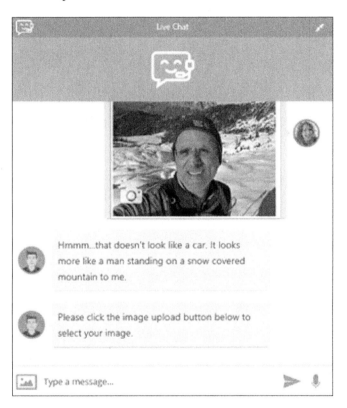

16. Once the correct picture is uploaded, the system has all the information needed in order to process the quote.

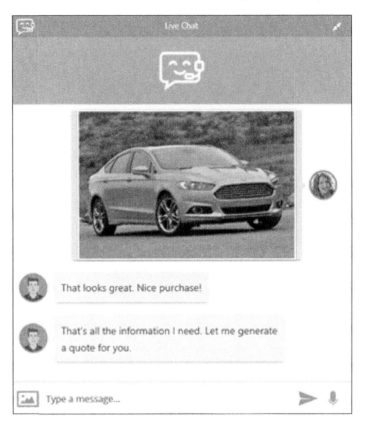

17. The system will now offer a personalized insurance policy based on the calculations from the previous steps.

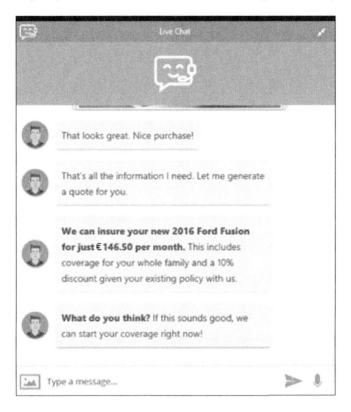

18. In our example, the customer rejects the offer, so the machine will now hand over the process to a sales rep.

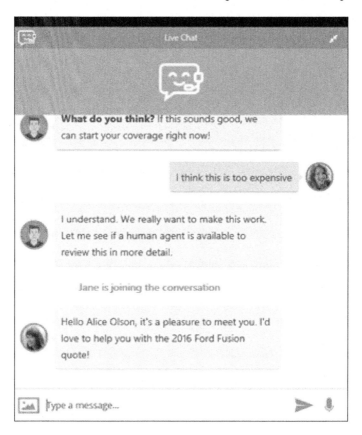

19. The history of the conversation is then also posted to the CRM application, in order to help the sales rep who has taken over this bot's conversation.

The solution we've just looked at is simple and powerful because it successfully automates the repetitive work with a machine, while enabling collaboration with customers and employees. The machine is also capable of learning and providing rich analytical dashboards, which will in turn help business leaders to improve products and services.

The example that follows shows what a great dashboard may look like:

Figure 5.4: Example of a dashboard for better business insight

This application does not need to be fully placed in the cloud in order to leverage AI technologies. For instance, a hybrid scenario combining cloud and on-premise applications can give you the ability to use AI, as *Figure 5.5* shows:

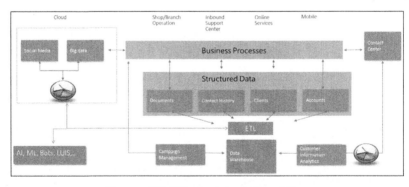

Figure 5.5: Hybrid cloud and on-premises solutions

We will dive deep into deployment in both *Chapter 8, Cloud Versus On-Premises Versus Hybrid – The Deployment of a CRM Platform*, and *Chapter 9, CRM Differentiators*, where we will explore the platform capabilities that are needed to build such solutions.

IoT

IoT, when combined with both AI and a CRM system, can provide better business solutions for today and tomorrow. IoT is transforming how people, devices, and data interact in every aspect of our daily lives.

While there have been numerous studies exploring the potential and opportunities presented by IoT, the focus is on service and maintenance management. It's not just about cutting-edge technology; it's about the digital transformation of industries and the reshaping of customer processes. While most experts expect IoT to go mainstream by 2025, early adopters have already acquired some experience from IoT deployments, resulting in some early experience being shared.

The immediate task of IoT is to connect the unconnected devices; the benefits being auto-diagnostics, asset tracking, connected vehicles, supply chains, and equipment maintenance. However, there is no doubt that IoT will provide huge opportunities in customer service and maintenance management, and that is where CRM will come into play.

The ATM case study in *Chapter 4, Architecting Your CRM Solution – Preparing for Today and Tomorrow,* is a very good example of such scenarios. A solution was implemented to manage the full life cycle of ATMs and automate maintenance through a CRM system, while improving process efficiency and reducing operational costs. Through communication with the CRM platform, the data is analyzed and captured as a case in the CRM system, where the maintenance team will then be dispatched and the case resolved. The same scenario will work with any small device that is IoT-enabled.

Another example is Shell's global energy business, which is leveraging IoT and AI in gas stations to improve customer experience, reduce operational risks, and improve business insight. An on-site video camera captures activities and images from a gas station.

A device inside the station running Microsoft Azure IoT Edge uses AI tools to pick out certain activities and analyze these images in real time. Out of all the cars coming and going, drivers cleaning windshields, and customers buying snacks, for example, the system is able to identify operational deficiencies or discover potential safety risks.

The data is quickly processed close to where it's collected, without accessing the cloud, and simple ML algorithms can dispense with anything that's not of interest. At the same time, the algorithms can also be trained to look for high-risk incidents, such as people driving recklessly, theft, and improper fueling.

Summary

AI and the technologies around it, such as ML, will help to improve customer experience and build stronger CRM processes by improving sales, marketing, and customer service operations. The examples in this chapter are just rudimentary and simple use cases, but they show the potential for process efficiency, reducing operational costs, and improving customer satisfaction.

AI today is used in almost all fields and industries, including consumer, healthcare, finance, government, and automotive. Every business and organization across the spectrum, from manufacturing to financial services, will be able to leverage AI technologies to improve operational efficiencies.

In this chapter, we learned about the most important elements of AI in regards to CRM solutions. We covered its history, its current state, and its future. AI is here to stay and it will expand functional areas. The opportunities AI presents are endless, from operational efficiencies to improved customer satisfaction and increased productivity and revenue. AI in combination with CRM processes will improve customer experience and business insight. This area is still a very untouched domain and many capabilities for AI in CRM are yet to be discovered.

Many companies I have been engaged with lately are experimenting with AI for customer service automation, increase marketing efficiency, analyzing social media data (and big data), to enhance sales processes, and fraud-detection.

As I highlighted, we can't afford to forget the ethical questions around AI technologies. Dealing with AI is not like dealing with another person but rather with an e-person. We need to modify our procedures and processes accordingly.

In the next chapter, we will be looking at something that is vital to any CRM solution: regulatory compliance. This topic will focus on the ethics of handling data and what you will need to take into consideration when designing your CRM solution.

CHAPTER 6

GDPR AND REGULATORY COMPLIANCE

The **General Data Protection Regulation** (**GDPR**) is a European Union regulatory policy that regulates the collection, storage, use, and sharing of personal data for all businesses dealing with clients that are based in the European Union.

In this chapter, we're going to take a look at regulatory compliance, with a focus on GDPR. We'll be looking at:

- Why GDPR is here.
- What GDPR is and its key elements.
- GDPR obligations and impacts.
- Mapping the key elements of GDPR to CRM entities.
- GDPR's effect on technology, tools, people, and processes.
- GDPR from a business point of view.
- Further reading into GDPR.

We'll talk about the design pattern that you would need to follow when implementing GDPR through a CRM platform. Specifically, we're going to look at a solution design that could be implemented on most CRM platforms in order to make your company GDPR-compliant.

The entire discussion around this regulation is a complex one. It will require significant investment from your end and will shape the way you manage personal data about both your clients and users.

 Important: This chapter is provided for informational purposes only and **should not** be relied upon as legal advice, or to determine how GDPR might apply to you and your organization.

GDPR is highly fact-specific, and not all aspects and interpretations of GDPR are fully settled yet, as the discussion is still ongoing. Therefore, we're going to approach this chapter from the perspective of understanding how being compliant with regulations may affect your CRM application.

Why is GDPR here?

We are living in a time where technology is having a profound impact on our daily lives, both in the way that we interact with each other as individuals and the way we interact with organizations. The volume of data that we are creating is rapidly growing and it's been estimated by multiple sources that there are, at the time of writing, 24 billion connected devices worldwide.

Just to show you how much data that produces, the **International Data Corporation** (**IDC**), has estimated that we will create and replicate 163 zettabytes, which converts to 163 billion terabytes, or around 167 trillion gigabytes, of data by 2025, a 10x increase from 2016.

With this increase in available data, the need to commit to securing and managing data in line with a company's legal and moral obligations is becoming an ever-increasing challenge.

Geography is also another issue and I encountered it when running a workshop with the Shanghai Pudong Development Bank in China. During my time there, I mentioned the option of the bank implementing regulatory obligations, such as the European Union law known as the **Markets in Financial Instruments Directive (MiFID)**, which is governed by the European Commission's Financial Services Action Plan.

The law's main objective is to protect investors through a set of processes and periodic reporting to the regulatory authorities. This provides harmonized regulation for investment services through the use of CRM.

Note: The law is outside the scope of this chapter; however, to understand more about it, the Wikipedia page provides excellent context: https://en.wikipedia.org/wiki/Financial_Services_Action_Plan.

In China, there are similar regulations to MiFID that are required by the **China Securities Regulatory Commission (CSRC)**.

One of the business leaders at the bank was incredibly surprised to hear anyone talking about the idea of implementing regulatory compliance and harmonizing the execution of these regulations through a CRM platform. That being said, the deployment option to do this is not an easy one. These solutions, which are offered by some major vendors, are extraordinarily complex, expensive, and lengthy to implement.

So, how did this banking executive respond to this proposal of using CRM to comply with the regulation? She admitted the idea, as a concept, was quite valuable to the company and should, therefore, be discussed in more depth.

Indeed, we explored this concept and we worked out how regulatory compliance rules could be implemented through the proposed CRM platform. In this case, this was done through the collective understanding that regulation is about automation in processes, keeping evidence of client interactions, and regular reporting to the regulatory authorities.

Though these principles can be applied to any platform, the example that follows is based on Microsoft's Dynamics 365.

What is GDPR?

GDPR covers personal data protection and privacy for the citizens of the European Union. No matter where they are in the world, all businesses dealing with European Union users and clients are affected by this law. For example, Facebook has its headquarters in California, in the United States; however, since you can use Facebook in European Union countries, the company must comply.

GDPR was adopted by the European Parliament on the 27th of April, 2016, and was enforceable throughout the European Union by May 25th, 2018. GDPR replaces the 1995 European Data Protection Directive.

The regulation aims primarily to give control back to European citizens and residents over their personal data, or **Personal Identifier Data** (**PID**). GDPR is designed to simplify the regulatory environment for international businesses by unifying the regulations within the European Union.

GDPR helps companies to regulate a number of processes that they'll face when it comes to dealing with and storing the personal data of clients. To work successfully, this requires people within your organization to be assigned roles, which I will identify later in this chapter, in the compliance process of GDPR.

The regulation itself consists of a set of rules that I will explain in detail later in this chapter. An example of complying with GDPR regulation is if your company applies the highest-possible privacy settings by default. This means that a user's data may not be processed unless this is done as specified by the regulation and that the personal data is not made publicly available without the explicit, and informed, consent of the user.

In *Figure 6.1*, you can see how GDPR is made up of three key elements within your company: the people (customers and those who have roles assigned to them), the data that you are managing, and the process that you're using to ensure your compliance with the regulation.

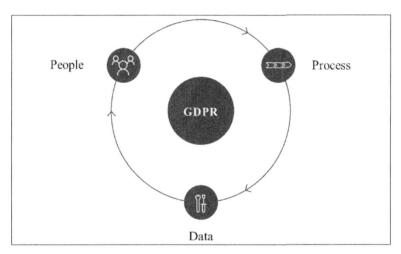

Figure 6.1: GDPR regulates the processing and use of the personal data of European Union clients

As a global leader in research and a key advisory firm in the IT and business applications sector across the world, Gartner believes that by the end of 2018, more than 50 percent of companies affected by GDPR regulation were not in full compliance with its requirements.

Personal data is defined broadly under GDPR as any data that relates to an identified or identifiable natural person. So, from where exactly would a company get personal data belonging or related to European Union residents? The list, as you can imagine, is quite large, but following I've highlighted some of the most common sources:

- Forms that have been filled out by customers
- The contents of emails
- Photographs
- CCTV footage
- Loyalty program records
- Human resources databases

If an organization deals with any of this information, then it needs to determine how GDPR applies and ensure that it complies with the regulation. This is why we're so interested in GDPR: CRM applications are one of the primary applications and data sources that needs to comply with GDPR regulation.

Let's now take a deeper look at PID.

PID

PID is a subset of **Personally Identifiable Information (PII)** data elements, which identify a unique individual and can permit another person to "assume" an individual's identity without their knowledge or consent.

Key examples of PID include:

- Birthdate
- Bank account number
- Fingerprint or voiceprint
- **Personal Identification Number (PIN)**

There is other European-defined sensitive data that is globally treated as PID and not just for citizens of the European Union. This includes:

- Racial or ethnic origin
- Political opinions
- Religious or philosophical beliefs
- Trade union membership
- Health or sex life
- Offenses, criminal convictions, or security measures
- Proceedings from crimes or offenses

GDPR also requires some organizational measures such as assigning a staff member as a data protection officer. This person will be responsible for the implementation and ensuring that regulations surrounding GDPR have been properly complied with.

While GDPR preserves most of the principles established in the earlier European Directive, it is a more ambitious law. Among its most notable changes, GDPR gives individuals greater control over their personal data and imposes many new obligations on organizations that collect, manage, or analyze personal data, or PII.

GDPR also gives national regulators new powers to impose significant fines on those who fail to comply with the law. This could be up to 4% of global revenue for organizations that breach the law. Companies that have been fined include Equifax (September 2018) and Facebook (October 2018).

GDPR obligations

GDPR extends the scope of the European Union data protection law to all foreign companies processing the data of European Union residents. As mentioned earlier, a single set of rules will apply to all European Union member states.

Each member state will establish an independent **Supervisory Authority** (**SA**), such as the UK and the Information Commissioner's Office, which will hear and investigate complaints, and sanction administrative offenses. In turn, each of these SAs will co-operate with those from across the European Union.

Under European data protection law, organizations harvesting personal data are divided into "controllers," or the entities that control and manage the personal data, and "processors," the entities that process personal data only on the instructions of the controllers, such as cloud providers.

Before we look at what each of these two roles involve, there are several significant obligations that a company must address when complying with GDPR:

- **Consent**: It must be as easy for the user to withdraw consent as it is to give it.

- **Breach notification**: The processors are obliged to inform both the controller and clients within 72 hours of a breach.

- **Right to access**: The data controller should provide an electronic copy of personal data for free to the subject of the data.

- **Right to be forgotten**: The data controller must erase personal data on request from the subject of the data.

- **Data portability**: This allows the data subject to obtain and reuse their personal data.

- **Privacy by design**: This ensures data protection from the onset of the design of the application.

- **Appointment of a data protection officer**: A role given to a qualified officer who is appointed by public authorities.

Let's now move on and look at both the controller and processor, two key roles that are vital to any compliance with GDPR.

Controller and processor roles

In the previous section, we introduced the roles of both the controller and the processor. In this section, we're going to consider each of those roles in detail.

It is important to identify and become familiar with these two roles, and their responsibilities, as they are accountable in the processes of compliance with GDPR and have obligations to the authorities.

In Article 4 of the GDPR regulation, three key subjects are defined:

- **Data subject**: Defined as "an identified or identifiable natural person." For the purposes of GDPR, that data subject is covered, regardless of the person's nationality or place of residence within the European Union, in relation to the processing of their personal data.

- **Controller**: Defined as "the natural or legal person, public authority, agency, or another body which, alone or jointly with others, determines the purposes and means of the processing of personal data." Within the context of the GDPR, a controller does not have to be located within the European Union for GDPR to apply to it. As a controller, you have two key roles to play:

  - ° Give data subjects a copy of their personal data, together with an explanation of the categories that their data is being processed under, the purposes of that processing, and the categories of third parties to whom their data may be disclosed to.

      ○   Help every individual to exercise their right to correct inaccurate personal data, erase data or restrict its processing, receive their data in a readable form, and, where applicable, fulfill a request to transmit their data to another controller.

- **Processor**: Defined as "a natural or legal person, public authority, agency, or another body that processes personal data on behalf of the controller." Here, the processor's main role is to implement the appropriate technical and organizational measures to assist in responding to requests from data subjects exercising their rights, as discussed.

GDPR applies to both controllers and processors of PID. If you are controlling and processing data about individuals in the context of selling goods and services to citizens in the European Union, then these roles apply to you.

In summary, the processors and controllers have to provide the customers (data subjects) with the following services:

1. Personal privacy for individuals, who have the right to:

      ○   Access their personal data.

      ○   Correct errors in their personal data.

      ○   Erase their personal data.

      ○   Object to the processing of their personal data.

      ○   Export personal data.

2. Controls and notifications, where organizations must adhere to:

      ○   Strict security requirements.

      ○   Breach notification obligation.

      ○   Appropriate consents for data processing.

    °   Confidentiality.

    °   Record-keeping.

3. Transparent and easily accessible policies regarding:

    °   The notice of data collection.

    °   The notice of processing.

    °   Processing details.

    °   Data retention/deletion.

4. IT and training, with a need to invest in:

    °   Privacy personnel and employee training.

    °   Data policies.

    °   A data protection officer (for larger organizations).

    °   Processor/vendor contracts.

What about the impact of GDPR? How do you ensure that your company is complying with the rules? In the next section, I'm going to list the people, processes, and tools that you'll need to consider.

GDPR impacts technology, tools, people, and processes

To ensure compliance and an ability to meet the responsibilities of GDPR, organizations must recognize that they will need to implement not only the right technology, or tools, but also the right people and processes.

People required are:

• Data subjects.

• People who understand that GDPR implementation is everyone's responsibility.

- Data protection officer(s).

- Information asset owners.

- People who will be responsive to inbound requests.

For processes, key questions are:

- How will you manage, process, and execute inbound requests to ensure you are meeting GDPR requirements as a data controller?

- How will you evidence your compliance? Consider factors such as being timely, auditable, and having the ability to report.

- How do you know how well you are performing against your requirements?

For tools, key questions are:

- Where will you track and manage the GDPR process and requests?

- How will you accept GDPR requests from data subjects?

- How will you allow data subjects to access or correct their data?

- How will you detail to your data subjects your transparency with respect to how you process their data?

- How will you know where data is stored within your organization?

We know that there are a lot of roles that must be considered when complying with GDPR. One such role that I've mentioned is that of the data protection officer. In the next section, we're going to break down that role and explore the tasks of someone who could describe themselves as a data protection officer.

Data protection officer

The role of a data protection officer and/or chief privacy officer becomes essential when working with GDPR. These people can set the policies that a company will need in order to meet regulatory requirements.

A data protection officer needs to take all necessary actions to enable GDPR compliance, including:

- Visibility and classification of data stored internally.
- Transparency to customers about opting in and data use.
- Effectively capturing route and fulfill requests.
- Handling evidence requests to or from regulators.
- Data governance, recordkeeping, and reporting.
- Preference center and visibility of data used.
- Self-service for customers and employees.
- Internal breach reporting.

But wait a minute! What about the chief privacy officer? Well, that's a good question. *Figure 6.2* will help you to recognize the key differences between the roles:

Chief Privacy Officer (CPO)   Data Protection Officer (DPO)

Responsible for establishing organizational guidlines for managing customer data, and for ensuring that all applicable legal guidelines of GDPR are followed. She or he is consulted for technology choice as well as overall accountability.

Responsible for informing employees of their compliance obligations as well as conducting the monitoring, training, and audits required by GDPR. She or he can be an employee or contracted from outside the company.

Figure 6.2: Responsibilities of both roles

Now that we've looked at the people involved with GDPR, it's time that we moved to looking at GDPR from the business point of view. This will be the focus of the next section.

GDPR from a business point of view

From a business point of view, you want to look at GDPR as an opportunity to optimize processes and build trust with your customers, while also improving their satisfaction level with your company.

For a minute, let's think about what GDPR could hold for your company:

- You can rethink how you engage with customers and customers' data.
- It can make you think, "How can I best use customer data with explicit consent?"
- It provides a platform to innovate on.
- It allows you to build a culture where GDPR compliance is not a burden but brings benefits to your company.

Indeed, GDPR provides an excellent opportunity to improve the loyalty of your customers, since if customers have visibility over the data you keep and process, their trust in your business will remain, if not improve. Because of that very fact, it is essential that you provide your customers with easy access to GDPR-related information services in order to increase your business volume with your customers, while still complying with the regulations.

There are three steps to take toward becoming compliant with GDPR:

- **Assess and manage compliance risk**: How will you understand your level of compliance risk on an ongoing basis, so that you know where you need to make improvements?

- **Protect personal data**: How will you manage data governance and the protection of your sensitive data across devices and apps, both on-premises and in the cloud?

- **Streamline processes**: What processes do you have in place to respond to inquiries and audits?

The idea of compliance risk is an important one. In fact, I want to dedicate the next section solely to assessing and managing those types of risk.

Assessing and managing the compliance risk

The first step toward GDPR compliance is to assess whether GDPR applies to your organization and if so, to what extent. This analysis includes understanding the data your organization processes and where the data resides.

Note: While these links are given as further reading, I want to remind you of them here, as they are excellent examples of how to evaluate your GDPR compliance.

How to assess your GDPR compliance: `https://www.microsoft.com/en-us/TrustCenter/Privacy/gdpr/default.aspx`.

A free Microsoft test to assess whether your company is complying with GDPR: `https://www.microsoft.com/en-us/cloud-platform/enterprise-mobility-security?ls=Website`.

Data controllers will be required to do a **Data Protection Impact Assessment (DPIA)**. Under such a CRM application is the data processor. If you have your own CRM application on your own premises, you are both the controller and the processor of the data within the CRM platform. DPIA includes the ability to ensure the ongoing confidentiality, integrity, availability, and resilience of your processing systems and services.

Figure 6.3 is an example of some of the possible elements that need to be considered in the processes of assessment and compliance. In most scenarios, and in most companies, the CRM platform is one of the few places where we keep sensitive customer information, including the PID and related activities:

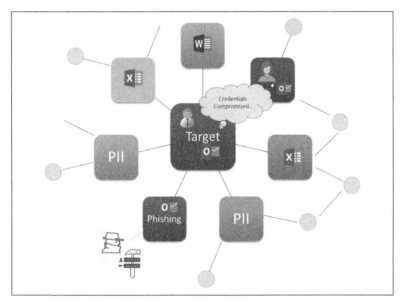

Figure 6.3: Typical scenarios in a company where the PID of customers is stored

As an exercise, why not try drawing your own mind map, like the preceding one, for your own company? It is a wonderful way to really get thinking about the specific PID that you hold on your customers!

This all begs one question, though: how do you, and your company, protect the personal data of your customers? We will find the answer to that in the next section.

Protect personal data

As you may have guessed, a CRM platform is not the only place where you can protect personal data and implement the GDPR processes and the procedures needed in order to comply with the regulation. The data protection officer plays a key role in the process of the assessment and protection of personal data.

The data protection officer could be the compliance officer. This person must be proficient at managing IT processes and handling data security, including dealing with cyber attacks, and other business-critical continuity issues around the subject of holding and processing customers' personal and sensitive data.

The skills needed to be a data protection officer stretch beyond simply understanding legal compliance with data protection laws and regulations. The appointment of a data protection officer in a large organization will be a challenge for the board as well as for the individual concerned.

There are a myriad of both governance and human factor issues that organizations will need to address. These issues can be specific to a company and the country it is in.

In addition, the data protection officer is not a singular role. The person must have a support team of people who are also responsible for continuing professional development, while being independent of the organization that employs them and effectively acting as a "mini regulator."

In regard to CRM design and protecting personal data, the business users from different business units should only be given access to data and entities they need to have access to in order to accomplish their daily jobs. They need to have sufficient privileges at an organizational, business unit, team, and user level, without having access to data they don't need to know about.

Another GDPR requirement is to establish an auditing mechanism in order to log all the user access requests to sensitive personal data. This has to be supported and implemented in your CRM, as users may access sensitive data on a daily basis and for good reason. But what if there is an attack and the credentials of a user are compromised? In this case, you need to know what exactly has been accessed so that you can report it.

You probably think that this is a lot to take on board, and you are right. Regulation compliance, in general, is a massive and complicated task to undertake. What if, with the aid of a CRM platform, we could make it easier? Let's do just that!

Streamlining Data Subject Rights processes

A number of GDPR articles require that organizations have robust processes in place to achieve and maintain compliance. One major element of GDPR requirements is the right of the data subject to transparency and privacy.

We're now going to focus on the **Data Subject Rights** (**DSR**) and service requests from your customers, which need to be managed and fully transparent according to GDPR regulations.

There are eight key rights that are relatable to the data subjects and that can easily be implemented through a CRM platform. In fact, my experience has taught me that a CRM platform can be the best place for handling DSR requests. Why? Because, in a CRM platform, there is a strong processes engine and a sophisticated case management functionality, which can typically be found out of the box in most CRM platforms.

So, what are the eight key rights? To make the conversation you could have with your customer more understandable, with each right, I've given an example of how a data subject might ask to enforce it.

- **The right to be informed**: "How do you use my data?"

- **The right to data portability**: "Provide me with my data so that I can use it elsewhere."

- **The right to rectification**: "Fix these inaccuracies."

- **The right to erasure (the right to be forgotten)**: "Delete my data."

- **The right to restrict processing**: "Store my data, but do not process my data any longer."

- **The right of access**: "I want to see my data."

- **The right to object**: "I disagree with the processing of my data."

- **Automated decision-making and profiling**: "I want decisions about me to be made by a human."

While these may appear to be quite simple, take a minute and ask yourself this: if a customer asked these questions, what type of response would they get?

Audit logging and GDPR

Auditing is the joint responsibility of both the data processor and data controller. The data processor's responsibility is to make available to the controller all the information necessary to demonstrate compliance with the latter's obligations regarding processing by a processor, while allowing for and contributing to audits, including inspections.

The processor is obliged to demonstrate that it has implemented technical and organizational measures capable of supporting the DPIAs. This involves assessing the appropriate level of security that is presented by processing. This is intended to cover accidental or unlawful destruction, loss, alteration, and unauthorized disclosure of, or access to, personal data that has been transmitted, stored, or otherwise processed.

The data protection officer's duties and responsibilities are to ensure that both the processor and controller fulfill their obligations, including:

- Data classification and accountability
- Client and endpoint protection, including notification and education of clients
- Identity and access management of all (not only CRM users)
- Application-level controls
- Network controls
- Application infrastructure
- Physical security

As explained previously, both data controllers and data processors will be required to complete a DPIA and provide the authorities with evidence of compliance, including audit logging as a mechanism to satisfy this requirement. In the following table, you can see a chart that outlines different obligations:

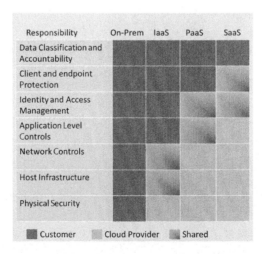

Figure 6.4: GDPR obligations and areas of responsibility

This extends to third parties. For example, has processing been outsourced to a processor, such as a cloud provider? If so, then processing by a processor should be governed by a contract or other legal act. That contract, or other legal act, must stipulate that the processor makes available to the controller all the information necessary for an inspection, which can be conducted by the controller or another auditor mandated by the controller.

There are also several application-level controls to be implemented, such as:

- **The CRM admin must be able to record and analyze unauthorized data access**. They must be able to identify all the clearly created and read actions by user X or customer Y in the system.

- **The CRM admin must be able to record and analyze the alteration of data**. They must be able to clearly identify all the update actions done by user X or customer Y in the system.

- **The CRM admin must be able to record and analyze the accidental or unlawful destruction of data**. They must be able to clearly identify any accidental delete action done by X's admin. They must also be able to identify the request origin clearly.

There are also some application events that should be audited:

- **Publishing customizations**: A developer or an admin publishes a new customization that overrides a change done by the previous person. The action requires auditing for analysis.

- **Attribute deletion**: An admin accidentally deletes an attribute; this action also deletes the data.

- **User management**: Who was added and who was deleted? What access rights a user or team has are important for analyzing the impact.

- **Configure instance**: Adding solutions to an instance.

- **Backup and restore**: Backup and restore actions at the tenant.

- **Manage applications**: A new instance added, an existing instance deleted, trials converted to paid, and so on.

- **Create, Read, Update, Delete (CRUD)**: Logging all CRUD activities is essential for understanding the impact of a problem and being compliant with DPIA.

- **Multiple record view**: Users of the CRM view the information in bulk, such as grid views, reports, and so on. Critical customer content information is part of these views.

- **Export to Microsoft Excel**: Exporting data to Excel moves the data outside of the secure environment, making it vulnerable to threats.

- **API calls via surround or custom apps**: Actions are taken via the core platform or surrounding apps that call the API to perform an action that needs to be logged.

For a CRM solution to support GDPR, there are two major functionalities that you need to implement:

1. Auditing

2. Request handling via DSR

Regarding auditing and reporting, these should be supported by the application platform, such as Dynamics 365, and managed by the CRM admin in collaboration with the compliance manager and/or data protection officer.

The key protagonists

I have previously described in this chapter the events that need to be audited and the controls that need to be managed. Regarding the DSR requests handling, the processes explained in this chapter are managed by business reps in collaboration with the compliance manager and/or data protection officer.

The key protagonists or process members are customers (DSRs), customer service (GDPR queue), the lead application manager (information assets), the data protection officer, and the CEO.

There are a few custom entities, forms, processes, and dashboards that you need to add to your solution in order to support and provide the necessary information and control panel for the key protagonists:

- **Including data assets**: This allows key protagonists to track and process data about information assets, where customers' PII data is kept, and what to do in the case of receiving DSR requests.
- **Exceptions**: As with other regulations, you may be mandated not to delete a certain type of data. Here you can track and process data about these exceptions with a flag (delete Y/N).
- **Requests processes**: You may attach this to case types and define processes; for example, who is the information's owner? Is this a data breach or simply a DSR? Is the service level agreement (SLA) attached to each request?

There are a number of fine-tunings to leverage in your daily business, such as counting the number of DSR requests and applying the information as needed. For example, a workflow process is grabbing the content of the roll-up field (number of cases) from the contact record. In this case, you may want to charge your customers for any additional request exceeding 10 per year or use this information in your next marketing campaign and trust-building activities.

Summary

This chapter has introduced you to some high-level solution design concepts for a GDPR implementation framework using a CRM platform. It's important to remember that the advice given in this chapter is not from a legal perspective. However, it will give you awareness of the impacts the regulation can have and how the use of CRM can ease the pain of compliance.

This chapter's sole purpose is to demonstrate to you how to implement a regulatory compliance solution such as GDPR on top of your CRM platform. As highlighted earlier, compliance with GDPR, or other regulatory rules, is not only a matter of implementing a software solution but also of managing people, processes, and organizational measures.

In my view, CRM is the best place to implement the framework that is needed for most regulatory compliances, particularly when it comes to protecting customers. Regulatory frameworks typically have three main pillars: processes, collaboration, and reporting, which are provided by CRM platforms such as Microsoft Dynamics 365, as we explored in *Chapter 1, What Is CRM?*.

Further reading into GDPR

As explained, I'm not a legal expert in GDPR and the topic is still moving at a rapid rate. Should you want to read more about the subject, the following links will provide you with more information that is concurrent with the latest developments of this regulation:

- **A brief, yet informative, three-minute overview video**: https://www.youtube.com/watch?v=n5WJOncaHt4.

- **The UK's Information Commissioner's Office guidance on data security breach management**: https://ico.org.uk/media/for-organisations/documents/1562/guidance_on_data_security_breach_management.pdf.

- **Microsoft's recommended practices for GDPR:**
  `https://www.microsoft.com/en-us/TrustCenter/`
  `Privacy/gdpr/readiness?&wt.srch=1&wt.mc_`
  `id=AID641639_SEM_w8IiEsqO&msclkid=b3875e8a2`
  `90114571c09042898f4a21b`.

- **How to assess your GDPR compliance:** `https://`
  `www.microsoft.com/en-us/TrustCenter/`
  `Privacy/gdpr/default.aspx`.

- **A free Microsoft test to assess whether your
  company is complying with GDPR:** `https://`
  `www.microsoft.com/en-us/cloud-platform/`
  `enterprise-mobility-security?ls=Website`.

- **The Wikipedia article on GDPR:** `https://`
  `en.wikipedia.org/wiki/General_Data_`
  `Protection_Regulation`.

CRM Integration Strategies

Managing customer interactions often requires integration with other enterprise applications, processes, and data sources. Building a 360-degree client view, managing a client's communication history, marketing campaigns, product holding, cross-selling and upselling processes, and the sales pipeline requires multiple integration strategies. In this chapter, we will look at these strategies and techniques.

When it comes to CRM implementations, integration, in general, is one of the most vital tasks for all stakeholders, both from a business and technical team's perspective. As we have already discussed in *Chapter 1, What Is CRM?*, and *Chapter 2, Getting to Know Your Customer*, quite often you'll find that CRM projects will provide the unique opportunity for companies to unify historically grown silos that have created multiple data sources, multiple process engines, multiple **User Interfaces** (**UIs**), and overlapping functionalities.

From previous chapters, you will be aware that there are a number of good reasons to bring in and combine data from disparate sources to create a single repository of customer and business data.

An example is when you want to build a comprehensive 360-degree client view or when you are automating client processes in sales, marketing, or a client service. Integration in CRM is often done to provide business stakeholders with the ability to slice and dice data. This can help with building valuable and efficient client processes and analytical capabilities.

Traditionally, a **Data Warehouse** (**DW** or **DWH**) solution provides a central repository of integrated data from multiple disparate sources within a company. What this solution doesn't do is provide the capabilities needed to manage all the different kinds of client processes.

Meanwhile, in addition to the DW concept, there are increasing implementations of data lakes. A data lake is a storage repository, such as Apache Hadoop. Apache Hadoop is a collection of open-source tools that leverage a network of many computers to solve problems involving massive amounts of data and computation. Data lakes usually hold a vast amount of raw data in its native form until it is needed for business. This is due to the fact that there is no time to process the vast amount of data using traditional integration tools.

Data lakes are an interesting concept because they increase the amount of data sources that companies can use to make better business decisions. As a matter of fact, these data sources can include:

- Social networks
- Review websites
- Online news
- Weather data
- Web logs
- Sensor data

All of these sources are resulting in rapidly increasing data volumes and new data streams that could be useful for business orchestration. Organizations are looking to optimize the ingestion and use of their data, so technology needs to adapt to the fast-growing business requirements that depend on these data streams.

With a CRM system, we need to not only integrate the external data from disparate sources and exchange information between other applications and CRM platforms, but quite often we must (re)build the business logic related to the data, including why, how, when, and the frequency at which information exchange will take place.

For example, the data integrated into the CRM application may need to pass through an operational data store first. This may require additional data cleansing to detect, correct, or remove corrupt or inaccurate data before the data is integrated into the CRM platform. This is done to ensure good data quality is attained before it's consumed by users and client processes in CRM.

On the other hand, the data lake approach, as mentioned earlier, will just collect the raw data. To create meaningful insights from it will require special techniques, which some platforms will be providing in time as an out-of-the-box capability. We will explore this in *Chapter 9, CRM Differentiators*.

In this chapter, we will explore all the different ways that we can integrate applications and data into a CRM platform. I will also highlight a few important elements regarding data integration within CRM systems, along with recommendations such as performance and security. In addition, we will discuss the initial data load, the regular data load – both daily and nightly – and data synchronization within a CRM, where we will be looking at batch versus real time, the frequency of data import, data profiling, standardization, scalability, and enrichment.

Building synergy to orchestrate business processes

I remember a CRM project that I worked on a few years ago. This was with a large enterprise company that had a large developer team, which had built some 50+ client applications for different business units over the previous 10-15 years.

All of these applications were related to customer interactions and they were each providing what a business unit needed at a given point in time. However, the company's growing challenge was simply how to orchestrate the business altogether, as all of these applications and data were isolated and not integrated.

Figure 7.1 best demonstrates the integrated CRM applications and processes:

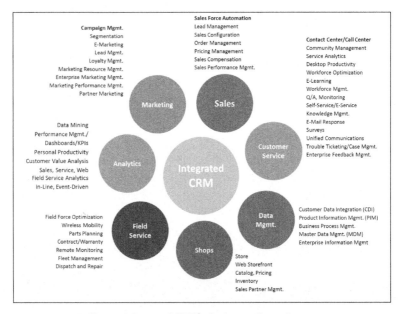

Figure 7.1: Integrated CRM for business orchestration

In CRM implementations, the integration element is done by linking various software components, business processes, data elements, and application screens (frontends) together. As a result, this delivers a selection of new tools or enhances an existing functionality in order to deliver a comprehensive business application for business orchestration. In simple terms, we can say that integration is like borrowing functionality and data from other systems in order to deliver new and improved functionality.

This borrowing approach helps us to create a synergy between systems instead of the replacement or reimplementation of existing systems. It also helps to eliminate silos of data and in some cases, it will help to eliminate some of the old legacy applications.

There are also some other elements that are adding complexity to the data integration process within CRM that you may need to consider, such as restrictions derived from compliance and regulatory constraints. A good example can be seen in *Chapter 6, GDPR and Regulatory Compliance*. In that chapter, we looked at the overall business requirements regarding related systems. One example is in banking, where regulations require any system that's consuming credit card data to be PCI-compliant, with credit card numbers having to be masked in non-PCI-compliant databases such as in a CRM. This requirement forces all system integrators to work with masked card numbers and add an additional layer of security and compliance in their implementations.

There are also other dependencies we need to consider when integrating applications and data sources, such as in situations where loan products and balances are uploaded on a daily basis within core banking systems. In these situations, implementing a real-time integration between CRM and the core banking system is not helpful.

On the other hand, if the core banking systems are not capable of sending real-time ATM transactions to a CRM system, then we must implement a middleware component to ensure that the CRM platform is notified of ATM transactions in the core banking system.

Unstructured data can be found anywhere, such as in emails, white papers, intranet portals, marketing collateral, and PDF files. Then there's also transactional data, such as data related to sales, orders, invoices, and service requests. Another type is metadata, which is data about other data, which may reside in a formal repository or in various other forms, such as XML documents, report definitions, table descriptions in a database, log files, connections, and configuration files. Lastly, there's hierarchical data, which stores the relationships between other data, such as company organizational structures or product structures.

These examples explain why data integration within CRM implementations is one of the most – if not the most – important activities and contributes to the success or failure of a CRM implementation. Integration is not only about technical know-how, writing web services, and importing or exporting data. Integration is about identifying processes, limitations, and constraints combined with new business requirements. This is important for defining a vision and strategy to connect your CRM solutions with other systems to achieve the required business outcome.

Factors relating to data integration

What is the information that you want to be considered in the integration architecture section of your Solution Blueprint? Well, some of the most important questions to consider are:

- Where has the data come from?
- What are the relationships inherited?
- What limitations are there?
- Is there any regulatory compliance to be considered?
- What's the value to the business?
- Is this data really needed within a CRM solution?
- What's the cost of integration?

Activities related to integration start as early as with the RFP and RFI processes. As explored in *Chapter 3, Conceptualizing the CRM Design from Business Requirements*, both RFP and RFI present preliminary requirements for the product or CRM platform. They define the business objectives and required functionalities, identify dependencies, and identify needs to varying degrees. Both processes happen early in the procurement cycle.

Having a clear understanding of the business objectives, functional requirements, and technical dependencies will drive integration requirements, and ultimately, identify the data needed to be integrated and the type of integration approach to be used. If you underestimate the integration requirements, then this will have a direct impact on your project deliverables, which eventually are translated into project success.

Defining integration requirements right from the start of the project enables the implementation team to drive integration activities from pre-sales phases to analysis, design, implementation, testing, go-live, and post-go-live phases.

Figure 7.2 illustrates factors influencing the integration strategy:

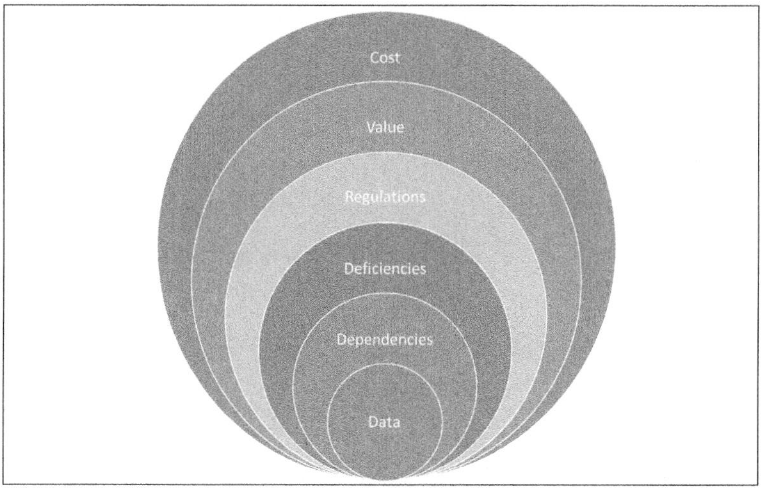

Figure 7.2: The factors relating to data integration

Analyzing CRM requirements will have a direct impact on the integration approach. Likewise, the integration strategy will have a direct impact on deliverables and functionalities within your CRM. The integration approach involves identifying business data, processes, external systems, and applications that need to be integrated with a CRM, including external systems.

This also defines the integration methods:

- Automated or manual.
- The frequency of integration.
- The integration mode and whether integration is synchronous or asynchronous.
- The data structure of integration messages.
- Security requirements.
- Audit requirements.
- Business rules.
- Transformation.
- Mapping information.
- Exception management.
- Capabilities.
- Scalability and high-availability requirements.
- Communication protocol.
- Tools and techniques required for integration.
- Constraints and limitations that may exist in an implementation integration strategy.

The golden rule is to keep it simple and use standard CRM platforms that will enable easy adoption, at any given point, within the process.

The ultimate architecture goal is to design a solution that supports the enterprise strategies and business requirements of today, while still having the ability to adapt to the needs and strategies of tomorrow.

In *Figure 7.3*, you can see an example of a universal banking solution that I implemented a few years ago for a mid-size bank in Europe. This shows the level of integration for all the different applications in the bank, such as card management, branches, and **point-of-sale** (**POS**) management.

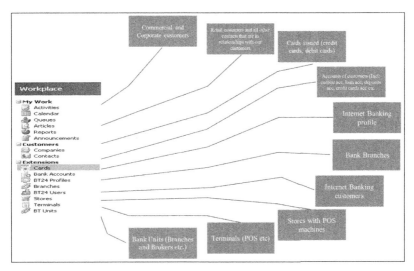

Figure 7.3: Example of a bank integrating branch operations into one CRM platform by leveraging several integration techniques

The bank needed to consider a broader integration of its applications, data, and processes as part of its steps for improving the operational costs by reducing the size of staff to two or three per branch. So, going forward, each branch's staff had to cover eight or more applications on a daily basis. To reduce the complexity and training effort needed for the staff, while still improving the data quality and customer service, we took a broader approach to integration.

We leveraged both data and application integration, and we improved some of the processes, along with leveraging unified service desk technology and other integration techniques across the company. This enabled the bank to provide a workplace that could satisfy all its daily business functions through a single unified application, with a single UI.

Integration is one of the main pillars of any CRM implementation; choosing the right approach will reduce both the cost and complexity of the implementation. To make this easier to understand, let's consider integration as a smaller element within a larger CRM implementation project. However, let's not forget that this is still an integral part of the CRM solution, as the example preceding can illustrate.

The ultimate purpose of integration is to enable various software components or data sources that are linked together to produce the desired business outcome in the form of either a new enhanced functionality or data insight for business users, or process automation.

Quite often, the complexity of integration causes a drastic increase in the effort required for CRM implementation. This is due to factors such as the nature of integrating systems, whether the integrating systems are based on proprietary standards or open standards, the nature and volume of data transferred in the integration processes, and the desired functionality of the system after integration. Other factors include the scarcity of resources that would allow you to implement the data integration, maintain it, and enhance it over time.

As mentioned in earlier chapters, a CRM implementation cannot be successful without onboarding all the stakeholders and gaining a shared vision among all the players. The same is very true about the stakeholders of the applications and data sources that will be integrated into your CRM solution.

Everyone needs to be on board, understand the scope, and know the business requirements in order to contribute to overall success. I always suggest that every stakeholder in a CRM project needs to ask what is in it for them. That's something that they should have an answer to.

Stakeholders

It's essential to agree that when it comes to integration, all identified stakeholders are sponsors and accountable for the design of the CRM system. This includes making sure that all the project team members, power users, end users, developers, and support team members understand and agree on what is being integrated.

Everyone will need to know why integration is needed, whether this is functionality, a set of data, or a screen from another application, as well as what the dependencies are, and the related and unrelated constraints, such as functional structures, processes, data centers, and system management.

Finally, a compliance officer should be included in discussions like the following:

- Do we need to track data in several systems or should we only use the master system to decrease the risk?
- Is the target system secured enough to track personal data and comply with regulations such as GDPR?
- What is the role and responsibility of everyone involved in the integration processes?
- What are the milestones and timelines?

In *Figure 7.4*, you can see an example of the stakeholders, the dependencies they have, and how they relate to each other:

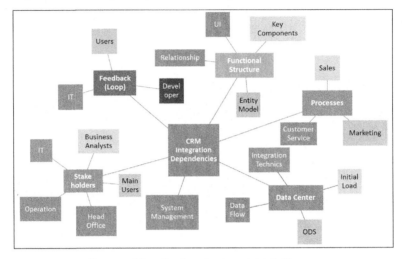

Figure 7.4: Integration dependencies and stakeholders

All of this information needs to be communicated and documented in the Solution Blueprint, as described earlier, along with the key decisions, design assertions, and open issues. The answers to the earlier questions will help team members to better plan their activities, contribute to the project, approve valid integration approaches, and set the right expectations for all those involved.

Reflecting on the fifth CRM case study implementation that we explored in *Chapter 1, What is CRM?*, at some point in the project, users will be asked to execute **Straight-Through Processing (STP)** transactions from the CRM platform. STP is a method used by financial companies to speed up the transaction process by allowing transactions to be processed without any further manual intervention, which is also referred to as the transaction going straight through. This requires the use middleware to allow the CRM platform to execute transactions in the back-office systems.

It's also important to note that in the bank example, there was a good deal of process integration needed to pass the record/request between different applications for processing and the UI integration, which was needed to simplify agent processes. However, with this case study, we had an aggressive deadline to go live in production, which did not allow us to include the STP requirement in the first release. In that case, we had to get agreement from all the stakeholders that this would not be part of the first release and that we would not compromise the go-live date for any new requirements, which was accepted by all members.

UI-level integration

Integration is not always about writing code or combining software modules. Sometimes, we need to think out of the box and come up with new ideas in order to deliver the desired outcome with the least amount spent on that process.

There is a common misconception that the best approach is always the most comprehensive and complicated, but that's not always the case. For example, call center agents often work with multiple screens and have up to 10 applications running at once, in order to obtain the necessary information to serve the caller's service requests. In such situations, integrating backend systems into one system, by combining application components and data, is not very feasible. This is because most of these are old legacy applications or data that is not related to any other CRM processes. In layman's terms, they have very little value to the CRM platform and/or to other business units separate from the call center agents.

However, using UI-level integration solutions that combine and unify the UI, such as **Unified Service Desk (USD)** from Microsoft, is a better approach for delivering an acceptable output with lower implementation costs for, in our case, the call center agent.

Using a UI-level integration solution to configure agent applications doesn't require you to write code for the most part, which reduces the lead time to design an agent application as per your business requirements.

With the addition of the **Computer Telephony Integration (CTI)** framework, which is a USD out-of-the-box functionality, organizations are able to build adapters to connect an agent desktop with the existing CTI infrastructure in order to support customer communication over various channels, such as chat, email, or telephone.

Figure 7.5 illustrates the UI-level integration and techniques that enable call center agents to have multiple customer conversations in parallel:

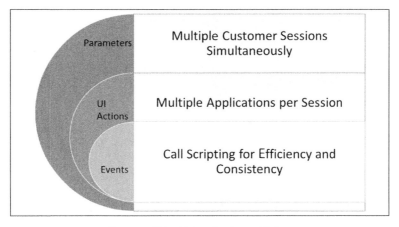

Figure 7.5: UI-level integration in a nutshell

As mentioned earlier in the chapter, good implementations are not the ones that are the most expensive and complex; they are actually the ones that deliver the highest value in the shortest time, with the lowest cost, enabling your business to adapt to the system a lot easier.

UI-level integration provides a good solution for multiple applications to serve desk personnel at a low implementation cost. For example, USD provides CTI integration and multiple sessions that can be handled in parallel, which is a very useful functionality in most call centers.

Integration techniques

Software implementors have come a long way from the early standalone programs, running originally on small computers, to today's modern applications connecting to multiple data centers and running on various devices. The need for early applications was limited, as were their integration capabilities. However, today old and traditional integration is not enough to serve the scale and functionality of the new applications that are being developed.

In the early days, integration requirements were met to connect two applications using custom development or **point-to-point** integration. Employees were writing code to handle scenario-based requirements. Software developers analyzed each customer's specific requirements and wrote a new integration component, which potentially used existing code, to integrate data and solution components.

In the early stages of integration, this involved the transfer of flat files between two systems. Here, both the sender and receiver had to agree on the type of transferred files, the format of the data in the files, the file exchange locations, the frequency of transfer, and the download and upload mechanism and triggers. This approach is still valid in today's integrations, despite some of the challenges it presents regarding the synchronization of multiple sources. The approach is often preferred for its simplicity and ease of implementation for certain types of requirements, such as the examples that we'll explore next.

An example of a point-to-point approach is the consolidation and transfer of payment files between an accounting system and reconciliation components running at the end of the day. After successful reconciliation, the company details in the CRM system are updated.

Another example of this approach is in loyalty solutions. All customer transactions are imported as flat files from various backend systems and partners into the loyalty engine, where loyalty points are calculated and awarded. Similarly, redemption points are imported from internal systems and partners into the loyalty engine, where customer records are updated back into the CRM system.

Another variant of point-to-point integration is **star integration**, which you can see in *Figure 7.6*. This is where each component integrates with all the other components using point-to-point integration. The effort and cost of this approach increases drastically when we want to integrate each point with all the other points. However, this is not very common and the approach is almost disappearing from application landscapes across the globe.

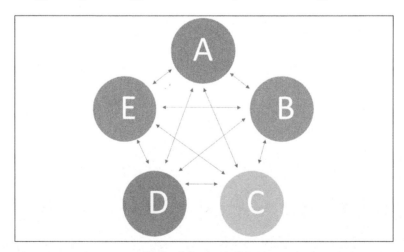

Figure 7.6: Star integration

Over time, as new technologies emerged, and more software components were added to a company's application landscape, the old integration approach based on custom solutions found it impossible to keep up with the pace. An increase in the volume and complexity of data being added to the integration layers was offsetting the advantage of reusable software components in custom integration applications.

The industry found the answer to the growing needs and complexity of integration in the **Enterprise Application Integration** (**EAI**) layer, which you can see in *Figure 7.7*:

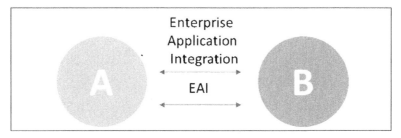

Figure 7.7: EAI software connects a variety of enterprise applications by letting them exchange data. It performs data conversion, provides messaging services, and gives access to interfaces.

EAI provides the architectural principles to integrate a set of applications in a structured manner. EAI is a collection of technologies and tools that form a middleware to support the complex integration of systems and applications in a company.

One approach used by EAI is **hub-spoke** architecture. In hub-spoke architecture, the integration component is composed of two sub-components: the integration engine and the message broker.

The integration engine will process requests and prepare responses, whereas the message broker is responsible for prioritizing, queuing, and dispatching requests and responses. The integration component plays a central role in managing and fulfilling integration requests and responses.

All the integrating components will only talk to the main integration component, whereas the integration component manages responses based on priority and response type. The limitation of this approach is that the integration component acts as a single point of failure. In the case of failure, all of the hub's connected components will lose their integration capability.

Figure 7.8 illustrates the hub-spoke integration:

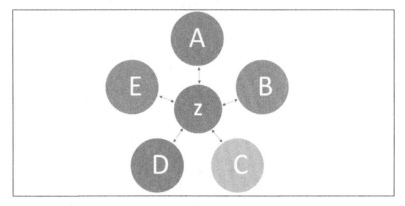

Figure 7.8: An example of hub-spoke integration

The performance and scalability of the hub play a vital role in this architecture. Yet, to overcome the scalability problem of hub-spoke architecture, the messaging service or message broker is separated from the integration engine.

Another important factor in this architecture is finding a common protocol that can communicate with all the proprietary technologies, which is sometimes difficult to find, hence we are pushed back to using the file transfer approach.

Service-Oriented Architectures (SOAs) are another technology that improved the integration technique and took it to the next level. The introduction of SOAs in the early 2000s changed the way that most software components were designed and delivered because the technology helped software vendors to offer software services in the form of web services.

This created interoperability, a common and understandable ground for integration points where each integration component can understand the language of other components among heterogeneous systems.

The use of SOAs, along with EAI, introduced the concept of the **Enterprise Service Bus** (**ESB**), which manages the message content, direction, destination, and protocols very much like a bus service. ESBs take care of **Quality of Service** (**QoS**) by applying security and managing throttling. Not only do they support legacy and new technologies, but they're typically configurable and extensible.

ESB implements a software architecture as depicted in *Figure 7.9*:

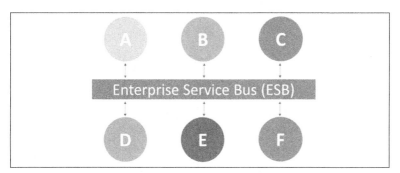

Figure 7.9: An ESB implements a communication system
between interacting applications in an SOA

In recent times, application landscapes have been widened by the introduction of cloud and mobile devices. Therefore, EAI, SOAs, and ESBs have become less relevant because these technologies are mainly for internal software components. The answer to this decline in relevance is that this growing integration needs better **Application Programming Interface** (**API**) management or an API economy.

API management proposes a new way of exposing business functionalities and data in a managed, accessible, monitored, and adaptive way. An API is a simple message format, usually leveraging HTTP, that can be used to transfer data between integration points in a lightweight manner. API management enables software vendors to publish APIs to external, partner, and internal components. However, we must not forget that an API cannot replace integration needs. Both APIs and API management are used to overcome some limitations of ESB and SOA. However, I would not consider them as a replacement of integration.

In addition to standard web technologies, we've seen the introduction of new concepts in the industry such as the Open Data Initiative, which is a partnership among Microsoft, SAP, and Adobe enabling data exchange across systems, making data a renewable resource that flows into intelligent applications.

Another example of emerging integration concepts that is perhaps more relevant to CRM implementations is the Microsoft Power Platform, which includes both PowerApps and **Common Data Service** (**CDS**). You can create and publish your own app in a figurative minute. You start with a simple app, before later adding components that share a common data service, allowing Microsoft Dynamics to share a common set of data elements and services for seamless integration.

Microsoft Dynamics 365 connects with other apps using native integration, but the story does not end here. Using Power Platform and Microsoft Flow, a Microsoft CRM solution can be integrated with 200+ external systems out of the box. This method overcomes limitations, effort, and costs that are required for integration between CRM and other Microsoft and non-Microsoft products, which in the end deliver a unique experience to support no-code/low-code integration. We will focus much more on the Microsoft Power Platform in *Chapter 9, CRM Differentiators*.

A CRM integration strategy might include all the preceding techniques, as depicted in *Figure 7.10*:

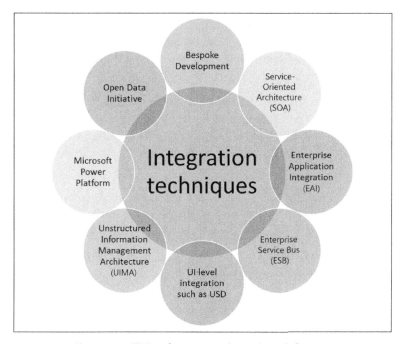

Figure 7.10: A CRM can leverage many integration techniques

Now that we have covered the integration techniques, let us explore other related issues with CRM integration that you'll need to consider in your integration strategies.

Master data management

Master data management (**MDM**) is a method used to manage the critical data of a business and to provide data management functionalities, such as a single point of reference, removing duplicate data, standardizing data, and incorporating rules to prevent incorrect data from entering the system.

It's important to mention here that a CRM is not a replacement for an MDM application, nor does it have any dependency on it. While data consolidation and integration are big subjects in every CRM project, there is always some customer data, such as demographical data or interaction history, that will end up being mastered in or by a CRM. This is by no means an MDM application.

I have seen this requirement come up sometimes in the RFI and/or RFP for CRM projects; therefore, it's worth talking about it here. In fact, there is sometimes confusion around what master data is and how CRM can help to classify it.

To be clear, MDM requires a more comprehensive and focused discussion about data integration and data management than any CRM project will, which is not within the scope of this book. However, there are a few common elements to address.

Typically, there are the same stakeholders involved and there are some similar discussions, such as data cleansing, duplicate detection, data ownership, data retention, and so forth. This is all either in a very limited scope or in a very small subset of how MDM is connected with data integration. It's fair to say that requirements must be agreed on and that the application for MDM itself is a completely different project than CRM.

In a nutshell, MDM has the objective of managing the processes for collecting, matching, aggregating, consolidating, cleansing, modeling, distributing, retaining, retiring, and archiving data throughout an organization. *Figure 7.11* covers the scope of an MDM solution at the very highest level:

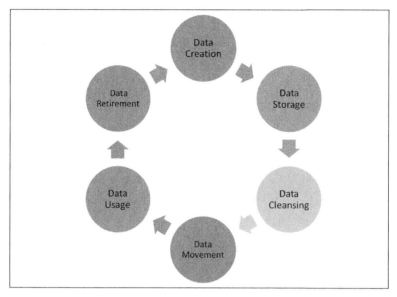

Figure 7.11: The MDM life cycle

There seems to be some overlap with CRM at this level, especially in regards to customer data. However, when we look a bit closer at what the MDM detail requirements are, then it becomes clear that they are very different requirements than a CRM system should or can provide, such as data governance, structure and the architecture of the data, data quality, and data security. These requirements are better off in an enterprise-wide MDM application.

A data management tool might include all the preceding functionalities and sub-functionalities, as depicted in *Figure 7.12*:

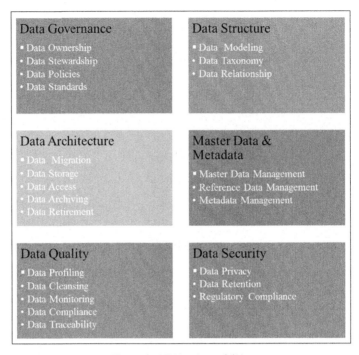

Figure 7.12: MDM main capabilities

As you can see, these are requirements and functionalities that MDM will provide that are traditionally not provided in a CRM system. With a new CRM system, you may have some common discussions about who will be the master of which data, especially the new data that was not in the enterprise before, and how to integrate, synchronize, and distribute this data.

There are some very easily identified master data items, such as the customer demographic data or products. There are even more soft areas, such as a customer's satisfaction level, that could be managed only by a CRM system and can be classified as master data by simply reciting a commonly agreed master data item list. Other areas that can only be managed by MDM include data standards, data modeling, data privacy, and data retention.

So, what if you already have MDM in your organization? Then it makes sense to leverage MDM and the information there, and load relevant data from it if it's available and is needed in the CRM processes. Actually, this will simplify some of the discussions and decisions regarding your CRM integration strategy.

MDM might be leveraged for CRM integration strategies as depicted in *Figure 7.13*:

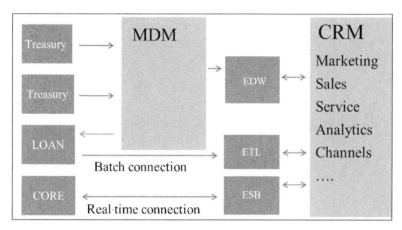

Figure 7.13: A combination of MDM and CRM data integration

An MDM tool supports MDM by standardizing data and incorporating rules for eliminating incorrect data, removing duplicates, cleansing, and storing data, along with rules for data policies, taxonomy, and compliance through data retirement. All of this will be useful in CRM integration discussions for both business and technical stakeholders.

Extract-transform-load or data hub?

Once the data, processes, and organizational issues have been clarified, and all stakeholders are on board, there are technical design decisions to be made by architects on how to best import or integrate these data and processes into your CRM system.

As described earlier in this chapter, one common approach to integrate data with a CRM platform is transferring customer data between systems using file transfer. This method is easy to implement because almost all modern CRM platforms support the import and export of data using files.

It's important to note that not all data managers approve of this, as they prefer to use an API-based approach. In this approach, the CRM solution, and other systems, will put the data into a file at a shared location for others to be able to use the **extract-transform-load** (ETL) method to load the data when needed and as agreed upon.

This method has been around for years, and many sophisticated tools, such as SQL Server Integration Services (SSIS) and Scribe, along with adapters, such as KingswaySoft, and other tools from IBM and SAP, exist to facilitate the integration. However, the file format, data types, location, privileges, and read/write coordination must be negotiated between the parties beforehand.

When a file integration needs additional extensive transforming, other approaches of data integration that could be leveraged are a shared database, the staging approach, or a data hub, in which applications can use a common database to populate and share data. This approach uses an intermediate database instead of files to store data in transit.

The benefit of this approach over file transfer is that the implementation team does not need to deal with unexpected circumstances that may occur in a file transfer with CRM. Also, in some situations, the approach may give an additional security layer for what data is exposed to the CRM software. It may also address some of the challenges of putting files in the correct directory, such as having read and write access by file reader processes and managing concurrency in operations.

Another benefit of this approach is the use of standard types in databases plus guidance from IT teams. In file transfer, all the data elements will be considered as text and therefore casting to the right data format is required. However, in this format data can be stored both as text and in a specific format, which will help implementation teams to use the right data format in their applications.

However, this approach may also bring some new challenges. For example, in one recent CRM implementation, the intermediate database was an Oracle database, whereas our CRM database was a SQL server. There was a business requirement to capture the creation date of each record in the CRM system. For records with an unknown creation date, both teams agreed to use a minimum date, supported by the database, as the creation date.

During the implementation, we realized that the way the Oracle database maintains a minimum date is different to how a SQL server will save the date. The earliest date possible in the Oracle database is "01-01-0001," whereas it is "01-01-1753" in the SQL server. It took us some time to realize where the issue was and how to fix it.

Simple object access protocol

The next approach of integration is application or process integration. In this approach, the data may or may not be shared among integrating systems. However, integrating systems can expose some functionality via a well-defined interface and other applications can invoke such functionality.

The result of calling the service can be an invocation of a function or a process in the invoked application or a return of processed data from it.

In applications with modern architecture, functionalities can be exposed using **Simple Object Access Protocol** (**SOAP**) or **Representational State Transfer** (**REST**) APIs. SOAP is a messaging protocol specification for exchanging structured data over web services. REST is an architectural design to define the constraints to be used for web services. However, in older architectures, you may see Remote Procedure Invocations called **Remote Procedure Calls** (**RPCs**). SOAP evolved as a successor of RPC.

SOAP provides extensibility, neutrality, and independence:

- SOAP, combined with HTTP, tunnels easily through existing firewalls and proxy servers, and doesn't require modifying the infrastructures and networks.

- SOAP's neutrality makes it suitable for use with any transport protocol, such as HTTP, but other popular transport protocols could be used, such as SMTP and message queues.

- SOAP allows processes running on different operating systems, such as Windows and Linux, to communicate using **Extensible Markup Language** (**XML**).

Technologies such as **Common Object Request Broker Architecture** (**CORBA**) were popular as RPC-style integration methodologies prior to SOAP and web service technologies. More recently, with the fast transformation of technology, we have seen the use of serverless computing.

Serverless computing, which is also known as serverless architecture or **Function as a Service** (**FaaS**), is a software design pattern where applications are hosted by a third-party service, therefore eliminating the need for server software and hardware management by the developer.

Regardless of the technology, whether it is RPC, REST, or FaaS, the core concept of this approach of integration remains the same: the execution of functionality in an application remotely. Examples of this approach can be an invocation of a dispatch functionality in the ERP system after the closure of an opportunity in CRM. In this example, the CRM is customized to call a web service provided by ERP to initiate a dispatch functionality on the closure of the opportunity after it is won.

Another example could be the execution of a debit transaction in a core banking system by a CRM in the service request entity. Usually, the API provided for use in CRM applications is managed in an ESB or API management tool. However, what is important in this approach is managing the infrastructure to maintain the API. Provisioning secure zones to give authorized parties access to the API, managing security, and building the API according to best practices are factors that implementation teams should consider while taking this approach.

Integration project phases

I suggest considering CRM integration tasks as their own mini project. This can start from the early stages of the CRM project, from diagnostics to initiation execution, stabilization, deployment, and operation. All of these stages define a horizontal set of activities that require various stakeholders to be involved in this process.

Parties involved in integration can be customers, partners, or regulatory agencies. It is vital for every stakeholder to understand what the outcome of the integration will be and what everyone's role is in making the implementation a success.

For instance, having a project champion from an internal team is one way to onboard everyone. In my experience, establishing a communication platform with everyone participating in the integration activities is essential and moreover, having someone from the internal team to champion the integration project internally is crucial for the success of the integration. They'll be able to help to gain support from various team members from business and IT teams.

Lastly, a top executive sponsor is needed for critical issues that may arise. Typically, after the first iteration of data import, that executive will be actively giving executive sponsorship in times of trouble. That is a vital support to the implementation teams.

The integration of project phases is depicted in *Figure 7.14*:

Figure 7.14: Classical integration approach

With an Agile approach, which makes the implementation and development cycle much shorter, coupled with delivering many releases, **Continuous Integration and Delivery (CI/CD)**, which was referenced in the Agile Manifesto, is visibly becoming mainstream.

This is an extension of Agile, as mentioned in *Chapter 4, Architecting Your CRM Solution – Preparing for Today and Tomorrow*, which is providing tools and processes needed to integrate smaller chunks of apps into the core apps quickly, while automating testing and delivering continuous updates that in turn enable a faster application development time.

The integration phases in the Agile project method are depicted in *Figure 7.15*:

Figure 7.15: Agile implementation approach

Once all the stakeholders are on board, the implementation team can begin work on the project and technical aspects of integration. The approach can be driven by the capabilities of the system, customer policies, and guidance. No matter what business requirements are gathered at the beginning of the project, the team has to understand what limitations/rules it has, what integration capabilities systems to provide, and what techniques to follow.

In one current project that I'm involved with, the company's system doesn't have an API, so that needs to be developed. IT has introduced a message broker as a common way to communicate between systems, so we have to follow this approach.

During all phases of the integration project, we dedicate some time to activities related to integration. For example, during the analysis phase, the solution architect dedicates sessions to analyzing integration requirements. Similarly, during the design phase, dedicated workshops are used for integration design. In these sessions, the presence of business and technical stakeholders is equally important. Here, each member from the business and technical teams will look at the requirements and analyze them.

Another important consideration related to integration is the inclusion of an integration effort in the project plan during the planning phase. Each integration activity requires resources – human resources, time, and a budget – and thus must be factored into all project management activities.

Analyzing integration requirements will help the project team to define an integration strategy. An integration strategy defines a set of principles for designing integration interfaces in order to support business processes in CRM.

The guiding principles in the CRM integration strategy include many factors, such as whether automation of the integration process is desired. For some type of requirements, using manual integration processes could be enough, whether using file transfer, a shared database, point-to-point integration using APIs, or the use of ESBs and middleware products. Likewise, the choice of integration techniques and the middleware product(s) is vital for CRM integration.

In the case of deciding on a middleware product, factors such as the cost of the solution, the readiness of the organization to procure and run an additional system in its IT landscape, and the training requirement for the implementation of the new product should be assessed.

Lastly, the choice of the CRM platform and its capabilities will define some of the integration strategies. This will be covered in *Chapter 9, CRM Differentiators*.

Even though following the guiding principles may require a lot of effort, failing to do so will have larger consequences for the project. In the absence of guiding principles, the integration costs can rapidly exceed the projected costs of the project, and in turn, this could delay the go-live date, which has a direct impact on the project health and the company.

We should base our strategy on the cost-value propositions of integration requirements. As more information impacting those cost-value propositions is received during planning, analysis, and design, the strategy should be refined accordingly.

As already explained in *Chapter 3, Conceptualizing the CRM Design from Business Requirements*, if we consider the cost of a particular integration to be very high when compared to the low value it provides to the business, then we may want to pause on this requirement and give it a lower priority in the process. If the organization agrees to use a manual integration approach, after assessing ESB products, then we can use manual processes to integrate CRM with external systems.

On the other hand, if the organization decides to go for an automatic integration approach, then we can consider point-to-point data integration, rather than an application layer integration, where too much risk exists, by bypassing business rules implemented in an application.

The next step after defining the integration strategy is to define the design constraints of each identified integration point. The design for each integration point should include integration approach details, as mentioned earlier, including data mapping and transformational requirements, data validation rules, business rules, security requirements, audit requirements, identifying technical methods of sending and receiving messages, a list of exceptions and exception handling details, and operational requirements, which will all go to the Solution Blueprint.

Every detail in that list is essential in order to execute a successful integration strategy. In recent integration workshops, I've tended to reduce the potentially high complexity by the classification of integration streams. The first question will be whether the integration is event-driven or in a batch mode. The event-driven approach enables organizations to evolve a process or data quicker compared to the batch mode. The event triggers sub-processes that impact customer processes, such as delivery timeframes.

Expect surprises and plan for additional time in the stabilization phase, as very often there are unexpected discoveries in the data you are importing. In one of the projects that I worked on, we had an agreement to master (own) the customer's birthdate in a CRM entity.

There was a requirement to integrate CRM with an external loyalty engine outside the CRM platform. Among other elements, it had to pass the customer's birthdate from the CRM platform to the loyalty engine.

The loyalty engine would calculate loyalty points using several parameters, including the age of the customer based on the birthdate received from the CRM platform. During the testing phase, we noticed that for some customers, the number of loyalty points was reducing after each data synch. Further investigation revealed that for customers without a birthdate, the CRM sent a null value to the loyalty engine.

In the loyalty engine, the null value on the birthdate is translated to "-1" as the customer's age. Therefore, the point calculated, which was a multiplication of the age factor with several other factors, would return a negative value.

In the platform, the birthdate could never be negative, but in the loyalty engine, the age was an integer and could be negative if it was null. These kinds of issues are normal and this is exactly why you need to plan extra time for integration testing. There can be a difference between what the developer perceives happening and usability, as depicted in *Figure 7.16*:

Figure 7.16: The application developer desktop

A successful integration requires iterative execution of analyses, design (both functional and technical), development, testing, and feedback. During the design phase, the implementation team can work with business users to define the requirements that are expected from the integration. These requirements can vary from displaying the customer location on the screen, to calculating the opportunity value outside the CRM based on some input parameters from the CRM entities.

It's important that this functional design is co-created by technical consultants and business users, and that it is in line with the project requirements. The content of functional design should contain:

- An expected outcome from the integration activity.
- Both a request and response messages format.
- Both input and output parameters.
- The exceptions.
- Both primary and secondary flows.
- Business rules.
- Pre-conditions and post-conditions.

All of these factors support good design. Once created and approved by business stakeholders, these functional designs act as an input for technical design. The goal of technical design is to identify and document all modifications and enhancements in the system in order to facilitate the integration.

The technical design will deliver the fit where the gap was identified and will act as a roadmap for the developer team, containing high-level solutions to functional requirements. During the technical design, the functional requirements are translated into the technical design by the technical team.

The result of this translation is either validation of both the effort and time requirement, or you obtain a new effort and time required to fulfill and implement the technical design. An incomplete or inadequate design can result in multiple remediation sessions. In addition to the solution design, special attention should be given to validating any additional security requirements that are identified while creating a technical design.

The next step after signing off on the functional and technical designs is to commence development and building of integration interfaces, which we often should integrate/test with stubs because development on the other systems is still in progress. The build and development effort should occur along with the creation of unit test cases to a level that supports functional testing.

The solution design and technical design documents are used as the primary source for development activities. The result of build activities may not always be production-ready. However, the result should at least support the architectural assumptions, as the design can be fully validated before completion of the interface.

Initial data load

Often, introducing a new CRM into a large enterprise with thousands of users and millions of customers will require a large amount of data to be loaded with the initial data load. This could include loading hundreds of millions of records for the first time.

Typically, a modern CRM platform leverages web services to manage records and entity relationships. The platform does, therefore, execute checks and balances for each record loaded to the system. Sometimes the platform creates not only one record but also all of its dependencies and related entities in the system, which is the so-called ripple effect. For example, creating a record would then create relationships, views, charts, and so on.

Creating a new record and its dependencies, along with the ripple effect, is depicted in *Figure 7.17*:

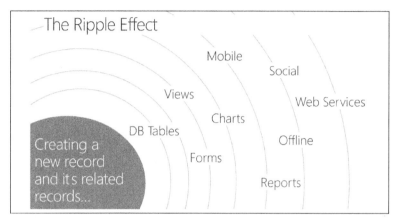

Figure 7.17: The ripple effect in action

Creating hundreds of millions of records in a reasonable time has some performance considerations that you need to be aware of and prepared for:

- Initial data load.
- Provisioning of a large number of users.
- Application performance (form load).
- Loading millions of records overnight.

There are a number of steps you could take to optimize the initial data load:

- Reduce the number of fields by removing unneeded fields from the default entity records.
- Consolidate all records before calling CRM.
- Optimize the data publishing on legacy systems before the load.
- Reduce the number of records to be processed.

- Pre-process the records that need to be loaded; for example, lookups or option sets.

- Allow continuous integration.

- Implement a fast **Operational Data Store** (**ODS**).

- Implement a high-performance CRM farm.

- Minimize any server processes (workflows, scripts, and plug-ins) prior to the initial load.

- Bring the users to CRM.

- Assign CRM roles.

The challenge of provisioning thousands of users includes bringing the users to CRM and how to assign individual roles to those users. The general recommendations are:

- Use existing automation processes provided by the platform, such as RACF for **Active Directory** (**AD**), and add a code (script) to bring AD users to the CRM platform, where you can allocate the security roles based on the AD groups. However, this could become complex depending on the security mode. **Resource Access Control Facility** (**RACF**) is an IBM security management tool and provides identification, access control, and auditing for the operating system.

- The use of script is recommended because that will let you define naming conventions and business-unit structures specific to your environment.

To increase the speed of the initial data load in an on-premises environment, you could increase the total capacity of the application servers that are responsible for the execution of the web-services calls, like in the following example:

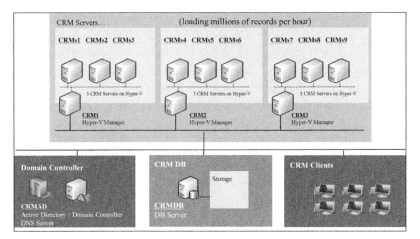

Figure 7.18: Increasing the number of application servers for the initial load

Figure 7.18 is illustrating a real-life project example for a large enterprise in Germany, where we had to import 100 million records over one weekend before opening the business at 9 am on the Monday. Here we were leveraging nine application servers to increase the speed of the initial data load to five million records per hour.

Loading data to the cloud follows the same principles and patterns as doing so in an on-premises environment; however, loading data to a cloud environment limits the project teams from accessing, modifying, or enhancing the infrastructure. Cloud environments have their own resource management and request/response handling mechanisms, which makes it very hard, if not impossible, to access the database server directly or customize the environment to suit all scenarios.

Since online cloud environments share resources among multiple clients, they don't provide much freedom to configure factors such as timeout periods. That being said, in a way, this is a good approach because it leads the implementation team to follow the best practices.

Due to the restriction on server resources in cloud environments, it is essential to plan data load activities in advance and mark the data load activities on the critical path of projects. The use of standard data load processes, such as out-of-the-box import wizards or data load products such as Scribe Online or KingswaySoft Adapter, will be a big advantage and allow you to implement faster. This is because they can validate types and fields, transform data, and load data from various sources, in addition to pushing data to CRM servers using the multi-threading capabilities of platforms.

However, the complex relationship between records, the number of records, and fields can impact the data load time. Because we cannot access the database directly or configure application server parameters, such as the maximum number of records in requests or timeout limits, we must follow the normal path without tweaking the settings.

System performance

The system performance, in general, affects user acceptance. There are a number of factors that affect the system performance that you need to consider in your design, such as form load. Loading a CRM form should not take more than five seconds; as everyone agrees, the speed of loading forms is an important issue when it comes to user acceptance.

Other factors that affect the performance of form load include:

- Client hardware and software. For example, with the Celeron type of CPU, it may have a bad impact on script processing, different browsers, and so on.
- The design of the solution in general (entities, fields, relationships, integration, and so on):
    - The number of entities (record types).

- ° Relationship of entities.
- ° The number of fields.
- ° Cascaded views.
- ° Processes.

- The type and architecture of the platform.
- Infrastructure (network, related applications, and so on).

Summary

In a nutshell, the ultimate purpose of integration in CRM is to enable various software components, or data sources, to link together and produce the desired business outcome in the form of new or enhanced customer data in CRM. This data will be used to improve customer processes across the company and in all interactions with the client. It will also be used to manage other business areas, such as product development and reporting.

In this chapter, I explained that while defining the integration strategy, the project teams should carefully choose the integration approach and select the best technique(s) in order to ensure deliverability and feasibility of integration. Integration can happen at different levels, such as data integration, application integration, or business process integration. Each of these methods has emerged to address specific requirements and can be used alone or combined in a single implementation.

The process of defining an integration strategy should start from project initiation, but it can also go on beyond the analysis phase. Unforeseen circumstances may lead us to make changes in our strategy, which correlates with the continuous architecture principle.

Data integration brings data from different sources into CRM and enables CRM to use this pool of data to form a consolidated view of customer information, which is helpful when managing and analyzing customer interactions, behavior, and intentions. CRM systems then help to gather sales, marketing, and service data.

However, customer relationships in today's world are about understanding interactions, offers, loyalties, purchases, social sentiments, surveys, emails, social marketing, and mobile self-service. CRM systems on their own are not capable of producing a customer's holistic single view, but they could provide a platform to enable the integration of data from all these sources. We will cover the platform capabilities in *Chapter 9, CRM Differentiators.*

As I've explained before, we are in the midst of the fourth industrial revolution and this is mainly powered by artificial intelligence (AI) at its core. AI, hyper-connectivity, the cloud, and big data provide huge opportunities for all of us. However, this has also created a challenging and dynamic economic and social environment for many businesses.

A CRM platform should be capable of integrating with an ever-growing ecosystem in order to consume data and information from all other sources, such as AI, social media platforms, and data lakes, to build a comprehensive customer view.

In the next chapter, we will explore CRM deployment options.

CHAPTER 8

CLOUD VERSUS ON-PREMISE VERSUS HYBRID – THE DEPLOYMENT OF A CRM PLATFORM

How you choose to host your CRM solution can significantly impact your business. Factors to consider include features and services that are available to you, regulatory compliance, security, portability, how and when you can access your data, and who is responsible for keeping your solution safe. Then there is the overall cost of the system, including the money you spend to buy, maintain, and operate the system, along with the ongoing costs that you'll encounter.

These are just some of the core factors that will directly influence your choice of CRM platform and the hosting method for your solution. In this chapter, we will be covering what the most important factors are in each method, before evaluating both the pros and cons of cloud, on-premise, and hybrid deployment.

You have already come a long way in your journey and you probably have, at this point, chosen your CRM platform. Alternatively, it might be that the deployment options provided by a vendor are critical for you to consider when choosing a platform. In both cases, the question would be, what is the best option for your business?

In this chapter, I want to look at CRM deployment options and compare them with each other to provide you with some great guiding principles for your CRM deployment. This discussion is not limited to talking about CRM. Most, if not all, business applications have the same considerations and questions as a CRM system. While CRM capabilities are very different in the cloud than on-premise, we are not comparing the platforms but rather the deployment options of the CRM solution.

This discussion will continue into *Chapter 9, CRM Differentiators*, where we will look at platform capabilities and compare them at a functional level. Some platforms, such as Microsoft Dynamics 365, provide you with all the deployment options that we'll discuss here, while others, such as Salesforce.com, will only offer you cloud deployment as an option.

 Note: It is important to mention that the information in this chapter is designed to give you visibility of the options that are available on the market and point you to some important parameters for your solution deployment. This chapter is not a vendor or a platform preference, nor does it provide a full list of the capabilities of a platform.

A mixture of the on-premise and cloud deployment options, referred to as a hybrid option, is also available today. You can use a mixture of cloud and on-premise services to deploy software applications, such as **Infrastructure as a Service (IaaS)** or **Software as a Service (SaaS)** deployment, both of which we will explore later in this chapter.

If you are still choosing your CRM platform, then I recommend having a meaningful conversation with your CRM vendor on the subject of deployment options. You will need to bring up the questions that we are going to discuss in this chapter with your vendor or your system integrator. You should ask them to give you detailed information on each of these topics.

My advice is don't go choosing a deployment method until you've also read *Chapter 9, CRM Differentiators*. Once you've read both chapters, you'll have knowledge of platform capabilities, along with their deployment options.

Your CRM platform will likely give you all the options that we are going to discuss in this chapter. As we discussed before, Microsoft supports multiple deployment options, including cloud and on-premise, mixed with a variety of sub-options, including public and private cloud. Alternatively, your platform may provide you with only one option, such as Salesforce.com, which only provides cloud deployment.

To ease you into this chapter, I find that the graphic that follows is a great way to summarize what we will be looking at. Over the course of this chapter, we will be balancing and weighing up each deployment option for a variety of situations, because as the saying goes, no one size fits all. Each option has its advantages and disadvantages depending on where you, your business, or your situation places you.

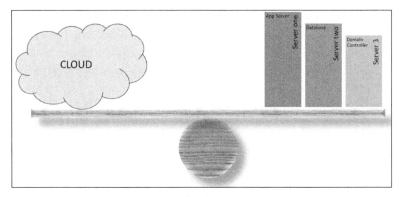

Figure 8.1: Cloud versus on-premises

I would strongly recommend that you read all the previous chapters before going any further, as the concepts discussed throughout the book will be critical in selecting your deployment option. But, for now, let's consider the most important criteria:

- The business requirements and fit-gap.

- The cost-value matrix (see *Chapter 3, Conceptualizing the CRM Design from Business Requirements*).

- User acceptance (see *Chapter 2, Getting to Know Your Customer*, and *Chapter 3, Conceptualizing the CRM Design from Business Requirements*).

- Technical matters including integration, compatibility, and deployment options.

- Explicit and implicit costs.

- Regulatory compliance (see *Chapter 6, GDPR and Regulatory Compliance*).

Factors influencing vendor selection

We will cover vendor selection criteria more extensively in *Chapter 9, CRM Differentiators*, but for the sake of our discussions in this chapter, the most critical influencing factors regarding vendor selection are:

- The overall capabilities of the platform in regards to the deployed option. For instance, the cloud has different capabilities than on-premise or hybrid.
- The overall cost of the system, including the money you spend to buy, maintain, and operate it, as well as the ongoing costs.
- Complexity and feasibility for customization, both initially and ongoing.
- Both portability and deployment limitations. For example, the freedom to move between cloud and on-premise or hybrid.
- The number of international data centers, including their location, compliance, and the regulations that they come with.
- Training and skills required for the users, admin, and developers.

Don't worry if you want more information, as that is the focus of the next, and final, chapter. Right now, let's have a look at cost and complexity, or the TCO/ROI factors.

Cost and complexity

In one of my past projects, I was working with a Swiss company that had implemented a CRM solution with the help of a major system integrator. At the point where I came in, the company had already had the system, which was based on a standard platform from a competitor and was deployed on-premise, for a couple of years.

However, the business leaders were complaining that the system was very expensive to maintain and that the users were not satisfied with it, nor were they using it on a regular basis because it was too complicated and time-consuming. By the time I was working with the company, it had gone through several very expensive updates and extensive customization based on its vendor's recommendations, but this had not helped to resolve the issues.

The company was seeking information from competitors to make an assessment about the total cost of ownership versus the TCO/ROI (see *Chapter 1, What is CRM?* and *Chapter 3, Conceptualizing the CRM Design from Business Requirements*) of the current system. There were three options:

1. Carry on with the current system and improve it by adding missing functionalities with in-house development tools.

2. Update the system to the latest release with new features and a system integrator.

3. Replace the platform entirely with a new platform.

Besides the challenge of user acceptance, the most pressing issues were the high maintenance, customization, and system upgrade costs. So, to solve this, it was decided, by top-tier management, that a TCO/ROI study was needed before making any decision about which pathway to choose.

In fact, as I mentioned earlier in this book, doing a TCO/ROI analysis works best if done prior to choosing and deploying a solution. However, doing it at any time later in the project lifetime, including when you're thinking about deployment options like we are now, is also very helpful, as requirements are changing, technologies are evolving, and vendor offerings are continuously improving.

The bottom line is that you need to conduct a TCO/ROI study at the start of your CRM journey, and continuously throughout the life cycle of the system, before any major improvement of the system is included.

In general, whenever there is a need for a major upgrade, extension, or improvements compiling a new TCO/ROI is highly recommended and I suggest that you make it mandatory, not only to secure the success of the project, but to innovate and improve processes. Innovation in CRM is no longer just a luxury; it is now an absolute necessity for the success of the business.

This Swiss company took the decision to re-evaluate the whole platform and innovate business processes in order to stay competitive and leverage the latest technology innovations that are only available in the cloud today. The company decided to do so by engaging third-party vendors to assist with compiling a comprehensive study that also considered the options of cloud and hybrid deployment.

The final outcome of the study was to implement a hybrid solution that provided a major improvement in the functionality and cost of the solution. At a very high level, these are the costs you need to consider:

- **The initial costs**: License, infrastructure, and so on.
- **The implementation time**: It needs to be short.
- **The degree of customizations**: Must be lower than 5%.
- **The control over the data and the solution**: Including backups and updates.
- **The ongoing maintenance costs**.

All of these points are summarized in *Figure 8.2*, which shows how they each interact and how they play their part in the overall costs that this Swiss company, and your company, would encounter.

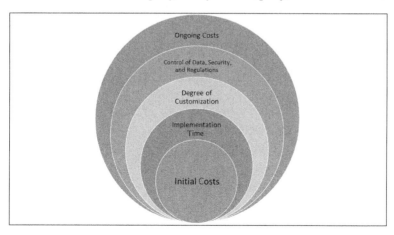

Figure 8.2: Factors for evaluating the cost and complexity of a platform

The cost-value matrix of a CRM system for every business will be very different and every situation will require a unique TCO/ROI assessment. The TCO/ROI (cost-value matrix) also needs to be considered when you're evaluating the deployment options of your CRM solution. This is, in general, not an easy task, as there are many factors to be considered, such as unnecessary subscriptions, excessive customization, and functionality features regarding the life cycle of the solution.

Besides all of this, some vendors also have hidden costs that you may not be aware of upfront. They may charge your company additional fees for enabling the sandbox environment where customers can experiment with the system's functionality, as well as develop and test new apps. Likewise, some vendors will charge more if a company needs additional integration via web service APIs, including REST and SOAP.

Applying knowledge to build sophisticated user interfaces, to configure, and to customize the solution in house is a non-trivial task for any business, no matter the size of the business. That's why some platforms can't do this without the assistance of professional developers, which, in turn, can be rather expensive.

For example, Microsoft Dynamics 365 supports common programming languages, such as HTML, .NET, and Java; meanwhile, Salesforce.com uses its own programming language called Apex. Besides all of that, most vendors rely heavily on partners that offer add-ons or resources to help companies to build a complete solution.

Cloud deployment

If you decide to go for cloud deployment, you won't be responsible for maintaining the infrastructure and the cloud-based software application, which in the long term may significantly save you both time and money. With that being said, there are several issues to be addressed first, such as:

- Solution capabilities
- Collaboration with internal IT
- Regulation
- Speed
- Security
- Portability

Some regional data regulations place a limitation on storing critical business and customer data in the cloud or outside the country of operation. For instance, this could include the use of personal data through GDPR.

With that being said, there are a number of benefits of the cloud, which can be seen in *Figure 8.3*:

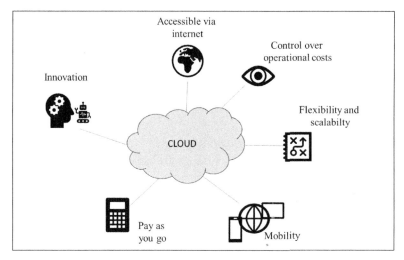

Figure 8.3: Benefits of the cloud

So, how does the cloud provider support you with the tools you need in order to help you to comply with the local standards and regulations? For businesses in different regions, countries, or industries, public cloud deployment might not be an option.

As I mentioned, this may be because some regulations do not allow you to store certain information (see *Chapter 6, GDPR and Regulatory Compliance*). The question is, then, does the platform support individual country regulations that you could be facing both today and tomorrow?

I remember working with a client in Reykjavík, Iceland. Regulations there did not allow businesses to store the financial data of customers in the cloud. At this company, the CEO initiated a successful campaign to change this regulation by connecting with political leaders and regulatory authorities. Yet, despite that, we designed a solution that would mask the customers' information before storing the data in the cloud. This served to satisfy the regulations, while leveraging the cloud services that the business needed to stay competitive.

Another important element to consider with the cloud option is ensuring that you have a data center closer to your company's location. Despite what you may think, this is not for increasing the speed of the application but for the response time, which depends on the location of the data center and its distance from the users.

In some countries, or geographic areas such as within European Union member states, there are regulatory issues with both customer data privacy and compliance that require companies to store their data in the country of operation or a regional data center. This extends across multiple industries such as healthcare, the public sector, or financial services.

Another important factor to consider is solution portability, as this could become important later on in your deployment, in the running of your CRM platform, or at exit time. It could also be a key factor if you want to move (transfer) your solution from one cloud provider to another, host a solution from a local partner, or bring the solution back to on-premise and manage it with your in-house team. This is a very important element to consider because Salesforce.com does not support public clouds, such as Rackspace, TelekomCloud, Amazon **Elastic Compute Cloud** (**EC2**), or Microsoft Azure, to name just a few.

For reference, Rackspace is an America-based company offering web application hosting. Meanwhile TelekomCloud is a German company offering a secure infrastructure as a service solution on the basis of OpenStack. EC2 is the foundation of Amazon's cloud-computing platform, and Microsoft Azure is a cloud-computing service created by Microsoft with an expanding network of Microsoft-managed data centers across the globe.

Users who employ the SaaS model can access innovative and continuously evolving technologies, such as machine learning and business intelligence tools, depending on the provider and connectivity method. With all that being said, there are still some misconceptions surrounding cloud services not being secure enough to protect intellectual properties and business data, or to prevent access by third parties.

Reports in the international media that revealed operational details about the global surveillance program of the **National Security Agency** (**NSA**) in the U.S. showcased a breach of trust back in 2013. Therefore, some providers such as Microsoft have taken action and have started to build data centers in different geographies that are protected by local laws and regulations; in this case, ones outside of the U.S.

In reality, your data and applications are almost certainly safer in the cloud than on your own servers if you do it right. For example, Microsoft Dynamics 365 employs multiple security features to ensure the safety of your business data, protect access to the data, and comply with regulations. All the connections made between users and data centers are encrypted, while public endpoints are secured with **Transport Layer Security** (**TLS**).

On-premise deployment

There is no doubt that the popularity of on-cloud deployment has been increasing in the last few years, with more enterprises now prioritizing public cloud. It's a crowded market, with top providers such as **Amazon Web Services** (**AWS**), Microsoft Azure, Google Cloud, IBM Cloud, and Alibaba all competing for the enterprise space. While AWS still is leading in both popularity and recognition, Microsoft Azure continues to grow quickly and is reducing AWS' lead, especially among enterprises.

But what if you are not ready to move to the cloud yet? Equally, what if, after reading the previous chapter, you encounter some business reasons to stay on-premise? For instance, say you've recently invested in your infrastructure, your local data regulations have changed, or you're in a particular country that has the benefit of on-premise having a lower cost of service compared to what you can get with cloud hosting?

It's important to understand that you don't have to think of the cloud as the ultimate solution. For some people, on-premise is a more viable option simply because they don't have access to a high-speed Internet connection in order to be able to utilize cloud services.

On-premise is what we would call the more traditional way to deploy software and the one that for obvious reasons has been with us for much longer. This option allows you to host your software either on your own servers or on those of an IT partner. This is just like how some larger organizations outsource their IT operations to specialized IT houses. This is a popular option, with examples being the UK's **National Health Service** (**NHS**), the Canadian train and plane giant Bombardier, or the Lloyds Banking Group.

Hosting on-premise means that you keep all of your data and applications in house. Because of that choice, you are responsible for all the housekeeping activities, including maintenance, backup, recovery, software updates, and hardware upgrades.

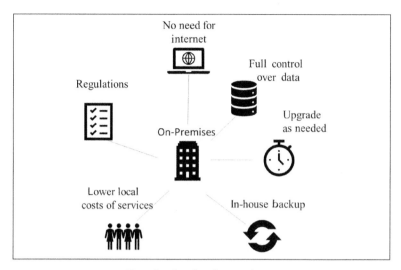

Figure 8.4: Benefits of on-premise

As I showcased for the cloud option, *Figure 8.4* is a great graphic that helps to showcase the six key features of on-premise deployment.

Cloud and on-premise mixed deployment

There are some mixed forms of on-premise and cloud computing that eventually (they're still being developed) will provide the benefits of both platforms. These include:

- **IaaS**: This is where underlying infrastructure, such as physical servers, physical location, scaling, security, and backup, is outsourced.

- **Platform as a Service (PaaS)**: This will allow you to develop, run, and control applications as a package, either using the provider's facility or in your own environment (on-premise).

- **SaaS** (also referred to as **on-demand software**): This is where software is licensed on a subscription basis and is hosted in the cloud.

The table that follows illustrates the ownership and responsibilities of each related component in your CRM application:

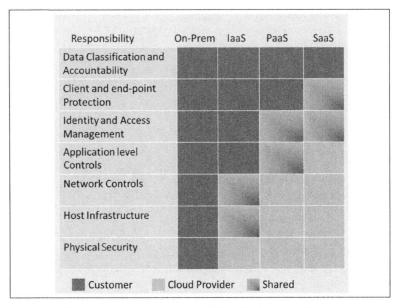

Figure 8.5: Ownership and responsibilities of deployment options

As you can see in the preceding table, all these options will split the ownership and responsibilities across both the customer and the cloud provider, and in some cases, both.

Hybrid deployment

A hybrid deployment is a mixed deployment of both the on-premise and cloud options, and in many ways, it takes some of the best elements from both. For example, through the use of this method, you could gain access to cloud-based services such as machine learning, business intelligence, and development sandboxes, but still have the ability to store your data on your on-premise infrastructure.

This hybrid will allow you to enjoy all of the benefits and services offered by both the cloud and on-premise solutions. However, because it involves two different deployment methods, you may find that it becomes more complex than choosing either cloud or on-premise.

In *Figure 8.6*, you can see a visualization of how you could split services between the two platforms:

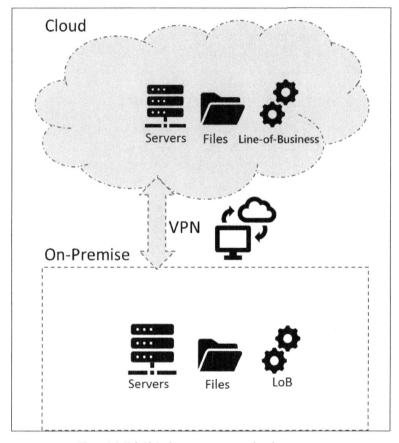

Figure 8.6: Hybrid, in theory, encompasses the advantages
of both cloud and on-premise deployment

For example, transactions are supported by local applications and the transaction data is hosted in house, with the option to sync it with the cloud in an anonymized form, just as the Icelandic company did. This is a great option for those businesses that need to have local business data for compliance purposes, but still want to be able to utilize cloud services, such as machine learning or Power BI.

As you can see in *Figure 8.6*, there is some complexity that may arise with a hybrid deployment. As an example, any data hosted locally on your in-house servers that is not backed up can still be vulnerable to corruption or loss.

So, what are your options?

You have all three options available to you. Depending on the platform capabilities that you have, as we will explore in the next chapter, there are some pros and some cons that could be encountered.

But, for now, let's have a closer look at the different options you have for hosting your CRM application and compare the benefits and shortcomings of each deployment option.

For this section, we will look at Microsoft Dynamics 365. I've chosen to look at Microsoft because it provides all of the preceding options and is, therefore, a very good case study. However, this table can be applied to any other vendor. To make it work, you simply need to ask your vendor to provide you with an up-to-date list of similar deployment comparisons:

Dynamics365	On-Premise	Cloud/Online	Hybrid	Partner Hosted
Releases/Year	One release	Two releases (April and October)	Mix	Mix
Upgrade/Update	By admin	Continuous Automatic Updates and Rollups. Automatic Upgrade after approvals	Mix	By admin
Skype (business), Yammer, Exchange, SharePoint	Yes	Yes	Yes	Yes
Office 365, Power BI, ML, Bots, Social,	No	Yes	No	Yes (federated)
Authentication	Active directory	Dynamics365 Authentication and Azure AD-Synch,	AD, ADFS, Azure Synch	ADFS, Synch Azure
Large Data Integration	Faster with low latency	Latency optimized by bulk API, or Azure-Server	Mix	Very fast
Mobile for Smart Phone and Tablet	Yes limited	Yes (online and offline)	Yes	Yes

Figure 8.7: Comparison of the benefits and shortcomings of each deployment option

The preceding table illustrates both the pros and cons of the deployment options and leaves you with a variety of options when deploying your system based on your specific aspirations, capabilities, and limitations.

Summary

All major CRM platform vendors offer multiple deployment options to their customers. As we've explored, these options can take the form of either, or both, cloud and on-premise deployments, as well as an array of mixed deployment scenarios. As we've explored, every deployment option has benefits and shortcomings, in addition to factors that your business itself has, such as Internet speed or location.

The business requirements, regulatory compliance, and TCO/ROI are all major driving factors for the decision process and the selection of the right deployment for your business. As we discussed, there is the possibility to mix cloud and on-premise deployment together, in what we call a hybrid approach, if the business requirements, or the IT and application environment, require it.

As we explored, there's no doubt that the popularity of on-cloud deployment has been increasing in the last few years, as more enterprises are prioritizing public cloud. There's also no doubt that most CRM platforms on the market are extremely powerful. There is fierce competition among the top vendors, such as Microsoft, Salesforce.com, and Oracle, surrounding the long list of functionalities and capabilities that they offer.

Yet, to leverage their platforms, businesses may have to customize and build numerous complementary components in addition to the integration efforts and other project costs. I would also suggest that the ecosystem is more important than the feature list of the CRM platform. This is something that will be the focus of the last chapter of this book.

In essence, and thinking back to the first few pages of this book, in the introduction, this topic may soon remind you of the building of the Taj Mahal in India, or the Sydney Opera House in Australia. They both started with a nice blueprint, a reasonable budget, and a time plan, but one architect spent a long time attempting to create a perfect solution that was able to satisfy the basic requirements, while the other tried to meet the budget and could change plans several times in order to adapt to future needs. In the next chapter, we will explore CRM differentiators.

CHAPTER 9

CRM DIFFERENTIATORS

It's not about the feature list; it's about the ecosystem

I n the last chapter of this book, I want to explore how CRM platforms differ in today's market. This will provide you with some insights into the essential elements and parameters for selecting a CRM platform for your business.

We are going to talk about the elements and characteristics that make a successful CRM implementation in today's environment. What we won't be doing, however, is comparing CRM products explicitly. Instead, we will explore the ecosystem that a new CRM solution should support in order to help business to successfully face the challenges of today and tomorrow.

In this chapter, I want to dive deep into some of the essential CRM differentiators that you'll encounter today, along with some examples from across the industry. I also want to share some personal thoughts on the current state of technological development in terms of managing customer relationships and where, I believe, that development is heading.

The innovation in CRM technologies has been so profound in recent years that we can expect even more fundamental changes in the way that we design and configure CRM solutions in the not-so-distant future.

Industry 4.0, or the fourth industrial revolution, is being driven by the current trend of automation, including data exchange within manufacturing technologies such as artificial intelligence (AI) and cognitive services, which has had a great impact on how we build CRM platforms.

We're going to start with a brief overview of the fourth industrial revolution and look at how this plays a significant role in business evolution today. As I highlighted earlier in this book, across both *Chapter 3, Conceptualizing the CRM Design from Business Requirements*, and *Chapter 4, Architecting Your CRM Solution – Preparing for Today and Tomorrow*, it's difficult to identify any industry whose business operations have not either been profoundly altered by new technologies or somehow affected by the big tech companies and start-ups that are entering new markets every day.

Regardless of which industry you are in, the market dynamics and the business challenges you face have changed with the arrival of new technologies, and this change has particularly been caused by digital disrupters. With this recent development in the market and the fundamental changes in the way customers do business today, CRM design criteria are looking very different to how they were just a few years ago.

The last 10 years have undoubtedly been remarkable years for technology innovations, but I expect that even more changes in the coming years will affect the way we manage our customer relationships and CRM platform decisions.

According to multiple surveys that have been conducted by the top market research and advisory firms, such as Gartner, IT spending trends confirm a powerful digital transformation across the globe, and CRM vendors are getting a significant part of this spending. I believe that the fourth industrial revolution is driving all this in the marketplace.

In this final chapter, we will cover the significant elements of the fourth industrial revolution regarding CRM strategies, including AI, big data, and machine learning (ML), before closing this chapter with a look at implementation tools.

The fourth industrial revolution and CRM

From my own personal observations, when compared with what we were facing a few years ago, there are two main drivers in the CRM market that are making a huge difference today:

- Digitalization and the way we all collaborate and connect with each other and our customers, along with how we partner in the marketplace today.

- Massive technology innovations and the democratization of technologies such as AI, big data, and ML, all of which are powering and spearheading the fourth industrial revolution.

All this development is changing the way we build a sustainable CRM strategy for tomorrow. You'll be hard pressed to find anyone who doesn't agree that AI is going to revolutionize CRM solutions in every business. Indeed, it is doing that already today, as we saw in the examples in *Chapter 5, Utilizing Artificial Intelligence and Machine Learning in Your CRM Strategy*, where we discussed how AI and ML could provide a semi-self-service solution for sales and customer service.

With AI, businesses are automating the repetitive and boring work in customer sales and service scenarios. AI is also enabling collaboration between customers and employees by providing rich analytical dashboards that can help business leaders to improve products and services.

When I talk about AI in this book, I am referring to the idea of training computer systems to complete intelligent human tasks through learning and automation. This ML leverages big data and bots to help us better understand the situation and support customer-facing staff in every interaction they have with clients.

AI and ML tools are very relevant to both CRM platforms and other business applications. Since CRM can leverage these technologies in most customer processes, it is becoming the core application for digital transformation in most traditional companies.

Digital transformation is all about how we leverage the latest technologies, and the vast amount of data that is at our disposal today, to manage more meaningful interaction and communication with our customers, make better business decisions, and be more competitive. Through the entire concept of digital transformation, companies will re-design the business processes and provide smarter tools to everyone in the organization to enable better customer service, design better products, create better business insights, and reduce operational costs.

In the process of digital transformation, CRM solutions are taking a more prominent place, for reasons we will explore later in this chapter. Across all modern industries, including healthcare, financial services, retail, and even manufacturing, there are companies that are going through digital transformation.

AI, hyper-connectivity, the cloud, and big data are providing enormous opportunities for all of us, such as higher operational efficiencies at a lower cost. However, these developments also have downsides, such as creating a challenging and dynamic platform of economic and social environments.

This new industrial revolution will bring tremendous opportunities to most traditional companies using a CRM strategy, as the examples in *Chapter 5, Utilizing Artificial Intelligence and Machine Learning in Your CRM Strategy*, showed us.

The traditional businesses that are not yet digitized are facing competition from big-tech companies, such as Google, Facebook, Amazon, Uber, and other start-ups that are leveraging the latest technologies in order to enter markets and take their market share.

Let's take a minute to look at the elements of the fourth industrial revolution in *Figure 9.1*:

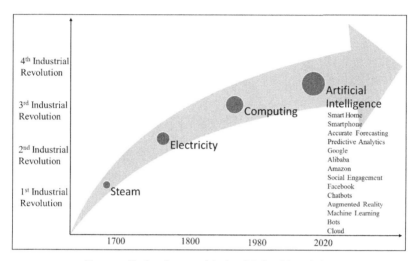

Figure 9.1: The key elements of the fourth industrial revolution

Big tech companies are typically taking market share from existing local businesses and traditional companies by leveraging all these new technologies to implement entirely new processes, which in turn allows them to have a competitive advantage. No industry, and therefore no company, will be unaffected by this new paradigm shift in the market.

As we explored in *Chapter 3, Conceptualizing the CRM Design from Business Requirements*, and *Chapter 4, Architecting Your CRM Solution – Preparing for Today and Tomorrow*, traditional businesses must go through a digital transformation in order to stay competitive.

Some of them are very successful in doing so, as the examples in *Chapter 2, Getting to Know Your Customer*, and *Chapter 3, Conceptualizing the CRM Design from Business Requirements*, showed us, while some are not so successful.

The most significant benefit of a new CRM platform could be a cost-effective digital transformation method for your business, as long as it can provide the ingredients of the fourth industrial revolution to your business processes, with the key ones being listed in the preceding illustration. In other words, it is not about a feature list anymore; it is about enabling your business to leverage the large ecosystem out there.

A CRM platform today could enable companies to leverage all these new technologies and support social channels to provide self-service and automated customer interactions, deliver recommendations and personalized customer experiences, carry out social selling, and use social advertising that is enabled by AI, big data, and cognitive services.

No doubt, such a CRM platform will expand your business abilities and accelerate your company's digital transformation. Later on in this chapter, we will be exploring what these platform components are and how they could work for your business and within your CRM strategy.

AI and smart cloud

By now, there is no doubt that the main driving power behind the fourth industrial revolution is AI. Yet, while AI is at its core, the revolution did not start overnight. Right now, AI is not the only component of the fourth industrial revolution. The revolution is taking place long after AI systems were first introduced in the 1980s.

I remember that during my computer science studies in Vienna, we had the first interactions with an expert system, which was a form of AI program that simulated the knowledge and analytical skills of human experts. Yet this system was not enough to power the fourth industrial revolution.

The revolution has mostly been driven by AI following advances in computer power and memory size. This is an industrial revolution because it is spreading across every industry, mainly through the democratization of cloud services. AI has become more mature and additional AI-based services, such as ML and the concept of big data, are providing the industrial scale needed to affect every business and power the revolution.

This concept is the smart cloud. I will explain this in more detail later on in this chapter, including what it is and how you can implement it, but, for now, let's take a visual look at the elements of the smart cloud, as depicted in *Figure 9.2*:

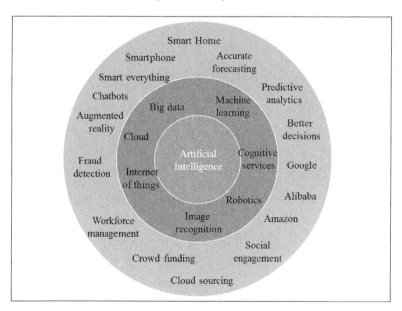

Figure 9.2: The concept of the smart cloud

With the democratization of AI and ML, combined with the mass spread of the Internet, the Internet of Things (IoT), and social media, we are witnessing a fundamental change in the way we do business, and how we communicate with our clients and partners today. All of this is directly affecting our CRM processes.

Since customers' expectations have changed, they not only expect that you have a 360-degree view of your relationship with them, as seen in *Chapter 2*, *Getting to Know Your Customer*, but they also expect your staff members to communicate over different channels, including social media. Therefore, your business applications have to adapt to this change. For example, you shouldn't ask for basic information, such as an address, when the customer already had an address-based transaction with your payment partner. In this case, the customer would expect that you have a full view of their entire history with your organization.

Customers sometimes even prefer to make a complaint about a product or service over a social media channel, rather than calling a contact center. Looking at *Figure 9.3*, you can see a customer's real-life complaint about the service of Qantas Airlines on its Facebook page:

Figure 9.3: Customer complaints today

As examples in *Chapter 5, Utilizing Artificial Intelligence and Machine Learning in Your CRM Strategy,* showed, you can achieve a lot of process efficiency in not only customer service but also in sales and marketing operations using AI and ML.

For example, OpenAI, a nonprofit research company, has developed a new AI model, called GPT2, that is a text generator. The system is fed with only a few lines of text (anything from a few words to a full page) and is then asked to write the next few sentences or pages based on its predictions of what will best match the subject of your text.

GPT2 is capable of writing plausible passages that match what it is given in subject. For example, given the first paragraph of *Nineteen Eighty-Four,* a dystopian novel by English writer George Orwell, which was published in 1949, GPT2 will write the next few pages of the book almost in context with what Orwell wrote in his book some 70 years ago.

By combining customer history, the product portfolio, and a 360-degree client view, you could use the same technology to support meaningful conversations with customers at a much faster speed. Eventually, this could move over to social media channels that are supported by bots and ML, as the examples in *Chapter 5, Utilizing Artificial Intelligence and Machine Learning in Your CRM Strategy,* showed.

The CRM market is growing and evolving very rapidly, with new vendors with new ideas entering the market to take a share of it, along with the market leaders, such as Microsoft, Oracle, SAP, SugarCRM, and Salesforce.com.

The competition among market leaders is no longer about the feature list, as the functionality of most available tools is continuously improving and is on a par for major vendors such as Microsoft and Salesforce.com. The differentiator between the vendors will be more about how the CRM platforms are able to leverage the broader technology innovations that are evolving today with the smart cloud. It's about which platform can provide a better ecosystem for companies to develop a successful CRM strategy.

The priority is no longer a CRM platform that can integrate easily with your business applications, both in the cloud and on-premise, in order to protect your know-how and your existing investment; the priority is how to leverage all these new technologies to build and extend a sustainable CRM strategy for your business of tomorrow.

Future CRM platforms will leverage the latest technology innovations, in combination with traditional applications, in order to process higher automation and achieve powerful business orchestration. This is associated with a much lower cost of implementation and maintenance caused by leveraging the smart cloud.

For example, your staff may prefer to use Microsoft Skype and Outlook when connecting with customers and partners, or prefer using LinkedIn for communicating with prospects and building sales pipelines. If that's the case, then why not let them use their preferred tools and let this information go to the communication history in your CRM tool without your staff needing to enter the data within the CRM solution?

If you want to go down this path, you won't need to build any more expensive integration tools; rather, your CRM platform will leverage seamlessly whatever tools your customers and staff use every day. Through this, your CRM platform will capture the information seamlessly, without the need for you to invest in expensive integration tools.

A good example of this can be seen with Microsoft **Common Data Services** (**CDS**), which has been built with the integration of 200+ external systems out of the box. The relationship between Microsoft CDS and a CRM platform is depicted in *Figure 9.4*:

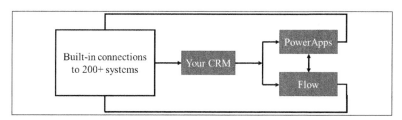

Figure 9.4: Microsoft CDS with built-in connections to the ecosystem

Later on in this chapter, we will explore how you can implement and build the apps and connections you see in *Figure 9.4*.

No longer is the focus on the feature list of the sales, marketing, or customer service module in your CRM. Instead, it's now about the ecosystem that is out there today and the ability to leverage it as a platform level within your CRM solution to lower costs.

To gain insights, businesses are harnessing data to drive intelligent business processes and business outcomes. They are adopting the cloud to store mass quantities of data (data lakes) and have become more efficient at collecting data and signals coming from a multitude of sources, such as web traffic, social media, and business systems, including both CRM and **Enterprise Resource Planning (ERP)** applications.

In a traditional application landscape, a CRM platform typically provides a marketing, sales, and customer service module, as referred to earlier. All of these modules are consuming other applications and data in your business, including retail management, ERP, reporting, business intelligence, and office applications.

We can explore some examples of traditional business applications in *Figure 9.5*:

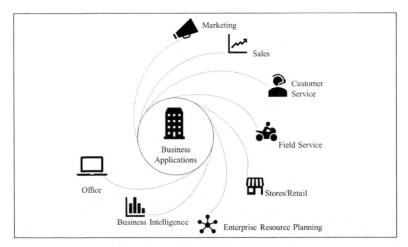

Figure 9.5: A traditional application landscape

In the business world of today, a traditional IT landscape consists of many applications that are well connected and integrated internally. Mostly, they overlap in functionalities and datasets.

The challenge is how to build a sustainable CRM platform that can best consolidate and leverage the existing investment in IT and applications, while at the same time taking on board all these newer technologies and tools, and leveraging them for your business and customers.

To cloud or not to cloud?

Just recently, I had a conversation with the business and IT stakeholders of a big retail chain. This business was evaluating whether to move its business applications to the cloud. It had to face the following questions:

- What options are there?
- What are the best practices?
- Should all applications move to the cloud or only some of them?
- What are the pros and cons of private cloud versus public cloud?

The company wanted to understand the integration and deployment options. This element was mainly focused on how to set up a hybrid application infrastructure in order to benefit from cloud services and on-premise.

We've covered all these topics in detail in *Chapter 7, CRM Integration Strategies*, and *Chapter 8, Cloud Versus On-Premise Versus Hybrid – The Deployment of a CRM Platform*, but you'll remember that the conclusion was that if a company wants to move completely to the cloud, but not all in one go, the best option is to choose a platform that can provide a hybrid deployment as a starting point.

Eventually, this solution gave the company the ability to experiment with business know-how and leverage the smart cloud in developing a better and smarter business environment. This is a cost-effective way to prepare for digital transformation.

From the business standpoint, the main reason you would move to the cloud is to be able to leverage AI and the technologies around it, including ML, cognitive services, IoT, robotics, and so on. The other option is using the smart cloud, as mentioned earlier.

My general advice is that if you move to the cloud, then you don't want to move all your business applications to the cloud at once. This is because there is a learning curve for every organization and moving one step at a time will be more successful and less expensive, coupled with the lower risks of not moving everything to a new system at once.

Obviously, to make such a decision, you'll need to do a total cost of ownership/return on investment (TCO/ROI) analysis on all three options you have, which are:

1. Stay where you are, on-premise, and improve what you have.

2. Move from on-premise and adapt to the cloud gradually. You can use a hybrid setting to leverage your existing investments and customer knowledge while building your experience within the cloud.

3. Move to the cloud entirely with your core applications, such as your ERP and CRM platform.

The TCO/ROI study you do will help you to justify your decision and enable you to measure your success.

In the example that I was involved in, the retail store was told by its technology vendor to move both the ERP and point of sales (POS) applications to the cloud, even though there was no hard evidence of any benefit that the company would receive by replacing the current and relatively new POS applications.

Leveraging smart cloud into CRM

In *Chapter 5, Utilizing Artificial Intelligence and Machine Learning in Your CRM Strategy,* we saw how you could leverage Microsoft's Azure Cognitive Services APIs to embed AI, including vision, speech, and text analytics, into your business application in order to build intelligent and automated services for your customers, and for your sales and marketing teams.

However, with Microsoft PowerApps and common data services, more integrated applications are looming on the horizon, with functionality coming already out of the box. A great example is the AI-driven relationship assistant from Microsoft; it is part of the new embedded intelligence suite of features you could leverage in Microsoft Dynamics 365.

The assistant keeps an eye on your daily activities and communications, then generates a collection of action cards (tasks) that are displayed prominently throughout the application, providing tailored, actionable insights. The assistant reminds you of upcoming activities, evaluates your communications, and suggests when it might be time to reach out to a contract that's been inactive for a while.

The relationship assistant identifies email messages that may be waiting for a reply from you and alerts you when an opportunity is nearing its close date. It's integrated into Microsoft Office and it enables Dynamics 365 for Sales to access your email in Microsoft Exchange to find and display messages that are related to your work in sales.

This makes it easy to see your relevant email messages, together with all of the other activities in your CRM platform that are related to a given opportunity in your sales pipeline. The message in Microsoft Exchange remains private and visible only to you, unless you choose to convert it to a tracked email in your CRM, which you can do with just one click if you want to make that email visible to the rest of your team.

The tracking is based on simple rules, such as the email addresses of any contacts in the stakeholders' list of opportunities in your pipeline or the open service requests of your accounts.

There are many more great business scenarios for CRM applications that are possible with these built-in technologies, such as:

- Routing cases by sentiment with cognitive services text analytics.

- The intelligent agent assistant, namely bots in the agent desktop that will provide insights, guidance, or alerts based on the current context, both proactively and reactively.

- Leveraging ML and AI to automatically extract metadata from audio and video files, including conversation keywords, a sentiment timeline, and a call transcript.

Big data

Another real challenge for businesses today is the rapidly growing amount of data, which has been expanding dramatically across all organizations. Through the mass adoption of the Internet and social media, there is even more data out there that companies want to leverage to improve their sales and marketing operations.

Big data, as a topic, is the new science for dealing with datasets that are too large or complex to be dealt with using traditional data processing applications. It's the science of leveraging AI and ML to analyze systematically extracted information from a variety of sources.

Companies are starting to adopt the cloud in order to store mass quantities of data, integrate with social media platforms, and leverage big data technology to slice and dice this data. This way, they can gain business insights through AI, ML, and cognitive services, all in order to gain a business advantage over their competitors and big tech companies.

So, now the question is, how would your particular business connect with the smart cloud to leverage big data techniques in order to improve your business outcomes with reasonable effort and cost?

A good example is Volkswagen, a German car company, which was the largest carmaker by worldwide sales in 2016 and 2017. The company started a digital transformation in 2018 for the same reasons as most other companies do so. In this case, it was mostly driven by digital disrupters and big tech companies, such as Google, Tesla, and Uber.

The cars of today have some 10,000,000 lines of code, mostly through embedded software, in various parts and micro-controllers in the cars. This makes it very challenging for a traditional automotive company, such as Volkswagen, to adapt quickly to market and technology changes. In comparison, a Tesla vehicle typically has a patch cycle of 30-to-60 days.

To face this digital disruption, Volkswagen is setting up a completely new organization and a software company for:

- Building new software architecture.
- Moving the company away from embedded software to application software.
- Creating separate software from hardware.
- Moving part of the software to the cloud for better manageability and lower maintenance costs.

According to Herbert Diess, the CEO of Volkswagen, 80-90% of innovation in the automobile industry will come from software in the cloud. The change is also driven by customers and their changing behavior. The result will be new models that will interact with the driver and passengers.

A digitally transformed Volkswagen is depicted in *Figure 9.6*:

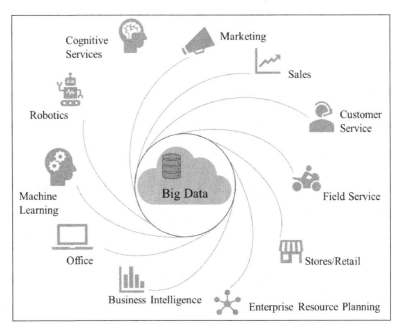

Figure 9.6: Leveraging big data in the cloud to improve operational efficiency

This is the first time that Volkswagen will have direct interaction with customers in its nearly 90 years of history. Its traditional business strategy was about engine, power, and brand, but now it is about software and customer experience. The company will own the software stack in the cloud, so it can deploy software updates to hundreds of millions of cars each year and be able to adapt to any change in the marketplace.

Social selling and advertising

Social selling is the process of developing sales over social network platforms and it is an integrated part of the modern sales process. This has been increasingly taking place via social networks such as LinkedIn, Twitter, Facebook, and Pinterest, and as a result, it is becoming an integrated part of CRM processes across most industries.

Examples of social selling techniques include branding and interacting directly with potential buyers and customers, which will help you to develop leads and opportunities with integrated social listening in your CRM strategies. The concept is gaining huge popularity in a variety of industries, such as financial advisory services, the automotive industry, and consumer products.

Social selling is the main source of income for a selection of social media platforms, such as LinkedIn, while social advertising is the main revenue source for Facebook. With LinkedIn having 675 million **monthly active users (MAU)** in 200 countries and Facebook having over 2 billion registered users, how would you best integrate these platforms to your CRM processes and benefit from them?

These companies provide a whole new set of emerging capabilities in terms of CRM through the smart cloud. For example, LinkedIn allows users to follow real news about their Facebook friends, LinkedIn contacts, and public companies, and can also help advertisers to reach businesses. For professionals, it provides surface insights about people in their network, right before they meet them. LinkedIn will also help you to leverage data science to close more sales, let salespeople share visual content with prospective clients, and provide employee engagement.

The idea of the social selling process is depicted in *Figure 9.7*:

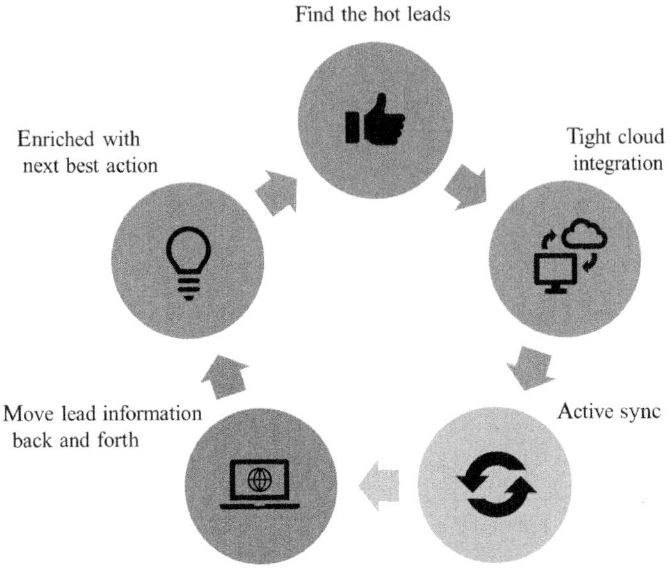

Figure 9.7: The social selling process

Companies have started to leverage social selling and social advertising in their daily CRM sales and marketing operations by targeting more and more of their own clients over such platforms. On the other hand, social media platforms have started to generate new business models by providing sales tools to companies in order to better integrate with their CRM strategies and data.

A good example is Sales Navigator from LinkedIn. Sales Navigator is available as a viewable widget within your CRM and can also be actively synced with your CRM to move sales information, including leads and accounts, from your CRM into Sales Navigator. The sync can also be enabled to send selected Sales Navigator information to your CRM. This will provide you with a whole new set of functionalities at almost no cost, which will have the added benefit of expanding your reach to a global network of companies and people.

Finding the right people and the most relevant prospects within your account portfolio will be easier, as the information about the right people on your target accounts is enriched with suggestions that have been customized for you.

Now, more than ever, organizations have embraced the value of using data to drive business outcomes. They've adopted the cloud to store mass quantities of data and have become more efficient at harnessing data and signals that come from a multitude of sources, such as web traffic, social media, and business systems, such as CRM/ERP applications.

You can see a CRM platform that leverages the ecosystem in *Figure 9.8*:

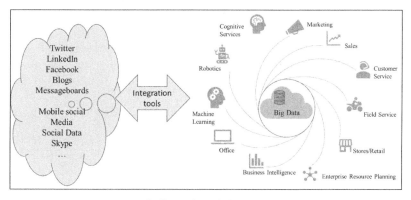

Figure 9.8: Social selling and social advertising with your CRM

Once you've implemented the infrastructure for harnessing data, how can you make that data work for you most efficiently? You'll need a layer on top of that data that lets your employees, regardless of technical ability, leverage it in a straightforward way to drive business impact.

That's what the Microsoft Power Platform does. It is a system that enables users to analyze, act, and automate. It does this with Power BI, PowerApps, and Flow, which all work together on top of your data to help everyone, regardless of their skill level, to drive the business with data.

Implementation tools

The challenge is to create a platform that is able to digest a vast amount of data and integrate it into your business applications and processes. Right now, there are only a few tools on the market to achieve this.

The Microsoft Power Platform allows your applications to share a common set of data elements to provide services for seamless integration with almost any other application in the cloud. CRM connectors will natively integrate with ERP applications.

The components of the Microsoft Power Platform have been visualized in *Figure 9.9*:

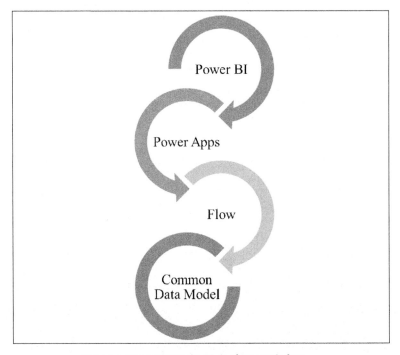

Figure 9.9: Components in the Microsoft Power Platform

Power BI is a business analytics service from Microsoft. It provides simple-to-use business intelligence and interactive visualization tools that allow users to create their own dashboards and reports on the fly.

Power BI offers a significant advantage by allowing your organization to connect to hundreds of data sources and it has deep integration with Dynamics 365 through PowerApps.

PowerApps is an application development environment that provides services, connectors, and a data platform. By using PowerApps, you can quickly build custom business apps that connect to your business data stored in the underlying data platform (Common Data Service for apps) or in various online and on-premise data sources (SharePoint, Excel, Office 365, Dynamics 365, SQL Server, and so on.) and data lakes. Just imagine how much power these tools could bring in future business scenarios!

In addition to all that, we can see a growing number of new integration concepts in the industry, such as the Open Data Initiative, which is a partnership among Microsoft, SAP, and Adobe to enable data exchange across systems and application. This makes data a renewable resource that flows into business applications.

As we saw in *Chapter 2, Getting to Know Your Customer*, companies have realized the value of building a comprehensive, 360-degree client view that is based on enterprise data and drives business efficiency.

The latest technological innovations and the vast amount of data in social media channels is providing a unique opportunity for businesses. Imagine what they could achieve with this data with the tools to build stronger business applications, including better dashboards, a 360-degree client view, data marts, mobile apps, and reporting.

The idea of leveraging a data lake and big data in your CRM has been depicted in *Figure 9.10*:

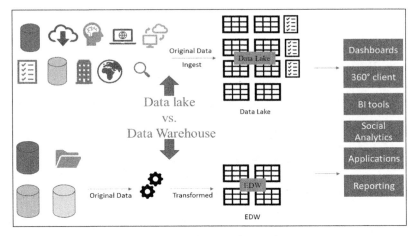

Figure 9.10: Data lake versus data warehouse

The data lake provides a unique opportunity to model, learn, integrate, and ingest signals from massive data integrated into your CRM platform, as *Figure 9.10* shows. All of this will provide significant advantages.

Your CRM can integrate with 200+ external systems out of the box. This method overcomes the limitations, effort, and cost required for integration with Microsoft and non-Microsoft products. This delivers a unique experience that will support no-code/low-code integration when building a new business application.

A sustainable CRM platform

The fourth industrial revolution is changing the way we do business today. Market leaders have integrated CRM with AI, IoT, and cognitive services, while staying focused on the CRM fundamentals, such as core sales, marketing, and services functionalities.

Smarter technologies, such as AI and robotics, will be driving the innovation in CRM; enterprise-level companies are demanding solutions that are easy to integrate with existing platforms both on-premise and in the cloud. The focus will be shifted toward ML, big data, automation, and other smart technologies that are tightly integrated with CRM and office productivity tools.

In designing a sustainable CRM strategy, it is legitimate to ask how CRM platforms today will differ tomorrow. The challenge is twofold; on the one hand, you need to integrate and leverage big data across the organization and on the other hand, you need to expand your applications into the cloud seamlessly. Your CRM platform must leverage cloud intelligent services (smart cloud) to expand and drive business outcomes.

As the example of Volkswagen shows, the possibilities are limitless. By leveraging social media platforms to onboard new clients or to develop a deeper relationship with existing clients and partners, you will not only improve sales, marketing, and services operations, but will expand into new areas, such as learning, hiring, and partner ecosystems. Ask yourself, how will your team's daily sales, marketing, and customer relationship processes integrate seamlessly with data in the cloud and social media platforms?

In a nutshell, you will need a CRM that applies big data, smart cloud, AI, and social techniques all together. A sustainable CRM platform is depicted in *Figure 9.11*:

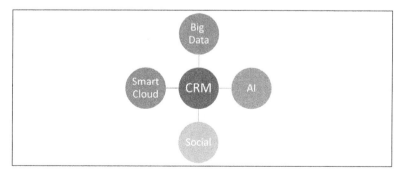

Figure 9.11: CRM ecosystems for today and tomorrow

Here you will need tools that provide a seamless, bi-directional, and tight integration with your sales, marketing, and service processes, such as the Microsoft Power Platform.

Technology vendors are spending billions on cloud infrastructure; they are building hundreds of data centers across the globe, with hundreds of thousands of kilometers of fiber, hundreds of terabits-per-second capacities, and thousands of sites providing cloud services. This is creating large connected commercial cloud networks.

These networks are offering **Software as a Service (SaaS)**, **Platform as a Service (PaaS)**, **Infrastructure as a Service (IaaS)**, and hybrid cloud platforms, along with virtually **Everything as a Service (XaaS)**, as I explained in detail in *Chapter 8, Cloud Versus On-Premise Versus Hybrid – The Deployment of a CRM Platform*.

AI and ML are some of the latest technologies that are no longer exclusive to Amazon or Google; they are available for everyone and all companies across the globe.

Summary

With the democratization of AI and ML, combined with the mass spread of the internet, IoT, social media, and big data, we are witnessing a fundamental change in the way we do business and communicate with our clients and partners today. All of this is directly affecting our CRM processes.

With most CRM systems, you can create a similar experience for users, as the functionality of most available tools is continuously improving and is similar for major vendors, but the true value to your business is in the ecosystem your CRM platform can provide. Being in the cloud is not the only differentiator; how your CRM platform can leverage new technologies, the smart cloud, and the services that are available through the smart cloud is important for your business.

Here you will need tools that provide a seamless, bi-directional, and tight integration with your sales, marketing, and service processes within your CRM platform, such as the Microsoft Power Platform. With such a tool, the future of CRM will be more like a Lego model: consisting of colourful, interlocking, functional modules accompanying an array of gears or connectors and various other services that are well integrated. Functional modules can be assembled and connected in many ways to construct a business solution, with all of them being supported by AI, ML, and bots. Anything constructed can then be taken apart again. The pieces could be used to make other business solutions easily, very much like the Taj Mahal example in the opening of this book. The building has changed its original purpose several times and each time it has changed successfully.

With platform like Microsoft Dynamics 365, you will be able to create an intelligent, adaptable, and flexible CRM that creates unique value for your business and provides you with a cost-effective digital transformation. You don't want to build the infrastructure, integrate applications, and hire the data scientists or security experts, but then only be able to leverage big data or AI to advance your business. You want your CRM to support your business strategy and fully leverage the limitless services that are in the smart cloud at an affordable price.

I'll leave you with my parting piece of advice: you want a platform that enables you to greatly increase your reach and to serve more customers, while reducing operational costs. Your CRM will have to leverage the cloud and XaaS (virtually everything as a service) in the smart cloud to scale and support customer interaction channels, including smartphones, mobile apps, and social media, in order to help your digital transformation strategies.

OTHER BOOKS
YOU MAY ENJOY

If you enjoyed this book, you may be interested in this book by Packt:

Mastering Zendesk

Cedric F. Jacob

ISBN: 978-1-78646-104-9

- Customize ticket channels such as Email, Twitter, Facebook, and Web-Widget

- Add business rules to create a more effective and automated Zendesk environment

- Use Zendesk apps to add more functionality to the Zendesk setup

- Extend Zendesk with JIRA and Salesforce
- Create custom metrics within GoodData in order to set up customized and automated reports
- Learn how to secure and troubleshoot Zendesk

Mastering Salesforce CRM Administration

Rakesh Gupta

ISBN: 978-1-78646-318-0

- Adopt Lightning Experience to improve the productivity of your organization's sales team

- Create and maintain service entitlements and entitlement processes

- Process Builder basic and advanced concepts

- Different ways to deploy applications between environments

- Best practices for improving and enriching data quality

Leave a review - let other readers know what you think

Please share your thoughts on this book with others by leaving a review on the site that you bought it from. If you purchased the book from Amazon, please leave us an honest review on this book's Amazon page. This is vital so that other potential readers can see and use your unbiased opinion to make purchasing decisions, we can understand what our customers think about our products, and our authors can see your feedback on the title that they have worked with Packt to create. It will only take a few minutes of your time, but is valuable to other potential customers, our authors, and Packt. Thank you!

Index

Symbols

A

B

C